MAKING WOMEN PAY

MAKING WOMEN PAY

THE HIDDEN COSTS OF FETAL RIGHTS

RACHEL ROTH

CORNELL UNIVERSITY PRESS

Ithaca and London

First published 2000 by Cornell University Press

Printed in the United States of America

Library of Congress Cataloging-in-Publication Data

Roth, Rachel.
    Making women pay : the hidden costs of fetal rights / Rachel Roth.
        p.   cm.
    Includes bibliographical references and index.
    ISBN 0-8014-3607-9 (cloth)
    1. Fetus—Legal status, laws, etc.—United States.   2. Pregnant women—Legal status, laws, etc.—United States.   3. Prenatal influences—Government policy—United States.   4. Women's rights—United States.   5. Conflict of interests—United States.   I. Title.
    KF481.R67   1999
    342.73′085—dc21   99-44982

Cornell University Press strives to use environmentally responsible suppliers and materials to the fullest extent possible in the publishing of its books. Such materials include vegetable-based, low-VOC inks and acid-free papers that are recycled, totally chlorine-free, or partly composed of nonwood fibers. Books that bear the logo of the FSC (Forest Stewardship Council) use paper taken from forests that have been inspected and certified as meeting the highest standards for environmental and social responsibility. For further information, visit our website at www.cornellpress.cornell.edu.

Cloth printing   10 9 8 7 6 5 4 3 2 1

for Helen Roth—

your memory is a blessing

Contents

Contents

Tables

Acknowledgments

When I first considered embarking on a Ph.D. program, I met with a graduate student who told me what a lonely experience it is: "Ultimately," she said, "it's just you and the text." I've been lucky to have people to share the writing process with, people who made sure it wasn't too lonely and who also made my work much better.

Three women in particular have been essential to the creation of this book: Barbara Blodgett, Alexa Freeman, and Eve Weinbaum. A writer could not ask for better critics: perceptive, concretely helpful, and unfailingly generous. Nor could I ask for better friends. Eve and I have known each other the longest, and for ten years she has been such an exceptional friend and teacher that I'm not sure how I could have done this without her.

Rogers Smith was also indispensable. As my advisor in the Political Science Department at Yale, he was always enthusiastic about my project and ready to share his time and ideas. Since then he has read new chapters and helped me navigate the entire publication process. Kathleen Clark, Kathleen Daly, Laura Gomez, Jane Levey, Tracy MacDonald, Julia Riches, Ian Shapiro, and Laura Wexler engaged in helpful conversation, read drafts, or did both. Lynn Morgan's passionate interest was a constant.

Two readers for Cornell University Press offered constructive criticism and valuable suggestions for improving the original manuscript. Both critic and advocate, Alison Shonkwiler at Cornell was all I could ask for in an editor. By reading the entire manuscript in two stages and making herself available, she helped me to write the book I wanted to. Whatever shortcomings remain are my own.

A second group of people also contributed to the book in important ways. Laura Orr of Yale Law School will always be the law librarian of my dreams. She initiated me into the mysteries of legal research with patience, humor, and an affirming interest in my work. The Hampshire County law librarians and Smith College reference librarians, especially

Sika Berger and Robin Kinder, were also wonderful, fielding countless questions. Thanks as well to Paul Frymer, Sandra Matthews, Marla Miller, my seminar students at Smith, and people around the country who shared information with me; Catherine Rice, Nancy Winemiller, and the many other people at Cornell University Press who labored to bring this book into being. Although I've never had the opportunity to work with her, Rosalind Petchesky's scholarship has so influenced the way I think about reproductive politics that I feel I owe her thanks, too.

Several institutions provided vital material and moral support along the way. I am grateful to the Woodrow Wilson Foundation Women's Studies grant program, the American Association of University Women Educational Foundation, and the Five College Women's Studies Research Center at Mount Holyoke College for assistance when I was doing the original research and writing my dissertation. The Graduate Employees and Students Organization (GESO) and its allies Locals 34 and 35 sustained me through graduate school at Yale. The Smith College Government Department extended privileges to me as a research associate when I wasn't teaching. At Smith and Mount Holyoke, Lea Ahlen, Robin Feldman, and Sheree Morgan deserve special thanks. The Center for Reproductive Law and Policy made my research easier and does the front-line work for women's reproductive rights every day.

Carolyn Ahearn tended to my muscles, and my extended family tended to the rest of me: Amil Roth, Ann and Ed Ferguson, Bob and Debbie Adler, David Roth and Debbie Reed, Josh Roth, Julie Holabird, and especially Peter Ferguson. Peter has lived twice through the maddening process of finishing a manuscript, encouraging and helping me to meet the challenge each time. Although my mother, Helen Roth, died when I was just beginning this project, I still hope that some of her insight graces these pages.

RACHEL ROTH

Northampton, Massachusetts

MAKING WOMEN PAY

1

How Women Pay for Fetal Rights

> For months, David was a victim of torture. He was kept in a small darkened room. His food was poisoned and his brain severely damaged. And then one day he was born.
>
> —Minnesota fetal alcohol syndrome public awareness poster

As government-sponsored materials depict fetuses as tortured prisoners, so do prosecutors hear fetal voices, psychologists dispense advice on behalf of fetal patients, factories exclude women lest they bring fetal visitors, legislators craft public policy for fetuses, and judges issue rulings based on fetuses' preferences, including one judge who denied a "surrogate mother" custody of a child she bore because there was "no evidence whatsoever" that the fetus had bonded with her (quoted in Hartouni 1997, 93). These are but a few developments in the expanding terrain of reproductive and gender politics that has come to be known as the politics of fetal rights.

People most commonly associate the term "fetal rights" with efforts to curtail legal abortion. Yet as the right-to-life movement's success in restricting women's access to abortion waxed and waned throughout the 1970s and 1980s, other targets of scrutiny and regulation in the name of fetal rights emerged: women who would be carrying their pregnancies to term and women who were not pregnant at all, but merely fertile.

The struggles over these women's lives are the ones explored here. Given their constructions of fetuses as autonomous, full-fledged persons, many doctors, lawyers, judges, employers, and lawmakers in the United States have perceived conflicts between women and their fetuses. This book examines in depth three areas in which such conflicts have been perceived and adjudicated, since the *Roe v. Wade* decision legalizing abortion in 1973 until 1992: at work, in medical care settings, and in government regulation of women's consumption of drugs and alcohol. In all three areas, proponents of fetal rights have misperceived the "conflict" and misdirected their policy solutions as a result.

Looking at how courts and legislatures have framed and resolved conflicts in all three domains illuminates the ways that fetal rights are used to structure constraints against women. When institutions assert or accept rights claims on behalf of fetuses, their stated reasons usually involve protecting fetuses from potential harm and enhancing their chances of healthy birth and survival. As I show, however, the strategy of creating fetal rights is not necessary to achieve those goals, is often counterproductive to those goals, and always undermines women's equal standing as citizens.

Fetal rights do not come free. When courts, legislatures, or other political and social institutions decide to award rights to fetuses, the award translates into costs for others. Women currently bear a disproportionate share of the costs of ensuring fetal health, relative to the rest of society. This unequal distribution burdens women and fails to provide a clear pattern of benefit to fetuses or to society as a whole.

American ideology and social arrangements assign to women the primary responsibility for reproduction. When I speak of primary responsibility for reproduction, I refer to women's disproportionate responsibility for the entire reproductive process, which includes timing pregnancies and rearing children as well as gestating fetuses and giving birth. Because all women are perceived as potentially pregnant for much of their lives, they are susceptible to having restrictions imposed on them because of what others think about that potential. Each of the three domains I examine has its own distinct pattern of distributing costs and selectively enforcing certain women's responsibility for fetal health. This is most often done according to class, race, or culture. By culture, I mean a range of influences on someone's life, including religion, national origin, or first language. In addition, the ideological message of fetal rights politics—that women are not entitled to be as self-determining as men because they can become pregnant—exacts a high price from women as a class. Taken together, the many forms of fetal advocacy politics place a heavy burden on all women's opportunities and pursuit of equality.

Because rights claims resonate so deeply with American political and cultural values, fetal rights claims have been taken seriously in the political arena, and courts and legislatures have granted rights to fetuses. Although she does not address fetal advocacy politics in her book *Making All the Difference: Inclusion, Exclusion, and American Law*, Martha Minow offers some insights about the power of establishing rights for fetuses. When people make rights claims, they assert their identity as individuals entitled to equality and liberty, and emphasize their essential sameness to others as persons and as members of the polity. Rights analysis further "treats each individual as a separate unit, related only to the state rather than to a group or to social bonds" (Minow 1990, 216). Fetal rights claims, then, present a rhetorically powerful strategy by giving the fetus an individual identity, asserting its equality with the woman, and establishing its independent relationship with the state that bypasses the pregnant woman.

The logic of fetal rights depends on certain rhetorical constructions. First, proponents of fetal rights oppose them rhetorically to women's rights, constructing a contest of equal antagonists with only one possible winner. Consider these representative titles of journal and newspaper articles: "Fetal versus Maternal Rights: Medical and Legal Perspectives"; "When the Rights of Mother and Fetus Collide"; "Maternal versus Fetal Rights: A Clinical Dilemma"; and "Fetal Patients and Conflicts with Their Mothers."[1] All set up a conflict between woman and fetus: a zero-sum choice.[2]

A second frequent formulation opposes fetal rights to women's responsibilities, as in this 1989 article in a medical journal: "Fetal Therapy and Surgery: Fetal Rights and Maternal Obligations" (Rosner et al. 1989). This title suggests that it is incumbent upon the pregnant woman to honor the right to surgery and medical treatment that doctors believe fetuses hold; in other words, women can be forcibly subjected to unwanted medical procedures. This kind of right is an entitlement enforceable against the pregnant woman. Its logic dictates that social institutions hold pregnant women accountable for the fulfillment of fetal rights. In this case, that means that pregnant women are responsible for ensuring the fetus's access to medical treatment, even though they themselves have no right to medical care.

These formulations have become so pervasive that supposedly objective news reporters use them freely. On National Public Radio's *All Things Con-*

---

[1] See Bowes and Selgestad 1981; Gorney 1988; Shriner 1979; and Dougherty 1985.

[2] All the titles also cast the pregnant woman in the role of mother. In our society, mothering connotes women's selfless devotion to children, a connotation that is at odds with any action that could potentially jeopardize the health of a fetus. I address this point later in this chapter.

sidered, news anchor Linda Wertheimer described a criminal charge of attempted murder against a woman who drank heavily during pregnancy as the latest chapter in the debate over how "to balance the rights of the woman against those of the fetus" (NPR 1996). This concept gains legitimacy through constant repetition in scholarly journals, popular media, and public discourse.

Creating individual fetal identities that are hostile to women's identities is not the only thing that rights rhetoric accomplishes. Rights rhetoric is also powerful because it obscures the question of costs. Both of the constructions I just described—maternal rights versus fetal rights and maternal responsibilities versus fetal rights—obscure the way that fetal rights function to distribute social costs. When a court or other institution decides to award rights, it has to assign the costs of those rights to some individual or group. That assignment—who should bear the costs of fetal rights—is a political question that has received very little direct public debate. It is the central concern of this study. The answer, explicit or implicit, has been to impose the costs of fetal rights on women.

These costs are tangible. They can't be measured solely in terms of money, although that is certainly at stake. Women also incur costs to their freedom, physical and mental security, identity, and privacy when they are denied jobs because they are fertile, when they are subjected to court-ordered medical operations against their will, and when they are given additional civil and criminal penalties for using drugs or alcohol during pregnancy that are never imposed on women who are not pregnant or on men. Women are assigned responsibility for taking care of fetuses without being given the resources they need to do so, and then penalized for falling short.

"There seems to be a qualitative difference between an invasion of privacy by your government and an invasion by a stranger," explain Ellen Alderman and Caroline Kennedy in their analysis of a class-action lawsuit women brought against the city of Chicago's policy to strip search every single woman brought to the jail, regardless of the circumstances of her arrest or the reason she was booked. "The women spoke of an abuse of a basic trust. They felt they had been violated by the very people who were supposed to be their protectors and expressed a sense of betrayal and vulnerability. All of them said they dreaded any future contact with the police" (1995, 13). The feelings of abuse and subsequent loss of trust that characterized the Chicago women's experiences also characterize the experiences of women whose privacy and bodies are invaded in the name of fetal rights. When forced to submit to unwanted surgery such as a cesarean or sterilization, or when jailed without due process, women may come to mistrust the medical and legal institutions that they rely on for care and protection.[3] Their mistrust, and that of their families and friends, in turn creates costs for all of society.

Women inevitably bear some of the costs of reproducing the species. They bear the physical, emotional, and time costs associated with pregnancy and birth. The Centers for Disease Control (CDC) reports that the maternal death ratio has held steadily at 7 or 8 deaths per 100,000 births since 1982, and that half of these deaths are preventable. The United States lags behind 20 other countries and has made no progress toward its goal of cutting deaths to 3.3 per 100,000 by the year 2000. The causes of death include ectopic pregnancy, hemorrhage, infection, blood clots, and pregnancy-induced high blood pressure (*MMWR* 1998). The CDC also estimates that for every woman who dies as a result of pregnancy, 3,100 women are hospitalized for complications each year (Leary 1996). In addition, there may be severe long-term consequences for some women. Women who have borne children appear much more likely than other women or men to get such autoimmune diseases as systemic sclerosis (Artlett, Smith, and Jimenez 1998).

Women also *evitably* bear a disproportionate share of the physical, emotional, and time costs in rearing children. Although new trends in paternal involvement in child-rearing make headlines, studies overwhelmingly show that women continue to shoulder most of the child care, as well as homemaking, even when they work the same number of hours outside the home as men.[4]

What is so troubling about fetal rights claims is that they make women bear almost all the costs, instead of distributing them more evenly across society. Consider, as an alternative model, how the demands of disabled people to participate fully in American life have led to newly articulated rights of access to education, housing, transportation, and work. In this case, when government actors and institutions decided that the rights claims of disabled Americans had merit, they distributed the attendant costs broadly to taxpayers, employers, and consumers. Rather than requiring disabled people to pay for their own access, Congress decided that society must share the burden, and enacted a series of laws culminating in the Americans with Disabilities Act (ADA) of 1990.[5]

[3] The poor treatment many women receive when they bring rape charges to the criminal justice system is perhaps the paradigmatic experience of such institutional betrayal. Women who press charges often speak of being raped twice: once by the accused, and again by the state. See, for example, *Real Rape* by Susan Estrich (1987).

[4] See Perry 1993 on the devaluation of women's reproductive labor.

[5] I would like to thank Eve Weinbaum for suggesting this contrast. Laura Rothstein's book *Disabilities and the Law* describes the requirements of the ADA, signed into law in 1990 (Rothstein 1992 and 1993 Supp.).

Reproductive costs can also be redistributed, and this book suggests many ways to do this. Moreover, the burdens that have been imposed on women in the name of fetal rights do not produce clear evidence of benefits to fetuses, calling into question the motives underlying fetal rights policy. By contrast, we can have more confidence that—if fully enforced—the ADA will improve the lives of its intended beneficiaries.

The notion of fetal rights is linked to another important rhetorical construct prevalent in public discourse—that of "maternal-fetal conflict." This notion is used to focus attention on women's behavior as the source of risk to fetal health and away from other factors. This study critically examines this construct, which rests simultaneously on two assumptions: (1) that all pregnant women are already mothers and (2) that they are bad mothers, for if they were good mothers they wouldn't be having conflicts with their fetuses.

Maternal-fetal conflict erases all other aspects of a pregnant woman's identity. All pregnant women are *expectant* mothers (unless they plan to place their future children for adoption), but only some pregnant women are already rearing children. Referring to pregnant women as "mothers" before they give birth evokes the qualities of selflessness and duty associated with motherhood and suggests that pregnant women have failed to demonstrate these important qualities. It also turns the fetus into a child. Cultural expectations and legal standards of parental duty then apply to pregnant women, and the fetus gains an independent identity that enables it to engage rhetorically in conflict with the pregnant woman ("mother"). Again, this serves to focus attention on the pregnant woman and away from her environment and the responsibilities that other individuals or institutions might have.

These rhetorical constructions are complemented by images that depict fetuses as independent. As Barbara Duden's book *Disembodying Women* aptly suggests, the politics of fetal rights has disembodied fetuses from pregnant women in visual culture and public discourse (Duden 1993). From Lennart Nilsson's famous *Life* magazine photographs of "the drama of life before birth" to prime time ultrasound scans, images of disembodied fetuses abound. Rosalind Petchesky explains how ultrasound imaging of fetuses presents the fetus "as though removed from the pregnant woman's body, as though suspended in space" (1987, 70). A 1991 Volvo ad does just this: A huge sonogramlike image of a fetus hovers above a tiny car at the bottom of the page; the text asks, "Is something inside telling you to buy a Volvo?" (Taylor 1992). In the television version of the ad, a voice off-camera asks the same question (Horovitz 1990). Janelle Taylor explains that fetal images "gain whatever power and meaning they may have precisely upon the strength of the ideological status of photographs as purely denotative, transparent representations of reality" (1992, 74). Political movements can deploy these supposedly neutral, self-evident images in a variety of ways.[6]

Even a recent collection of feminist essays called *Expecting Trouble: Surrogacy, Fetal Abuse, and New Reproductive Technologies* recapitulates this problem on its cover (Boling 1995). The cover design features the profile of a pregnant woman in front of the Supreme Court; she is merely a dark blue silhouette, while the fetus is rendered in intricate detail, its tiny features and fingers giving it the distinct human appearance the pregnant woman lacks. (Never mind that the term *fetal abuse* is not in quotation marks, implying it is an acceptable and unproblematic category.) As all of these examples show, the more the fetus is aggrandized, the more women tend to be diminished.

Hmn

The Pervasive Influence of the Discourse of Fetal Rights

The dominant image of the fetus as distinct and individuated from the pregnant woman has become so pervasive and powerful that it affects even the way many women's advocates cast their arguments. Nancy Rhoden (1986), credited with publishing one of the first feminist legal analyses of court-ordered medical intervention, uses the expression "maternal-fetal conflict" throughout. In his book criticizing fetal protection policies in the workplace, political scientist Robert Blank speaks of something called the "maternal uterine environment" and contrasts it with "extramaternal environmental factors" (1993, 51–52, 46). Blank seems to use the expression "fetal environment" to refer interchangeably to women's bodies and to all the things to which pregnant women themselves are exposed (see p. 79, for instance).

This language is even more surprising when it comes from nationally recognized women's health experts and opponents of fetal rights. Wendy Chavkin and her colleagues describe state intervention during pregnancy in the case of *In re Steven S.*: "That case involved the detention in a hospital of the fetus and the mother, based on the mother's mental illness"

[6] Echoing the idea that fetal rights politics and the construct of "maternal-fetal conflict" locate problems of fetal safety within pregnant women themselves, Taylor argues that the ad presents the pregnant woman "as potentially dangerous to the fetus, [whose] safety can be ensured only by enclosing it (and her) within a car. The Volvo ad implicitly suggests that the pregnant woman is herself a sort of transport vehicle, and a relatively unsafe one at that: the steel body of a Volvo is needed to encase her, if the fetus is to remain safe" (1992, 78).

(1992, 303). They suggest that the fetus could somehow be detained all by itself in the hospital, but authorities decided to keep the "mother," too. Consider also the first paragraph of an article by Lisa Maher that criticizes the harsh governmental response to "crack pregnancies": "The subjugation of a woman's right to privacy, autonomy, and bodily integrity to that of her fetus is no longer the futuristic scenario of feminist fictions. It is fast becoming one of the harsh realities of post-Reagan America" (1990, 111). By treating the fetus as an independent, rights-bearing individual, these writers implicitly concede the very ground they seek to challenge.

Self-identified feminist writers also objectify pregnant women, talking about "the pregnant form," "the pregnant body," or "pregnant bodies," as if severing them from the personalities that animate those bodies (see, for example, Condit 1995; Daniels 1993; Stabile 1992). Similarly, a legal news story sympathetic to pregnant women is entitled "Prosecutors' New Drug War Target: The Womb," when clearly the targets are women (Jacobus 1992).

The problem explored in this book might be thought of as one of distributive justice. Under this framework, we can conceive of reproducing and caring for future generations as a social good. Justice requires that the costs be widely shared, as the benefits will be. But the framework as traditionally conceived is inadequate because it recapitulates the very harm that I criticize—that is, it makes women disappear. The eminent figures associated with theories of justice have precious little to say about women, especially outside the context of family.[7] Gender cannot be submerged as a category of analysis when investigating the politics of fetal rights. Rather, analyses must foreground women's experiences both to avoid perpetuating in theory the same injustices practiced against women in life and to design effective policy. In her book *Justice and the Politics of Difference*, Iris Young argues that "instead of focusing on distribution, a conception of justice should begin with the concepts of domination and oppression" (1990, 3). I use the concept of distribution as a window onto relations of domination and oppression. In other words, I demonstrate throughout this study how women's socially allocated burden of responsibility for reproduction contributes to their oppression. And so while I argue for reallocating the burdens of reproduction, I have framed this study as one about equality and gender justice rather than as one about distributive justice per se.

---

[7] For example, Rawls 1971; Nozick 1974; Sandel 1982; and to a lesser extent Walzer 1983. For a critique of the way these and other major theorists treat families, see Susan Moller Okin's book *Justice, Gender, and the Family* (1989).

While traditional justice theorists ignore gender, feminist theorists who rely on an essentialized concept of gender difference can still make real women disappear. Cynthia Daniels's book is a prime example. *At Women's Expense: State Power and the Politics of Fetal Rights* quickly became the standard in the field, winning an award from the American Political Science Association for the best book on women and politics. Daniels organizes her book around three high-profile court cases that each reflect a different dimension of her model of political power: the power of self-sovereignty; the power to transform public structures, called *political agency*; and the power of authoritative moral discourse.

Perhaps Daniels's greatest contribution is her analysis of the politics of science. Daniels demonstrates how cultural values and assumptions affect the interpretation and media representation of scientific data to create a "sense of social and political crisis" (1993, 107). She deftly analyzes the myths and synthesizes the findings of research on threats to fetal health, exploring the methodological limits of current research, and paying special attention to the role of men in reproduction.

This important discussion, however, is embedded in a theoretical framework that weakens the book as a whole. Daniels seeks to advance both a new theory of the state and a new theory of citizenship, but she does not fully articulate either one. Unresolved tensions prevent her from doing so, especially the contradiction between advocating a notion of citizenship based on the specificity of "the pregnant body" and concluding that women succeed politically when they cast their claims in gender-neutral terms. On the one hand, Daniels argues that "liberal citizenship redefined to include the pregnant body" requires "the redefinition of the principle of self-sovereignty" to encompass women's "right to consensual sex," "freedom from rape and domestic violence," and "right to voluntary pregnancy" (138). On the other hand, she argues that women succeed politically when they reject gender-specific claims. Daniels identifies women's victory in an employment discrimination case as their most successful use of political power to counter claims of fetal rights. Women won, she argues, because they successfully de-gendered the issue of protecting fetuses from toxic exposures and broadened the scope of the case to include male-mediated risks to fetal development (see chap. 3). (The briefs filed by the workers reflect this strategy, although the Court's opinion does not emphasize it.)

This tension between universal and gender-specific claims has a long history and may be familiar under another name: the equality/difference problem. In simplest terms, the problem is whether, when devising strategy to achieve gender equality, it is better to insist that women be treated exactly the same as men or to insist that social policy recognize real differences between the sexes. The dilemma is also sometimes cast in terms of equal versus special treatment. A widely debated example asks whether covering pregnancy and childbirth expenses in an employee medical plan, thereby increasing the overall cost of the plan, constitutes "special" treatment of women (as only women get pregnant) or equal treatment (as all employees get the medical care they need).[8] The equality/difference problem is not easily solved; Ann Snitow calls it the central divide in feminist theory and practice (Snitow 1990). It is not surprising, then, that Daniels does not resolve the theoretical tension. But by failing to acknowledge its presence in her own work until her last chapter (and then presenting it only as a paradox for women), she leaves readers with a vision of a "new body politics" stressing gender difference that is at odds with her entire analysis of how women can only win in the political realm by degendering their claims.

To pose the choice as one between "equality" and "difference" further implies that equality demands sameness. Yet I believe we can have a conception of equality that honors difference. As Michael Walzer puts it, "The aim of political egalitarianism is a society free from domination. . . . It is not a hope for the elimination of differences; we don't all have to be the same" (1983, xiii). In a related vein, Catharine MacKinnon (1987) argues that the equality/difference debate asks the wrong question; instead, we should focus on the way that "difference" becomes a justification for domination by the powerful. Eliminating domination is what matters, and that may require a number of strategies rather than a choice between two mutually exclusive alternatives.

Daniels invests pregnancy with deep symbolic meaning. Pregnant women stand in for all of humanity as the bearers of life, against the forces of capitalism and masculinity: "The pregnant body is trouble in the workplace as well. The pregnant body doesn't punch a time clock and doesn't listen to the directives of bosses. . . . It represents life over profits, health over production" (139).[9] But pregnant women do punch time clocks and listen to their bosses—if they want to keep their jobs. Daniels's heavy investment in the meaning of pregnancy flows from her position at the outset of the book, when she asserts, "At stake in the new politics of fetal rights is not control over fetal health but the mediation and consolidation of the ultimate power that women have: the power to give birth" (2). I disagree;

[8] Compare, for example, Krieger and Cooney 1983 to Williams 1984–85, both excerpted in Weisberg 1993.

[9] See similar comments on pp. 55, 83, 98, 140, and 143–44.

there is far more at stake in fetal rights politics. Fetal rights politics is part of a struggle over women's prospects for equality with men and women's power in any realm of social or political life. The question is whether women will continue to be disempowered by being forced to bear the primary responsibility for reproduction.

A troubling outcome of Daniels's line of reasoning is evident in her contrast between the traditional liberal citizen and the pregnant woman: "Whereas the good citizen enters politics to defend individual self-interest, the pregnant woman represents the interdependence of human life and the difficulty, even impossibility, of distinguishing self from other" (139). To be connected to others in a web of relationships is one thing (134). To lose any and all claim to individuality is quite another, and more reminiscent of women's political past than symbolic of any "new kind of polity." In contrast, I do not try to identify a necessary relationship between pregnancy and citizenship. Instead, my work emphasizes how political decisions and social structures have shaped women's experiences and range of choices.

Throughout these pages I argue that misdiagnosing the problem of fetal harm has quite often had dire consequences for women *and* their fetuses. Policy solutions to improve fetal health have taken largely two forms. One conceives of women as the biggest threat to fetal health; the other provides assistance but tends to render women invisible by designating the fetus as the recipient of needed services. These two approaches are linked in the sense that even the beneficial measures treat pregnant women themselves as unworthy of help.

A debate currently taking place in many state legislatures also centers on whether women or fetuses should be the subjects of public policy. Many state lawmakers are contemplating changes to their criminal codes in order to make attacks on pregnant women a specific crime. Some propose enhancing penalties for assault against a woman when the perpetrator knows, or could be reasonably expected to know, that she is pregnant, and she miscarries as a result. This type of measure is positive and seeks to recognize that the woman has suffered an extra loss. In addition to the pain, fear, and anxiety about future safety that all victims of violence may experience, a woman who has suffered a miscarriage is also robbed involuntarily of the opportunity to raise the child her fetus was to become. "Holding third parties responsible for the negligent or criminal destruction of fetuses," as legal scholar Dawn Johnsen says, "is therefore consistent with, and even enhances, the protection of pregnant women's interests" (1986, 603).

In contrast, another set of proposals takes the form of codifying a new

crime of feticide. These laws do not vindicate the pregnant woman and society for her loss but reify the fetus into an independent legal entity with
its own rights that have been violated. Some people may argue that these
laws are good because they give the state an extra weapon to prosecute violent criminals, who can be charged with two separate crimes and hence
be given longer sentences. But the trade-off is too great. There is no reason to think that the creation of rights for fetuses can be contained in this
one realm, without potentially adverse effects on women, especially if the
laws are not written explicitly to exempt pregnant women from their
reach. The active participation of anti-choice organizations in shaping
these proposals should give women's advocates pause (*RFN* 1996a).[10]

Unfortunately, fetal rights advocates' concern with fetal health contrasts
sharply with the unduly low concern for children in U.S. society. Historically, the United States has tolerated high levels of child neglect and abuse
and low levels of child support; the latter problem is something Congress
tried to correct in its 1988 Family Support Act. But even as child support
enforcement has improved in some parts of the country, welfare politics
have deteriorated. The 1996 welfare law ending poor families' entitlement to cash assistance is expected by the Clinton administration's own estimates to throw at least one million children into poverty (Mink 1998, 3).
One in five American children is already poor. Poverty is responsible for
the high rates of infant mortality in the nation's capital and urban centers,
rates that rival or surpass those of developing countries. For the fetuses of
poor and low-income women, then, the traditional slap at birth is indeed
a rude awakening into a life of diminished prospects. Some critics argue
that fetal rights appeal to politicians because they make the government
look as if it's doing something for children without having to commit any
resources (see, for example, Field 1989). In Katha Pollitt's words, focusing
on women's behavior and fetal rights "allows the government to appear to
be concerned about babies without having to spend any money, change
any priorities, or challenge any vested interests" (1990, 410–11).

The logic of fetal rights and the social construction of "maternal-fetal
conflicts" do not simply privatize responsibility for the next generation but
instead locate responsibility specifically with women, burdening their opportunities and pursuit of equality without providing the resources necessary to carry out their socially ascribed maternal duties. To argue against
the government's creation or sanction of fetal rights in no way deprives
government of a meaningful role in promoting fetal health. It does not

[10] *RFN* stands for *Reproductive Freedom News*, published by the Center for Reproductive Law
and Policy in New York City.

mean the state should not value potential life. Rather, it means that the best way for the state to express its compelling interest in potential life is by creating conditions for healthy wanted pregnancies and by helping families to meet their basic needs.

Fetal Rights in Action

Chapter 2 places contemporary fetal rights conflicts in the historical and political context of struggles over women's reproductive autonomy in the United States. Chapters 3–6 address fetal rights politics in three different arenas. My goal is to analyze fetal rights policies and practices on their own terms and to analyze their impact on women, the fetuses they may bear, and prospects for gender equality in the United States.[11]

Courts and legislatures are the major political institutions that actively participate in the allocation of reproductive burdens, and yet most literature on fetal rights politics focuses on court decisions. The literature on legislation is often partial, anecdotal, or inaccurate, often because it relies on secondary sources. This study provides a fuller picture of fetal rights politics as it actually plays out in the United States by presenting the first systematic study of policy patterns across several fetal rights domains. In the legislative sphere, the vast majority of battles are fought at the state level. Congress has rarely entertained bills related to fetal rights. In contrast, some two hundred measures were enacted in the states between 1973 and 1992.[12]

[11] Because this book focuses on situations in which fetal rights are asserted in conflict with women, it does not include such topics as tort law and criminal fetal death laws. There are a handful of court cases involving the use of tort law to sue a woman for injury she inflicted on her fetus, but these so far are the exception. Tort law is more commonly a tool used by women to attempt to recover damages from doctors, hospitals, and other such third parties. For a discussion placing more emphasis on the potential uses of tort law against women, see Blank 1993, esp. 145–49. Fetal manslaughter laws date back at least to the nineteenth century. Although their numbers increased after 1973, their language and history make it clear that legislatures were inspired to adopt them to punish third parties who injure pregnant women, not to punish women themselves, as some prosecutors want to do. Feticide laws have become a fiercely contested issue in the 1990s. Chapters 6 and 7 describe homicide prosecutions against women whose infants are stillborn or die shortly after birth.

[12] While there are some good overviews of specific policy areas (such as English 1990 and Larson 1991), the literature on fetal rights policy is often inconsistent (Benton and Dyke, for instance, both published in 1990, conflict in nine instances in their surveys) or incomplete (failing to give citations so that the reader can pursue the subject on her own). Relying on secondary sources can also lead authors to mischaracterize the political implications of particular laws, because they misreport the era when they were passed (for instance, Condit 1995). The bibliography gives citations to state statutes analyzed in this book, reflecting the state of the law in 1992, and the Appendix excerpts selected statutes.

Chapters 3 and 4 analyze women's challenge to corporate "fetal protection policies" that deny women jobs involving exposure to potentially hazardous substances unless they can prove they are infertile. As a result of these policies, women have gotten sterilized in order to keep their jobs. In a society already structured to assign the costs of reproduction to women, corporations can do the same and come out looking socially responsible for championing the cause of healthy babies. Hence officials of the Bunker Hill Mining Company publicly stated that the company "is willing to be criticized for not employing some women—but not for causing birth defects" (quoted in Kenney 1992, 304). In a 1983 article on fetal protection policies, American Civil Liberties Union attorney Joan Bertin said that corporations adopted fetal protection policies to avoid the costs of nondiscrimination—that is, to avoid the costs of making women equal participants in their workforces (Bertin 1983). What this means is that corporations sought to avoid certain *perceived* costs; after all, running a potentially dangerous business always entails some costs, whether of providing a safe work environment, insuring against liability, or hiring workers of both sexes. The corporations misperceived the costs of hiring women as unduly high, because they wrongly believed that women could not control their fertility and that only women could expose a developing fetus to the risk of harm, when men's exposure can also pose a risk. They perceived the problems of dangerous workplaces as either/or: Either women could be employed, or the health of potential fetuses could be protected. This false dichotomy is characteristic of the "fetal protection" debate.

I want to make it clear at the outset that objecting to sterilization as a condition of employment is not a romantic claim about women's fertility. Surgical sterilization is the most popular form of birth control in the United States among women over age twenty-five (CARASA 1988, 26). It is clearly a fertility-control option many women choose, and it is neutral in and of itself. What is objectionable is when women subjected to economic coercion go through with such a serious and irreversible procedure when they do not want to do so. The women employed or seeking work in hazardous jobs had reasons for not wanting to be sterilized. Former American Cyanamid workers speak of the devastating loss of self-esteem after their ordeal with the company, of not feeling like a woman anymore (Faludi 1991, 437–53). While it is certainly possible to critique the women's position as an unfortunate manifestation of patriarchal ideology that values women only as sexual and reproductive objects, the pain they experienced is nevertheless real, and was inflicted for no justifiable reason.

Chapter 5 examines the practice of forcing pregnant women to submit to medical interventions against their will. Typically, these situations arise when doctors cannot convince pregnant women to accept their recommendations, and, along with hospital attorneys, turn to the courts for authority to treat women over their objections. Women's objections are often but not exclusively religious in nature, such as when Jehovah's Witnesses refuse blood transfusions. Women decide to reject medical advice for a host of reasons that make sense in the context of their lives but seem irrational to physicians and judges. The chapter also analyzes the tendency of state legislation governing patients' rights to disempower women and substitute the state's value judgments for women's decisions. These policies *KC ?* and practices undermine women's standing as equal citizens, putting their bodies to use for others in ways unparalleled in American society.

Chapter 6 explores the ways that government institutions have sought to regulate pregnant women's consumption of drugs and alcohol. It focuses primarily on two types of institutions—the criminal justice system and state legislatures—but notes also the role of civil courts in deciding whether women can keep their children. Between 1973 and 1992, thirty-three states and the District of Columbia passed legislation of some kind in this area. None of these states has passed a law creating "special or additional penalties for becoming pregnant while addicted to drugs" or alcohol, and yet more than 150 women in 28 states have been prosecuted for the crime of "fetal abuse" (Paltrow 1992, i). The power to create new crimes rests with legislatures, not with courts.

These prosecutions function on two important levels. Many scholars see the prosecutions as examples of the state's power to wield moral images of good and evil (see, for example, Daniels 1993 and Maher 1992). Criminal trials in the United States often serve as a kind of public theater or modern-day morality play, and so it is right to point out this symbolic function. In this sense, we can compare the prosecutions of women to the reinstatement of chain gangs. Brent Staples argues that the new chain gangs in the South feed "the American appetite for spectacles of punishment and humiliation" and serve no purpose other than political profit (1995, 62). Similarly, the charges brought against pregnant women give the American public a focal point for anger and resentment about social problems, and they often help to boost prosecutors' careers.

Nevertheless, we should not underestimate the significant material impact that prosecutions have on women's well-being and on the rule of law. The prosecution of women for their conduct during pregnancy has real effects—in addition to the trauma of being drawn into the criminal justice system for something that is nowhere in law defined as a crime, the fear of prosecution can scare other women away from medical care.

This book has two principal aims. First, it seeks to improve upon existing research by providing a broader and more thorough empirical base to examine the way that institutions have allocated the burdens of fetal health and to examine the consequences of fetal rights policies and practices on women. To this end, I present the first comprehensive nationwide picture of policy outcomes in key fetal rights contests. Just as scholars have shown that medical and popular visual imagery erases pregnant women, this work demonstrates the same process in law. The policies enacted by states around the country have made women disappear. These struggles play out at many levels—in federal and state courts, in corporate medical offices and individual factories, in statehouses, and in local hospitals and district attorneys' offices. An impressive array of political and social institutions has been shaping the direction of fetal rights politics and the outer limits of women's freedom.

The book's second goal is to provide a way to understand this complicated picture. The dynamic of rights and costs provides a framework that unifies the distinct arenas of fetal rights politics, while also making clear the different patterns that predominate in each and the differential costs that various groups of women are made to bear in each.

My overarching goal throughout this book is to shift the debate away from dead-end arguments about whether a fetus is a person, to arguments about the real impact of current practices on women and the children they may have. Even if we knew definitively when life begins or whether a fetus is a person, the answers still wouldn't solve the problems I describe in this book. Only by thoroughly informing ourselves about the consequences of the current regimes can we properly evaluate them and go about the task of reconstruction. Only then can we rethink the relationship between reproduction and equality.

2

Backlash and Continuity
The Political Trajectory of Fetal Rights

C onflicts over fetal rights can only be understood in terms of the struggles over women's reproductive autonomy in the United States. Placing these conflicts in historical and comparative context dispels the notion that they are driven by changes in technology. They are fundamentally political.

In 1973 the *Roe v. Wade* decision legalizing abortion created new conditions for women's autonomy, provided a legal framework for thinking about fetuses, and realigned abortion politics by satisfying many people working for abortion reform while galvanizing the fetal rights movement in opposition. Yet the fetal rights politics of the *Roe v. Wade* era did not emerge out of a vacuum. Rather, this activity is part of a long tradition of reproductive politics in the United States, a tradition of subordinating women by controlling their reproduction. As this chapter shows, the politics of fetal rights is best understood in terms of historical continuity as well as backlash.

The creation and promotion of fetal rights in situations besides abortion has led to a highly demanding set of expectations about how women ought to behave during pregnancy for the sake of their fetuses. Disseminated through popular media, advice books directed at women, and legal scholarship, these expectations politicize pregnancy itself. In other words, it is not just the decision whether to continue a pregnancy but the entire period of pregnancy that has come under political scrutiny.

The Abortion Connection

Legislative Impact)

Roe v. Wade was a tremendous victory for women: The nation's highest court legalized abortion across the country, granting women the authority to decide whether to carry a pregnancy to term. In many parts of the United States women had access to hospital abortions before World War II. After the war hospital abortions fell sharply as the medical establishment narrowed the health indications for abortion and state laws continued to permit abortion only to save women's lives. Many women who were able to obtain abortions had to agree to a "package deal" of simultaneous sterilization (Solinger 1993). Other women lived in communities where skilled illegal abortionists ran thriving practices, operating under a tacit agreement with law enforcement: no death, no intervention. But their availability, too, dropped after the war (Solinger 1994). The Supreme Court's decision in 1973 thus gave women a new power over their reproductive lives, one that ended the need to resort to dangerous back-alley abortions and also the humiliation of trying to secure permission for an abortion from all-male hospital committees in those states that had liberalized their abortion laws (Kaplan 1995).

According to Laurence Tribe, nineteen states changed their abortion laws between 1967 and 1973. Most of the reforms did little to improve women's access to legal abortion, however, because the states imposed so many restrictions and because illegal abortions often remained cheaper. In Colorado, for instance, a sponsor of the reform bill lamented how it was working in practice: "Nineteen of every twenty women seeking legal abortions are being turned away" (quoted in Tribe 1992, 43). The most fortunate women lived in or near states that repealed their criminal abortion laws outright, something only four states did: Alaska, Hawaii, New York, and Washington. (Washington repealed its law as a result of a popular referendum, not legislation.) Only the wealthiest women could afford to travel to Alaska and Hawaii, and Hawaii imposed a residency requirement to prevent becoming known as an "abortion mill" for mainland women (Tribe 1992, chap. 3).

Despite its benefits, the *Roe v. Wade* decision has always been problematic for political and jurisprudential reasons, for it set the very terms of its own unraveling. The opinion grounds women's constitutional right to abortion in terms of privacy. The right of individual women to choose abortion was deemed a private matter, one understood in terms of decision-making. Furthermore, Justice Harry Blackmun speaks throughout the opinion of a woman's right to choose "in consultation with her doctor." This phrase foreshadows the importance of medical authority in the courts' resolution of disputes over reproductive decision-making, the subject of Chapter 5. One line of feminist critique has always assailed the decision to regard abortion as a matter of privacy instead of as a matter of equality. A group called New Women Lawyers filed an amicus curiae brief supporting Jane Roe that defended abortion rights as a matter of sexual equality and full participation in society (cited in Copelon 1990). Legal scholars like Rhonda Copelon, Sylvia Law, Catharine MacKinnon, and Supreme Court Justice Ruth Bader Ginsburg all advocate equality over privacy. Equality claims provide a way to demand resources from the state that privacy claims do not. The idea of equality also more accurately captures what is at stake for women in being able to control their fertility (Copelon 1990; Ginsburg 1985; Law 1984; MacKinnon 1989). The logic of privacy—understood as the right to be left alone—made it possible for the Supreme Court to uphold a federal law to fund poor women's childbirth expenses through the Medicaid program but not to pay for their abortion expenses (*Harris v. McRae* 1980). The Court delineated women's right as the right to choose, not as an entitlement to the means to carry out their choice. As a result of this decision, by 1992, only thirteen states paid for Medicaid recipients' abortions (Sollom 1993).

MacKinnon in particular argues that privacy is inadequate on its own terms, because women don't have privacy in the sense the Court assumes; that is, women do not have control over what happens to them in the "private" realm, including sex (1989, 184–94). Rosalind Petchesky affords women more agency than MacKinnon but makes a related point. Petchesky argues that the critical abortion issue for feminists "is not so much the content of women's choices, or even the 'right to choose,' as it is the social and material conditions under which choices are made" (1984, 11). This insight is equally true of other forms of reproductive politics.[1]

Roe v. Wade established a three-part framework of "separate and distinct" competing interests and set up a particular formula for balancing those interests. During the first trimester of pregnancy, a woman's funda-

---

[1] In contrast, Dorothy Roberts wants to hold on to the value of privacy jurisprudence. She attempts to rehabilitate privacy as grounds to challenge the prosecutions of pregnant women who use drugs and to affirm Black women's right to procreate, drawing on the positive dimension of privacy that relates to personhood and forging an identity. But her arguments fall short of showing how to overcome the state's tendency to turn privacy to women's disadvantage (1991, 1462–81).

mental privacy right encompasses her decision to terminate a pregnancy without state interference. Women obtain at least 90 percent of abortions within the first three months (Petchesky 1987, 65). During the second trimester, the state may regulate abortion in ways reasonably related to its compelling interest in protecting women's health. The Court found that a woman's privacy right is not absolute, and so after viability, during the final trimester, the state may regulate and even prohibit abortion to further its compelling interest in "the potentiality of human life," except where abortion is necessary to preserve a woman's life or health.

The Court also ruled that a fetus is not a person within the meaning of the Fourteenth Amendment. This ruling is consistent with the Anglo-American legal tradition of treating a fetus as part of a pregnant woman, not as a separate entity with rights of its own. According to Dawn Johnsen, when courts first conferred rights on fetuses, their decisions were narrow exceptions to the general rule, predicated on the live birth of the subsequent child. That is, the rights accrued to the child upon birth, but could be used to make claims about something that happened prior to birth. In 1887, for instance, a Connecticut court deemed for the first time that a child had a right to inherit property left by someone who died after a fetus was conceived but before it was born. In 1946 a federal court first recognized a child's right to sue someone for injuries inflicted on him or her as a viable fetus. It was after 1973 that courts, and legislatures, too, increasingly began to recognize rights for "the fetus qua fetus" and not "only in those cases where it is necessary to protect the interests of the subsequently born child and his or her parents" (Johnsen 1986, 603–604).

In response to *Roe v. Wade*, the anti-abortion movement has sought to establish rights for fetuses in a vast array of contexts. Its fundamental goal is to abolish abortion, something it has sought by resisting the reform efforts of the 1960s and by pursuing a "human life amendment" to the Constitution, the appointment of federal judges who disagree with *Roe*, and policies at the state and federal level that interfere with abortion. Unable to achieve this bedrock goal, the movement has successfully limited women's access to abortion services while also shaping the cultural and political terrain for other fights over fetal rights. Some organizations, such as the Chicago-based Americans United for Life, lobby for both parental consent laws and homicide laws that endow fetuses with independent rights. Although these groups tend to support anything that would enhance the legal status of fetuses, some are concerned that criminalizing behavior during pregnancy will backfire by encouraging women to have abortions.

The year 1992 marked a turning point: As the Court diminished women's constitutional right to abortion, abortion became even more potent politically, driving electoral politics and contributing to Bill Clinton's presidential victory. In 1992 the Supreme Court reconsidered its decision in *Roe v. Wade* and replaced the trimester framework with an "undue burden" standard in *Planned Parenthood v. Casey*. *Casey*'s undue burden standard recasts the state's interests, holding that the state has a profound interest in protecting fetal life throughout pregnancy, not just at the point of viability. The state can therefore enact obstacles to abortion as long as they are not so substantial as to be unduly burdensome. Pennsylvania's mandatory twenty-four-hour waiting period after a state-scripted counseling session designed to discourage abortion passed this test. Although it still requires a significant interpretive leap to read these restrictions on women's ability to terminate a pregnancy as permitting restrictions on their conduct during pregnancy, *Casey* creates a new point of departure for analyzing fetal rights claims, one that is arguably more favorable to those claims.

The fetal rights movement galvanized by the *Roe* decision found its greatest allies in the Reagan and Bush administrations. Clinton's election in 1992 signaled a new era in reproductive politics at the executive level. One of the first things Clinton did as president was sign four executive orders reversing Reagan-Bush policies limiting access to abortion and another lifting the moratorium on fetal tissue research (Segers 1995, 231). He issued these orders as anti-choice protesters gathered for their annual march on Washington on January 22, the anniversary of *Roe v. Wade*. As I show, most fetal rights struggles take place at state and local levels, and those that occur at the federal level are likely to be fought out in the courts. Still, when Clinton made it clear that his administration would no longer be an ally to the right-to-life movement, he closed the door on an era when the highest level of government promoted fetal rights at women's expense.

The Historical Connection

People often describe fetal rights as a function of backlash. Fetal rights politics provide evidence of several kinds of backlash: against the changes wrought by second-wave feminism, the civil rights movement, and the War on Poverty and social spending. Certainly hostility toward feminism and toward people of color, welfare recipients, immigrants, and others in need of social services can be seen everywhere—in reverse discrimination suits brought by disgruntled white male employees and unsuccessful white applicants to undergraduate and professional schools; in California's successful voter initiatives to end affirmative action, bilingual education, and benefits to illegal immigrants; in Congress's repeal of the sixty-year-old Aid to Families with Dependent Children (AFDC) program; and numerous other political conflicts. These multiple attacks on social equality and on the welfare state help to fuel the fire of gender subordination that is at the heart of fetal rights politics.

I also want to emphasize that fetal rights politics is continuous with a long history of reproductive politics in the United States. Reproductive control of women has taken many forms. On plantations, slave owners and overseers wielded tremendous power over female slaves and their families by raping women and deciding whether to sell off their children (Davis 1983; Roberts 1991). In the nineteenth century, all states passed laws making abortion a crime (Petchesky 1984). Around the time criminalization was consolidated, campaigns against "vice" successfully restricted women's access to birth control devices and information that might have reduced the need for abortion (Gordon 1976; McCann 1994). The eugenics movement succeeded in institutionalizing and sterilizing masses of "unfit" persons, ranging from developmentally disabled individuals to sexually promiscuous women (May 1995; McCann 1994). The legacy of sterilization abuse continued throughout the twentieth century, shifting primarily to African American, Native American, and Puerto Rican women (Davis 1983; Lopez 1993; May 1995). In Puerto Rico, women have been the subjects of contraceptive experimentation as well as aggressive sterilization policies; more than one-third of all Puerto Rican women have been sterilized (Davis 1983; Lopez 1993). The stigma associated with out-of-wedlock births operated as an effective mandate for white women to relinquish their children in the years following World War II (Solinger 1992).

Ever since abortion was legalized in 1973, Congress and a majority of state legislatures have enacted barriers to access, including spousal consent, parental consent for minors, public funding cuts, and mandatory waiting periods. Courts have upheld many of these measures. The anti-abortion movement has become emboldened in the past decade, with groups such as Operation Rescue staging mass demonstrations outside health clinics to intimidate women seeking abortions. In the climate of accelerating violence, scores of clinics have been bombed, torched, or vandalized, and many people have been injured and even killed escorting women to clinics and working in them. Consequently, it is harder and harder for women in many parts of the country to find anyone willing to provide abortion services where they live (Fried 1997). Poor women dependent on government assistance have much higher rates of sterilization

[handwritten: current stat of __?__]

than other women (Petchesky 1984, 180). The federal government subsidizes sterilization costs for Medicaid recipients, but not abortion, constraining poor women's reproductive choices (see Petchesky 1984 and CARASA 1988 on the Hyde Amendment).

Women's rights advocates have been actively challenging the social relations of reproduction since at least the 1840s, when white, middle-class women first called for "voluntary motherhood" (Gordon 1982). The demand for voluntary motherhood was part of a larger movement for women's rights that valued motherhood but recognized that women would not be able to exercise their hard-won political rights if they were incessantly burdened by pregnancy and childrearing. The voluntary motherhood movement promoted women's right to decide when to become pregnant, giving women the right to refuse their husbands' sexual advances (Gordon 1982). Early twentieth-century feminists continued the demand for motherhood on women's terms but added a positive sexual dimension. Where their Victorian counterparts had advocated abstinence and refuge from predatory male lust, these activists, including Crystal Eastman, Emma Goldman, and the young Margaret Sanger, demanded birth control, claiming for women a lust of their own (Eastman 1918, 1920).

A contemporary illustration of reproductive politics is the way Norplant, the first major new contraceptive device to hit the U.S. market in more than twenty years, quickly played into class, race, and gender politics. Norplant is a 99-percent-effective hormonal contraceptive that lasts five years when surgically implanted under a woman's skin. Approved by the U.S. Food and Drug Administration in December 1990, Norplant immediately became a proposed means of legal and economic coercion. Within the first month of its availability, an editorial in the *Philadelphia Inquirer* called for implanting all welfare mothers with the device, and a judge in California made Norplant a condition of probation for a woman who pled guilty to child abuse. Legislatures quickly entertained measures to give AFDC recipients cash bonuses for using Norplant or to make it a condition of receiving benefits; some considered establishing mandatory Norplant as a condition of probation for women convicted of child abuse or drug possession (Mertus and Heller 1992, 362–67). These proposals raise serious constitutional concerns, including equal protection, because men are nowhere subjected to similar treatment and because Black women rely disproportionately on welfare for support. The health implications of coercing Norplant use are especially troubling for African American women, who are more likely to have high blood pressure, diabetes, and heart disease, all of which contraindicate Norplant (Mullings 1984; Mertus and Heller 1992, 360). Finally, in 1993, the Michigan legislature earmarked

$500,000 to distribute Norplant in family-planning clinics. The program's champion, Senator Vern Ehlers, described it as "totally voluntary" but added that the program targets prostitutes, drug addicts, and teenage mothers. Ehlers explained that the Norplant program was "developed strictly on the standpoint of rights—every child has a right to be born normally" (*State Legislatures* 1993). Rather than facilitating women's right to control their fertility, Ehlers sees the Norplant funding as safeguarding fetal rights.

Many of today's biggest political battles are ultimately battles over reproduction—conservative welfare reform and even crime prevention strategies seek to control the conditions under which women reproduce and advocate the patriarchal, heterosexual, two-parent household as the answer to poverty, violence, and social change. Charles Murray maintains that "illegitimacy is the single most important problem of our time—more important than crime, drugs, poverty, illiteracy, welfare or homelessness— because it drives everything else. Reversing the current trend should be at the top of the American policy agenda" (Murray 1993; see also Murray 1984). Writers who identify themselves to the left of Murray on the ideological spectrum also see "restoration" of the nuclear family as an essential social policy (Kaus 1992; Wilson 1987).

As Adolph Reed points out, no matter how chroniclers of the "underclass" define that term, most of the core characteristics are associated with women—teenage childbearing, out-of-wedlock births, single motherhood, and welfare dependence (1990). Although poor women have borne the brunt of this line of argument, the reproductive and family decisions of other women have also come under attack. Recall how former Vice President Dan Quayle condemned the television character Murphy Brown for "glamorizing" single motherhood and blamed single motherhood for the Los Angeles riots following the verdict in the Rodney King beating trial (Quayle 1992). Political theory professor and Clinton advisor William Galston promotes his case for the two-parent family in op-eds and policy journals; his ideas include making it harder to get divorced (for instance, Galston 1995).

Globally, reproductive rights has also emerged as a central issue in human rights campaigns. Feminists organized to put reproductive rights on the agenda at such events as the 1992 Earth Summit in Rio de Janeiro, the 1994 International Conference on Population and Development in Cairo, and the 1995 World Conference on Women in Beijing. They successfully organized to include "forced pregnancy" by rape as a crime against humanity in the 1998 treaty to create a permanent international criminal court (CRLP 1998). And feminists around the world have widely debated the extent to which new reproductive technologies such as in vitro fertilization serve to control women and reinforce traditional roles (for instance, Stanworth 1987 and Corea 1985).

What all these examples underscore is that reproduction has always been a site of political conflict. Reproductive arrangements are social rather than natural, given, or inevitable. Women may be biologically destined to conceive and gestate fetuses, but it is human power relations that shape their ability to decide whether and when to bear children and constrain them to take on the primary responsibility for child-rearing after they give birth. Many studies have demonstrated how fights to restrict legal abortion are really fights about changing gender roles and women's dual commitments to family and work, as more and more women enter the paid labor force (see Ginsburg 1989; Luker 1984; and Tribe 1990).

Current struggles over fetal rights fit into this political history. Ultimately, it should be clear that the debate about fetal rights is not so much about fetal personhood as it is about women's personhood. Notice the dehumanizing language that fetal rights advocates commonly use to describe pregnant women: Women are called "maternal hosts" and even the "fetal environment" (Raines 1984; Blank 1993). Pregnant women's drug use is referred to as "gestational substance abuse," an expression that reduces women to incubators (Flannery 1992; Lowry 1992). These advocates also describe pregnant women's bodies as inanimate objects: The title of a scholarly article calls the "maternal abdominal wall" a "fortress" against fetal health care (Phelan 1991). In his role as "lawyer for the fetus," the public guardian in Chicago asked the court to order a pregnant woman to submit to a cesarean against her will. He argued in court that the judges had to decide whether the fetus is "a real life form being kept prisoner in a mother's womb" (quoted in Terry 1993, A22). This language makes two things clear: that pregnant women are not considered full-fledged human beings, but merely better or worse vessels for fetuses, and that the pregnant woman's body, once thought of as a nurturing sanctuary, is now often seen as a form of solitary confinement for the fetus.

Politicizing Pregnancy

The experience of pregnancy today, at least among middle- and higher-income women, is governed by doctors' appointments, expert advice books, and classes, as well as cultural norms about the ever-narrowing bounds of appropriate behavior that affect all pregnant women. Pregnant women are told what to eat, how to exercise, when to stay in bed, and whether to work or have sex. Lisa Ikemoto calls this "the code of perfect pregnancy" (1992b).

Helena Michie and Naomi Cahn argue that middle-class women internalize the code by consuming advice books that teach them to police their own conduct, while the state polices poor women, disciplining them and sending a symbolic message to all others. They deftly reveal the way the best-selling "yuppie bible" *What to Expect When You're Expecting* constructs an autonomous fetus who monitors and ultimately effaces the pregnant reader, ironically producing a "homeless fetus, a baby without walls," even as it is deeply invested in domesticity (Michie and Cahn 1997, 31).[2]

In addition to advice books, actual advisors are acting on the code. Two mental health experts were given a hypothetical case about a "large, close-knit group of siblings whose father just died" and asked whether they should tell their youngest sister, eight months pregnant and three thousand miles away, about the funeral, or wait until after she gives birth. A psychology professor favored waiting, insisting, "Your sister's baby has a right to be born as healthy as possible, and this takes precedence over all other considerations." Listen to how Dr. Peters elaborates his answer: "None of us would condone a pregnant woman taking drugs that would have an adverse impact on this unborn child's life, and none of us ought to overlook this unborn child's right to be born free from preventable stress-related complications" (quoted in Hall 1998, 7). The psychologist clearly considers the fetus his patient, and gives its "rights" precedence over the woman's emotional well-being and any rights she may have to be informed and included.

Moving beyond exhortation to enforcement, a Boston-area health club owner canceled a woman's membership when she became pregnant. The member was a longtime bodybuilder and was consulting with her obstetrician about her training activities. The owner hinted at fears of liability should the bodybuilder injure herself, but she told a reporter that she didn't understand why a "mother" would want to burn calories or "overheat." Renee Solomon interprets these remarks as evidence of the owner's sense of entitlement to replace her client's motivations with her own sense of concern for the fetus (1991, 421). This sense of entitlement to make unilateral decisions for pregnant women politicizes disagreements over fetal health in a way that simply giving unsolicited advice does not.

Just as some feminist writers speak the language of fetal rights, so they have been influenced by the code of perfect pregnancy. This makes them

---

[2] As Michie and Cahn recognize, male partners can also play a policing role. In the realm of popular culture, the television show *Party of Five* anchored its fall 1998 story line around Daphne and Charlie's clashes over her conduct during pregnancy.

reluctant to stake a strong claim for women's reproductive autonomy when confronted with countervailing claims that fetal rights impose limits on pregnant women's potentially harmful behavior. For instance, Cynthia Daniels says employers who discriminate against women assume that they "will not place the interests of fetal health before their own economic interests" (1993, 86). Daniels thus assumes in turn that, if confronted with such a conflict of interest, women would always place "fetal interests" first. But what if they do not? What then? Does opposition to fetal rights depend on being sure that women will always do the "right" thing—that is, make the choice the author approves of? Daniels defends women against fetal rights advocates who argue that women "can no longer be counted upon to put the interests of the fetus first" (117). Implicitly, she suggests that, yes, women can be counted on to do this. But what exactly does this comment mean? Does it make historical sense to claim that women used to be trusted to "put the fetus first," or is this a distinctly late twentieth-century way of thinking?[3]

Consider also comments by Deirdre Condit, who argues forcefully that the creation of fetal personhood as a political identity depends on making pregnant women invisible. But then at the end of her article, Condit says, "Those fetal images will not be easily willed back into the bodies of pregnant women. *Nor should they,* because in fact fetuses do have value and material reality" (Condit 1995, 43–44; my emphasis). No one disputes that fetuses are real, but people do dispute what value to attribute to that material reality and who should make that determination. The question is why women shouldn't be the ultimate arbiters of their fetuses' value.

Feminist ambivalence is most apparent in writings about pregnant women who drink or use drugs. These women's conduct poses an agent/structure dilemma: How much personal responsibility do women bear for their situation, and how much is determined by factors outside their control? The way some feminist scholars deal with their ambivalence is to create a monolithic construct of "the pregnant addict" whose entire life story is one of structural victimization: Before she was victimized by drugs she was a victim of physical and sexual abuse by parents or partners, of poverty, of a culture that never cared about her as a child, and of a host of other ills.[4] Couple this with the idea that pregnancy is a "window of opportunity,"

[3] See similar statements on pp. 35, 69, and 146. This defense resonates with Daniels's emphasis on birth as women's ultimate power and borders on saying that social reproduction should be considered women's responsibility (and women's true calling). Her argument suggests that only when something goes wrong, such as becoming addicted to drugs, do women get sidetracked and does their essential nurturing nature get perverted into something else.

[4] For example, Daniels 1993, 129–31; compare with Knapp 1996, 46, on other paths to addiction. Daniels's construct also has a geographic dimension: "Most addicted women," she

a time of intense motivation for women to get clean, and you may come up with a politically palatable drug-addicted pregnant woman who can inspire compassion rather than punishment.

But the downside of this construct is that its adherents may lose as much as they stand to gain. Other feminists have criticized the return to maternal instinct embedded in this claim as dangerously essentialist and reactionary. Lisa Maher and Richard Curtis criticize what they call a dominant myth in the drugs literature that pregnancy is the ideal time for treatment intervention: "The 'natural' instincts of the woman toward her foetus are expected somehow miraculously to surface and to over-ride the psychosocial realities of women's lives" (1992, 237). This myth can lead researchers to downplay important findings. For instance, Wendy Chavkin and her colleagues surveyed pregnant women and mothers of preschoolers who use crack or cocaine. They found that women were motivated to embark on treatment because they were concerned about their pregnancy and future child. Although they make less of it, they also found that women enter treatment out of "concern for self" (Chavkin, Walker, and Paone 1992, 319–20). This finding is cause for optimism, and it is perhaps the more important one, given other findings that some women whose primary concern is for fetal development will stop using drugs during pregnancy but will start again after birth.[5]

It is certainly true that many, perhaps most, drug-addicted women are impoverished and have been abused. And surely part of the definition of addiction *is* losing control over at least some of one's actions and decisions—that is, experiencing a loss of agency. But the construct of "the pregnant addict" depends on women having little or no agency to begin with.

This construct ignores a middle ground between women's total agency,

---

states, "have little or no access to health care or prenatal care. As a result, poor inner cities experience extremely high rates of infant mortality" (129). By collapsing these two issues, Daniels constructs women's drug addiction and unmet health care needs as an essentially urban phenomenon, playing into the dominant imagery of drug addiction as an urban—that is, Black—problem. This construction of the problem erases the fact of suburban women's drug use and denies the very real difficulties that poor rural women have obtaining rehabilitation and medical treatment. Daniels deploys this construct despite arguing that in order to displace any prevailing policy approach, challengers must "demythologize" the constructs on which the policy rests.

[5] See, for instance, Marsha Rosenbaum's classic study *Women on Heroin* (1981). As for drinking, "pregnancy is a time of incredible motivation for women," according to Dr. Barbara More, director of Boston University's Fetal Alcohol Education program (quoted in Rosenthal 1990, 61). Claire Dineen also quotes social work experts who say that pregnancy is "the one time in a woman's life when drinking decreases spontaneously and substantially" (1994, 64).

which carries with it full responsibility for the consequences of their actions, and women's total victimization, which relieves women of any responsibility. There are reasonably independent women with average self-esteem who actively initiate recreational drug use but then succumb to addiction, as opposed to those who were driven by "hopelessness and despair" to "self-abuse" (Daniels 1993, 130). What concerns me is making public policy and the provision of needed services depend on the reasons why someone became addicted, and on judgments of that person's responsibility (guilt) or victimization (innocence). While it may not be politically or ethically possible for everyone to defend women's illegal or harmful actions, that should not temper the commitment to service provision, fair treatment, and due process for pregnant women.

Such willingness to abandon standards of due process is just what we see in fetal rights scholarship. Like many others, John Robertson argues that women have both legal and moral duties to protect the fetus. Because his scholarship has been so influential, it is worth considering in some detail. Robertson situates his argument for controlling pregnant women and for punishing those who do not comply within the context of a sweeping defense of procreative freedom. He does this by distinguishing between the right to procreate, which he supports, and women's "right to bodily integrity *in the course of* procreating," which he does not (Robertson 1983, 437; emphasis in original).

In his most famous declaration, Robertson claims that "once she decides to forgo abortion and the state chooses to protect the fetus, the woman loses the liberty to act in ways that would adversely affect the fetus" (437). Put somewhat differently, he says, "Although she is under no obligation to invite the fetus in or to allow it to remain, once she has done these things she assumes obligations to the fetus that limit her freedom over her body" (438).

The loss of freedom that pregnant women experience under Robertson's scheme is almost total. He argues that women can be compelled to take medication or submit to surgery on the fetus as well as to be force-fed in the case of anorexia, to be civilly committed to an institution in the case of mental illness, or to be subjected to any other intervention that poses "reasonable" risks to their health and safety (444–47). Decisions about where to give birth (home or hospital), how to give birth (vaginally or by cesarean), and whether to submit to electronic fetal monitoring, episiotomy, or other procedures should be subordinated to expert opinion about the "child's well-being" (453–58). Robertson also asserts that the state may validly prohibit women's use of alcohol, tobacco, and drugs, as well as their employment in potentially harmful workplaces (442–43).

Mincing no words, he declares that a pregnant woman "waived her right to resist bodily intrusions made for the sake of the fetus when she chose to continue the pregnancy" (445).

Robertson's efforts to establish women's legal duty to the fetus are tenuous and poorly substantiated. He misreads the state authority to intervene in pregnant women's lives under *Roe v. Wade* and misreads child abuse laws to apply to fetuses (439, 442, 445). He treats a pregnant woman's duties to her fetus the same as a parent's legally enforceable duties to a child who has been born. He extends tort principles holding third parties accountable for injuries to a fetus in utero to pregnant women themselves (438). And he argues that "this preference for fetal interests over maternal freedom during pregnancy is rooted in an enduring criminal law tradition" that punishes the injury or killing of a fetus, saying, "the fetus' mother is as much subject to liability under these doctrines as anyone else" (438). Robertson cites no case law from this centuries-old tradition (most of his arguments are speculative), but even if his description was accurate, two problems would remain. One is that the existence of such a tradition does not necessarily imply a commitment to fetal rights per se. The other is the presence of a competing legal tradition that does *not* recognize independent fetal interests or rights. Dawn Johnsen's research shows that American law has historically treated the fetus as part of the pregnant woman, not as a distinct entity with rights independent, and potentially hostile, to hers (1986). Florida made it clear in 1868, for instance, that the crime of fetal manslaughter could only be committed by a third party attacking a pregnant woman, not by a woman herself (Fla. Stat. Ann. § 782.09).

According to Robertson, if women choose not to exercise their constitutionally protected right to have an abortion, then they become liable for less than perfect outcomes of their pregnancies. The meaningfulness of women's "choices"—in the case of a poor woman, for instance, whose state Medicaid program does not pay for abortions—or the timing of women's decisions to carry to term is ultimately irrelevant, because women are held accountable for their actions from the moment of conception. Robertson retreats from his claim that a woman's "obligations to the fetus arise only after she has already exercised her procreative rights by choosing to bring the child into the world," arguing later that a woman who has not yet made up her mind "should have a duty to avoid the harmful activities in case she decides not to abort. Similarly, she should be penalized for failing to use a fetal therapy before viability, so that the infant will be healthy if she decides to go to term. If she does not want the therapy, her choice will be to abort or to risk the penalty" (442, 447n129).

Under this regime, women have no room for error or indecision. Robertson's attitude toward women is nothing short of callous and, if implemented as policy, would probably result in women feeling pressured to abort pregnancies they would rather bring to term, for fear of the consequences. Waxing philosophical, Robertson concludes that freedom "provides meaning only through the acceptance of constraint" (464). For some reason, this applies only to women.

Doctor-lawyer Margery Shaw agrees with Robertson but goes a step further to add a eugenic spin (1984). Fetuses don't just have a right to life, she argues; they also have a right to a certain quality of life, a right that imposes on women the responsibility to undergo genetic testing and to accept medication and surgery on behalf of the fetus. Shaw also suggests that pregnant women have an obligation to abort fetuses with abnormalities. If women refuse, and give birth to children suffering from preventable diseases or "defects," then they can be sued by their children for prenatal torts. Neither Shaw nor Robertson makes clear the purpose of these tort suits. If the parents are already financially responsible for the child, what good is served by suing them for money? The only likely beneficiaries would be the creators of a new insurance industry in parental malpractice coverage. Shaw's perspective on mandatory abortion clearly puts her at odds with other fetal rights proponents and with defenders of women's civil liberties and the rights of the disabled.

Sweeping Aside "the Iron Curtain" to Reveal "the Mystery of Life"[6]

Scholars have theorized that several political and social trends contributed to the emergence of fetal rights ideology and practice. The factors most commonly included are the abortion controversy and a perceived crisis in women's commitment to motherhood; the war on drugs, especially crack, and the depiction of drug addiction as a problem of racial minorities; advances in medical technology such as fetal surgery and neonatal intensive care; and especially the development of such imaging technologies as ultrasound and intrauterine photography (see, for example, Blank 1993; Daniels 1993; Condit 1995; and Gomez 1997).

No matter which factors they choose as especially significant, most analysts have overestimated technology as a force driving fetal rights politics,

[6] Dr. Ian Donald, Scottish ultrasound pioneer (1969), quoted in Oakley 1984, 182, and Alida Brill 1990, 77.

endowing technology with a causal power of its own. In his book on fetal protection policies, Robert Blank insists that we should not fall prey to the technological imperative common in U.S. thought, and yet he focuses on the important role of technology in his opening paragraphs, arguing that new biomedical "technologies force a reevaluation of maternal responsibility for fetal health" (1993, 3). Later in the book he repeatedly invokes changes in medical technology as causal factors—or the cause—of changes in judicial doctrine (see especially chap. 6). Nancy Rhoden's description of forced medical treatment is gender-neutral and apolitical: The "[forced cesarean] dilemma is generated by advances in medical technology," and "its resolution is a part of the broader question of how society should respond to medical technology" (1986, 1952).

Further illustrating this tendency, Jeffrey Phelan argues in *The Southern California Law Review* that "for centuries, the fetus existed in an isolated environment, somewhat like a recluse, essentially unnoticed from conception to birth. The law similarly gave little notice to the unborn child. . . . As a result of [such] advances in fetal care [as ultrasound], the fetus can no longer be characterized as a hermit" (Phelan 1991, 463–64). Surely the fetus did not go unnoticed by the pregnant woman who carried it. Nor did her family and community, at least once she began to show, fail to notice her pregnancy, regardless of the state of medical care or imaging technology in centuries past.

If we want to understand the conflicts erupting over fetal rights, I believe we would do better to focus more on the social relations of technology and less on the technology itself. Though technological capabilities are not altogether irrelevant, if the United States was not a place where struggles over gender equality and abortion in particular were so intense, longstanding, and seemingly intractable, then new medical technologies might not have been put to use in a campaign to achieve fetal rights. As Rosalind Petchesky argues, "The presumption of fetal 'autonomy' . . . is not an inevitable requirement of the technologies. Rather, the technologies take on the meanings and uses they do because of the cultural climate of fetal images and the politics of hostility toward pregnant women and abortion" (Petchesky 1987, 64).

Rickie Solinger investigates how in the 1950s and 1960s a particular segment of the medical and psychiatric community developed a notion of pregnant women and fetuses as separate (1993). Hospital committees charged with deciding whether to grant women's requests for abortions used a moral mechanism of separation, not a technological one. That is, psychiatrists were influenced by ideas about women's duty to fulfill their feminine destiny by bearing children, not by images of fetuses. William

Arney dates the separation even earlier. He argues that the medical profession actually "discovered" the fetus in the 1940s, noting that in 1941 *Williams Obstetrics* first used the term "fetal distress" instead of referring to conditions that originate in the pregnant woman herself (Arney 1982, 134). In both Arney's and Solinger's studies, focusing on the fetus helped the medical profession to shore up power at a time when women were trying to assert control over reproduction. Arney writes, "Obstetricians could leave their treatment of the mother-to-be out of the debate entirely, for now they had the fetus, which they could defend against all the bad consequences that they claimed might result" if they accommodated women's demands for a more natural childbirth experience (136). In neither study do doctors cast their new interest in the fetus in terms of protecting fetal rights.

Solinger calls Lennart Nilsson's 1965 *Life* magazine photos of fetuses against a starry background "the most perfect iconic expression" of the new way of seeing fetuses and pregnant women as distinct beings (1993, 255). Analyzing Nilsson's work has become a feminist cottage industry, but Karen Newman argues that such images significantly predate the 1960s. She identifies medical illustrations dating from the second century that feature a fetus (homunculus) in a simply drawn uterus unmoored from any female body. She traces these images to their culmination in seventeenth- and eighteenth-century illustrations, which feature an idealized, autonomous fetus that effaced pregnant women, to argue that these images "contributed to Enlightenment conceptions of individualism" (Newman 1996, 44).

Carol Stabile compares the text accompanying two Nilsson photo essays, from 1965 and 1990, and finds that pregnant women play a much larger role in the original 1965 story—represented both in the photos by the placenta and other evidence of the fact that fetuses grow in women's bodies and in the text's many references to what the "mother" is experiencing as the pregnancy progresses. The 1990 version excised visual references to the pregnant woman and emphasized fetal autonomy by describing the embryo's "separate" blood supply (Stabile 1992, 187). The changing narrative demonstrates that photographs don't speak for themselves, that they need to be interpreted to make sense to the viewer; technology alone does not tell a story. Both Stabile and Newman note the irony that all but one of Nilsson's original photos—used by clinic protesters and books for expectant parents alike—were of aborted or stillborn fetuses.

What's significant, then, is not simply the technology that shows a fetus or even the idea of a fetus separated from a pregnant woman. Rather, it is the way that these images and concepts are becoming embedded in law. As fetuses attain independent legal status, women are finding themselves not only erased as important social beings but also disenfranchised as people entitled to fair, equal treatment. New fetal rights claims get layered on top of older moral claims and increasing cultural demands, all in a context in which pregnancy is highly medicalized, enhancing professional and state authority over women.

A look abroad lends further support to the political primacy of fetal rights. Australia, Canada, and Great Britain have the same kinds of prenatal technology as the United States does. Indeed, the use of ultrasound in pregnancy was developed in Scotland in the 1950s and 1960s, and the first "test-tube" baby was born in England in 1978 (Oakley 1984, chap. 7). And yet while government officials in these countries take children away from mothers who use drugs, they do not prosecute women for crimes of "fetal abuse." Reports of forcing pregnant women to undergo medical procedures against their will are also fewer and farther between. Belinda Bennett explains in a 1991 article that there are no reported cases of "fetal abuse and neglect" in Australia, which was also a pioneer in reproductive technology research and development. Furthermore, the only two relevant British cases concern civil proceedings initiated after birth, not criminal ones, and in those cases the courts were extremely reluctant to become involved in regulating women's behavior during pregnancy (Bennett 1991). Similarly, Avril Taylor's study of Scotland describes how pregnant women and mothers who use heroin fear losing their children, but it never mentions the possibility of criminal actions (1993).

Susan Boyd describes criminal sanctions against women for conduct during pregnancy as uniquely American, contrasting the United States with the Netherlands, England, Scotland, and Canada. She reports that in Canada there have been several cases in which social service agencies have sought to take custody of a fetus, but an appellate court ruled in 1988 that only "live children" can become wards of the court (Boyd 1994, 187). The 1988 ruling was issued in the context of a doctor's unsuccessful request for permission to force a woman to undergo a cesarean (see Dawson 1990 on this case). It was only in 1992 that a British court imposed "for the first time a public duty on pregnant women," by authorizing a hospital to perform a cesarean on a woman over her objection in *Re S* (Hewson 1992, 1538). More recently, the Court of Appeals in Manitoba, Canada, has ruled that a pregnant woman cannot be forced into drug treatment and that a fetus does not have an independent legal identity, and a provincial court in Ontario reached the same conclusion on an attempted murder charge against a woman who shot herself while pregnant (*RFN* 1996c; *Lancet* 1997). As these examples show, something besides the simple availability of technology must account for the degree of fetal rights activity in the United States: the heightened intensity of reproductive politics.[7]

Anthropologist Lynn Morgan makes an argument that is more subtle, interesting, and, I think, accurate than the one about technology. Morgan argues that a child in the United States is now born twice, and that its social birth often precedes its physical birth. "As a result of reproductive imaging technologies, the commodification of babies, and other social changes," she explains, "the attribution of personhood (what I call 'social birth') can now precede biological birth" (1996, 59). "The result is a new, unprecedented category of fetal persons," gendered and named, their pictorial representations hanging "(in the form of ultrasound scans) on walls and refrigerators" (59).

And yet despite these insights, Morgan's development of this line of reasoning becomes problematic when she argues that the "rhetoric of birth as the moral dividing line between persons and non-persons is simply unconvincing in an era when ever greater social value is being attached to fetuses (especially wanted, viable, third-trimester fetuses). Furthermore," she continues, "arguments for the 'moral significance of birth' are doomed to be politically ineffective because they do not resonate with the experiences of women who desire and create fetal personhood through their avid consumption of infertility treatments, amniocentesis, ultrasound, and in-utero video services" (59–60).

There is a lot going on in these claims, including the collapsing of the categories "moral," "social," and "political." Most pregnant women probably do desire and create fetal personhood by imagining the person their fetus will become, whom it will resemble, and so on, whether or not they consume such services as genetic testing and ultrasound. Women's personal actions and attempts to make meaning, and broader social efforts to attach meaning to pregnancy and fetuses, are not the same as political decisions to award personhood to fetuses through legal status. These efforts can create pressure to recognize a fetus as an autonomous person, but they tell us little or nothing about whether we ought to.

What principles, then, should guide the body politic in determining how to regard pregnant women's fetuses? Many people have argued that new medical technology has made the fetus knowable, opening the

[7] It is interesting to note that, unlike American law, English statutory law treats infanticide as a lesser crime than homicide. Conviction under the Infanticide Act of 1938 tends to yield sentences of probation and counseling, rather than imprisonment (Mackay 1993; Wilczynski and Morris 1993). England's lenient treatment of women who kill their infants doesn't mean the country places a lower value on human life. British social policy choices, including health care for all, suggest just the opposite.

mysteries of women's wombs. But how we "know" the fetus through scientific images and information is still a matter of interpretation, mediated by politics and culture.[8] As Justice Blackmun noted in his opinion in *Roe v. Wade*, medicine, religion, and common law all give different answers. Pregnant women might offer yet more answers of their own. The political question—rather than the epistemological or ontological one—turns on what the state should do when confronted with the many meanings that fetuses hold for different constituents. In the rest of this book, I provide answers to this question.

[8] See generally Hartouni 1997; Morgan 1997 on fetuses' liminal status in Ecuador; and Mitchell and Georges 1997 on the different meanings of ultrasound examinations in Canada and Greece.

3

Fighting Fetal Protection Policies

Women and Corporate Risk Management I

When the first women were hired into production jobs at the American Cyanamid chemical plant in Willow Island, West Virginia, in 1974, the foreman protested that women's breasts would get caught in the equipment, and someone put up a message reading "Shoot a Woman, Save a Job." The women persevered, and productivity went up. Then four years later, the plant manager told the women that their work was dangerous for fetuses. If they were under age fifty they could not keep their jobs unless they proved they were incapable of becoming pregnant by getting surgically sterilized. This policy effectively forced the women to choose between their fertility and their financial livelihood. Those who stayed endured the taunts of male co-workers, who said they'd been "spayed" by the veterinarian, and later expressed regret. In a cruel twist of irony, the women who got tubal ligations were all laid off the following year anyway, when their department in the plant was closed.[1]

What happened to the women at American Cyanamid was not an isolated incident but one of the earliest and most insidious manifestations of fetal rights ideology. This chapter focuses on how corporations and courts used the notion of fetal rights to discriminate against pregnant and fertile

[1] See Faludi 1991, 443, 448. The events at American Cyanamid are discussed more fully later in this chapter, in the section entitled "The Occupational Safety and Health Model."

women workers, burdening women's pursuit of economic equality and diminishing their integrity as full human beings, without ensuring real protection of fetal health.

"Fetal protection" policies stand at the intersection of two important domains in women's lives: wage labor and reproduction. Control over both is central to women's autonomy, to freedom from dependence on men or the state for economic security. In the United States there has long been a socially ascribed tension between seeing women as economic actors and seeing them as mothers. This tension is evident in everything from turn-of-the-century limits on women's wage work to current debates about whether children in day care develop adequate attachment to their mothers (there is no corresponding debate about fathers) (Chira 1996). The idea that women are wives and mothers first and workers second persists today, as women's second-class position in the economy reflects.

Fetal politics in the workplace vividly demonstrates the ways that fetal rights translate into costs for women. When businesses exposing their employees to dangerous substances began to fear they might one day be sued if their female employees had children with birth defects, they responded by asserting that fetuses had a right to be protected from occupational hazards. Corporate managers did not translate that right into action to make the workplace safe for everybody, including a fetus. Rather, they passed the costs of ensuring fetal safety onto women, saying that a woman could not earn a living in a way that might expose her fetus to harm, should she ever actually be pregnant. It is not necessary to look for explicitly misogynist motives to account for these decisions, because corporate managers operate within a context of institutional sexism. The corporate climate, informed by the cultural climate at large, identifies women (and exclusively women) with reproduction. This identification makes it easy to assign women all reproductive responsibility.

The costs of fetal rights are literal and substantial: the higher wages, opportunities for advancement, health and retirement benefits, and union representation that the restricted jobs typically provide. For some women, the costs also included their fertility. In the name of protecting fetuses' rights, corporations have insisted that women give up even the possibility of bringing a child into the world. Other costs are less tangible. Women subjected to fetal protection policies have been deprived of the ability to make their own decisions about employment, risk, family, and priorities. This denial of normal freedoms diminishes women's identities as autonomous human beings negotiating a complex social world.

Throughout the 1980s, as awareness of fetal protection policies grew, the federal government took almost no role in the ensuing public debate.

Instead, both Congress and the Reagan-Bush executive agencies abdicated their responsibility to enforce equal employment opportunity and occupational safety and health laws.[2] By creating a policy vacuum and leaving the issue to the courts, the other branches of government were in effect complicit in burdening women with the costs of fetal rights. Not only did women bear the literal costs of seeking redress for discrimination, but they faced years of litigation with uncertain outcomes.

The politics of fetal rights burdens women with the responsibility to ensure fetal health but fails to provide the resources necessary to do this. Because the United States has no national health care program, most people depend on their work (or welfare) for access to health care. Women often seek out industrial jobs for the income and benefits they provide; when they are deprived of these jobs, they find it harder to support themselves and any family members for whom they are responsible. Moreover, when women who are actually pregnant find themselves fired out of purported concern for their fetus, they are extremely unlikely to be able to obtain health insurance on their own, because pregnancy is a "pre-existing" condition that most insurers will not pay for.[3]

It is ironic that corporate fetal protection policies equate all women workers with reproduction and family even as they undermine women's power to meet their family's needs. But the other material realities that the policies ignore are that women can control their fertility and that men play a role in reproduction. Most women do become pregnant at some point during their work lives, but they are not perpetually pregnant. Fetal protection policies place tremendous obstacles in women's path to financial independence on the assumption that women are in a constant state of pregnancy, instead of accommodating all workers during times of actual conception and pregnancy. Corporations should be held accountable when they endanger the health of their workforce, instead of being permitted to hide behind a facade of false benevolence toward future gener-

---

[2] See Samuels 1995 for a thorough discussion of the administrative paralysis of agencies such as the Equal Employment Opportunity Commission (EEOC) and the Occupational Safety and Health Administration and the lack of engagement on the part of other relevant agencies such as the Environmental Protection Agency. Samuels draws on a congressional investigation of the EEOC (House Ed. and Labor Comm. 1990). Laura Oren also details the failed interagency attempt to formulate anti-discrimination guidelines for the disposition of fetal protection cases at the end of the Carter administration when Eleanor Holmes Norton was in charge of the EEOC (Oren 1996, 356–62).

[3] Typically, health insurance plans deny new members maternity benefits for up to a year. Only six states (Massachusetts, Minnesota, New Jersey, New York, Vermont, and Virginia) require all policies to cover these expenses, which average $5,000 for a routine pregnancy and delivery (Brown 1994).

ations. Otherwise, reproductive potential comes to eclipse all other potential a woman may have.

In this chapter and the next, I challenge the legitimacy of fetal protection policies, reclaiming for women a space in the economy and rejecting the limited construction of women's lives these policies help to enforce. Work is important politically as well as economically; in Carole Pateman's words, paid employment has become "the key to citizenship" (1988, 237). After brief overviews of women's economic position in the United States and of the historical roots of judicially sanctioned gender protectionism in the workplace, I show that fetal protection policies are not complete anomalies. Rather, these discriminatory policies play a role in maintaining the sex-segregated labor market in the United States. Next, I review the ways in which women workers and unions have fought the implementation of fetal protection policies, including going to court to secure the right to a safe workplace.

As these strategies encountered obstacle after obstacle, sex discrimination emerged as the dominant paradigm to challenge fetal protection policies. Chapter 4 examines these cases, as well as state legislation directed at reproductive discrimination. The litigation of fetal protection policies shows how cultural assumptions about women, work, and reproduction have led courts to undermine women's legal guarantees of occupational safety and equal employment opportunity alike. Setting fetal protection policies in the context of practices toward pregnant employees in general exposes corporations' purported moral concern toward fetuses for what it is—concern for liability and the bottom line. Finally, considering policy alternatives to safeguard workers' health and promote the well-being of future generations, we will see that the range of possibilities for achieving this goal is far broader than proponents of "fetal protection" suggest.

Women in the U.S. Economy

Wage-earning women in the United States experience widespread discrimination, and discrimination against pregnant women is on the rise (Shellenbarger 1993). Despite the fact that the majority of women, including mothers of preschoolers, work for wages, women still occupy an inferior place in the workforce (Schlichtmann 1994, 347). Women tend to be concentrated in service jobs. When they hold factory jobs, they are most likely to work in a few industries, such as textiles, electronics, and food processing. Economic trends in place since the 1980s will only reinforce women's marginal status. The federal government predicts that fully half of all employed Americans will be contingent workers by the end of this century (Weinbaum 1997, 326). These trends fall most heavily on women, who are over-represented in temporary and part-time work.

Occupational segregation by sex and women's insecure labor position are linked to another important economic phenomenon: wage disparities between women and men. Women who work full time still earn considerably less than men do. Women have earned between fifty-seven and seventy-one cents to a man's dollar in the 1973–92 period, and the narrowing wage gap is attributed to declines in men's earnings (NCPE 1998). The service-sector jobs in which women are concentrated (and where job growth occurred in the 1980s) pay on average only 72 percent as much as manufacturing jobs, and they rarely provide health benefits, pension programs, or union membership (Amott 1993, 33; 1989 data). The lack of retirement benefits poses long-term economic problems for women, who account for a disproportionate number of the elderly poor. Only one in five women over age sixty-five received pension income in 1992 (Steckenrider 1996, 5). Rates of union membership fell throughout the 1970s and 1980s, so that by 1990 only 14 percent of working women were represented by a union, as compared with 22 percent of men (Amott 1993, 65). Purchasing power also fell: Minimum-wage workers saw theirs decline by nearly 40 percent during the 1980s, when fetal protection policies were in full swing (Amott 1993, 41). All of these conditions make traditional, blue-collar work extremely important to women as an avenue to economic independence. Fifteen to twenty million jobs involve exposure to toxins that have been targeted by fetal protection policies; hundreds of thousands of them were closed to women by 1990 (House Ed. and Labor Comm. 1990, 11).

These general statistics do not demonstrate whether any particular group of women is disproportionately affected by fetal protection policies. Many writers have pointed out how little concern employers have for people concentrated in hazardous, low-wage jobs such as hospital work; these workers are predominantly women and men of color. These analysts often move from this observation to the conclusion that fetal protection policies harm women of color more than white women, but there is no evidence of this specific claim.[4] White and Black women (at least) have been

[4] Both Blank 1993 and Daniels 1993 advance this claim. In an otherwise excellent article, Laura Schlichtmann oversimplifies her statistics to argue that blue-collar workers are disproportionately women of color, compressing the jobs of almost forty-five million workers into six categories (Schlichtmann 1994, 357). What we really need is a racial breakdown of the composition of the female and male workforce in specific occupations by industry. In

plaintiffs in lawsuits. In addition, the ideology advanced by corporations and courts does not include the racial bias that is seen in the prosecution of pregnant women who use drugs and the multiple cultural biases seen in the forced medical treatment of pregnant women (the subjects of Chapters 6 and 5, respectively).

What can be said with more confidence is that these policies have their greatest impact on working-class women and on any women transgressing gender boundaries into "men's" jobs. Regardless of the class position they were born into, many women have sought to make the transition from white- and pink-collar jobs to blue-collar work.[5] By limiting women's access to industrial employment, fetal protection policies effectively foreclose a major route to economic independence.

Women Workers and the Next Generation

Regulation of wage-earning women is not new and has often turned on women's capacity for reproduction and motherhood, ensnaring women in what Judith Baer has called "the chains of protection" (1978). States have variously prohibited women from working as lawyers and bartenders and from working at night. In 1873 Justice Joseph Bradley of the U.S. Supreme Court expounded that "the paramount destiny and mission of woman are to fulfill the noble and benign offices of wife and mother"; "the domestic sphere [is] that which properly belongs to the domain and functions of womanhood." Throughout the twentieth century the Court worried about women's "peculiar and natural functions" and the "moral and social problems" that women's unregulated presence in the market might unleash.[6]

Historically, "protective" discrimination has been justified for women's own good and because it benefits the next generation. In its 1905 decision *Lochner v. New York*, the U.S. Supreme Court struck down a maximum-hours law as unconstitutional interference with a worker's right to contract. Then three years later it upheld an Oregon law specifically prohibiting *women* from working more than ten hours per day, because their role as mothers allegedly rendered them weak, dependent, and inferior. The Court reasoned in *Muller v. Oregon* (1908):

---

other words, we need to know what occupations women fill in each industry, so that we do not inadvertently count all the women who work as secretaries, accountants, janitors, and so on in a given manufacturing sector. I am not aware of any such detailed data.

[5] For examples, see Faludi 1991, chap. 13; Moore 1990 on women coal miners; Neimann 1990 on women who work the rails; and Schroedel 1985 on women in the trades.

[6] See Goldstein 1988 for excerpts of *Bradwell v. Illinois* (1873), *Radice v. New York* (1924), and *Goesaert v. Cleary* (1948).

That woman's physical structure and the performance of maternal functions place her at a disadvantage in the struggle for subsistence is obvious. This is especially true when the burdens of motherhood are upon
her. . . . [A]s healthy mothers are essential to vigorous offspring, the physical well-being of woman becomes an object of public interest and care in
order to preserve the strength and vigor of the race.

[T]here is that in her disposition and habits of life which will operate
against a full assertion of [her] rights. . . . [S]he is so constituted that . . .
her physical structure and a proper discharge of her maternal functions—having in view not merely her own health, but the well-being of
the race—justify legislation to protect her. . . . The limitations which this
statute places upon her contractual powers . . . are not imposed solely for
her benefit, but also largely for the benefit of all. (416–17, 421, 422)

Interestingly, the ideology of protection did not always hold when it came
to other kinds of employment regulation, like minimum wages. The Supreme Court ruled in *Adkins v. Children's Hospital* (1923) that the District
of Columbia's establishment of a minimum wage for women unduly inter-
fered with their freedom of contract. The Court claimed that the matter
of wages could be distinguished from the matter of hours, which were legitimately concerned with women's unique physical limitations. In addition, the Court specifically argued that the Nineteenth Amendment,
granting women the vote, forbade singling women out for such special
protection. Chief Justice William Howard Taft dissented, criticizing the
Court's reliance on the myth of free contract. Taft wrote that legislatures
adopting minimum wages "proceed on the assumption that employees in
the class receiving least pay *are not upon a full level of equality of choice* with
their employer," and therefore need government protection from ex-
ploitation (562; my emphasis).

Whatever interest the Court had previously displayed in the well-being
of women workers' children seems to disappear here, for surely the
amount of money a woman could earn would have an impact on the
"strength and vigor" of her children, and hence "the race." Although
the Court did not use the language of fetal rights, its reasoning is familiar
today: Society protects "children" while they are in the womb. Once they
are born and therefore actually *become* children, their "rights" cease to exist and instead become the mother's exclusive responsibility. The thinking
in these early decisions resonates with explicit and implicit assumptions
in contemporary fetal rights cases.

It was not until later in the century that women gained any promise
of legal protection from policies that discriminated against them on the

basis of sex, and later still before the ban on sex discrimination guaranteed protection from pregnancy discrimination. During the 1960s, Congress passed comprehensive civil rights legislation aimed at guaranteeing voting rights, integrating public schools, and removing barriers to employment. Title VII of the 1964 Civil Rights Act prohibits discrimination in employment on the basis of race, color, religion, sex, or national origin. It makes it illegal to discriminate in hiring, firing, compensation, and other terms of employment, as well as to "limit, segregate, or classify" employees "in any way which would deprive or tend to deprive any individual of employment opportunities" (42 U.S.C.A. 2000e-2[a][2]). Title VII has been an important tool to dismantle structures of discrimination against women workers.

Martha Gilbert and other female employees of General Electric used Title VII to launch a class-action sex discrimination suit against the company's disability benefits policy, which did not cover routine pregnancy care. Gilbert argued that the exclusion of pregnancy from coverage discriminated against her and other women workers because of sex. The lower court ruled for Gilbert, but the Supreme Court did not. Quoting from an earlier decision, the Court asserted that, "while it is true that only women can become pregnant, it does not follow that every legislative classification concerning pregnancy is a sex-based classification" (*General Electric v. Gilbert* 1976, 407). Rather, it found that "an exclusion of pregnancy from a disability benefits plan providing general coverage is not a gender-based discrimination at all," because "for all that appears, pregnancy-related disabilities constitute an *additional* risk, unique to women" (408, 410; emphasis in original). This logic exposes the androcentric bias in law: Women are being measured against a male standard, and any way that women deviate from men is considered extraordinary, or at the very least "extra."[7] Biased benefits packages such as GE's reflect the lingering assumption that men are primary breadwinners and women merely supplemental workers.

After the *Gilbert* decision, a coalition of feminist and labor groups lobbied Congress to make it clear that treating women workers differently on the basis of pregnancy *does* mean treating them differently on the basis of sex. The coalition succeeded, and in 1978 Congress added the Pregnancy Discrimination Act (PDA) to Title VII. As the House Report on the PDA

---

[7] The earlier case was *Geduldig v. Aiello* (1974), in which women employed by the state of California posed an unsuccessful challenge to a similar benefits policy under the Fourteenth Amendment. For discussions of the male standard in law, see MacKinnon 1987 and Kenney 1992, chap. 2.

explained, "Until a woman passes the child-bearing age, she is viewed by employers as potentially pregnant. Therefore, the elimination of discrimination based on pregnancy . . . will go a long way toward providing equal employment opportunities for women, the goal of Title VII" (quoted in *Grant v. General Motors Corporation* 1990, 1307). Specifically, the PDA prohibits discrimination against workers on the basis of "pregnancy, childbirth, or related medical conditions," and requires that pregnant or potentially pregnant workers similar to other employees in their "ability or inability to work" must be "treated the same" for all employment-related purposes (42 U.S.C.A. 2000e[k]). Discrimination on this basis is supposed to be upheld only under very restricted circumstances.

Reinforcing Women's Economic Marginality: Fetal Protection Policies

Tammy Nedzweckas quit her job as a restaurant cook in 1995 and began working at a Ford Motor Company plant in Wayne, Michigan, installing air-conditioning valve caps on Broncos and pickup trucks. Her income went from $10,000 a year to $31,000, including five months of paid leave when she gave birth to her second child. Nedzweckas estimates she walks twenty-one miles each night (she drives each truck around the corner after installing the cap and walks back to do the next one). Despite the physical demands of her night-shift assembly job, she is excited about the change in her standard of living: "I can afford to have my own house—I can afford to have a reliable car" (quoted in Meredith 1996, F3). In contrast, Pat Grant was derailed from this kind of upward mobility when she found herself a casualty of a fetal protection policy barring women's exposure to lead. Grant was involuntarily transferred from her position as an iron pourer at General Motors' foundry in Defiance, Ohio, at a loss of nearly $8,000 per year; she was also denied the opportunity to become a licensed hot metal crane operator, at a projected loss of up to $32,000 per year (see *Grant v. G.M. Corp.* 1989, 1264).

Modern fetal protection policies have been in force since at least 1972, when the battery plants of General Motors' Delco Remy division stopped employing women (Stellman and Henifin 1982, 119). Fetal protection policies have restricted women from jobs working with an array of common industrial substances, such as vinyl chloride, benzene, cadmium, toluene, carbon disulfide, and lead.[8] There is no comprehensive data on

---

[8] These compounds are associated with high blood pressure, strokes, organ damage, cancer, and heart disease in adults and with impaired development of the brain and central nervous system in fetuses. There is no known safe exposure level for vinyl chloride, a car-

how many employers have such policies. In 1985 the Office of Technology Assessment (OTA) estimated that at least 15 percent of Fortune 500 companies had implemented some kind of fetal protection policy (OTA 1985). In 1987 a survey of chemical and electronics manufacturers in Massachusetts found that nearly 20 percent of companies using substances considered hazardous to reproduction restricted women's employment in some way. All these companies restricted pregnant women, and others restricted all women or those trying to conceive. The restrictions were enforced according to substance (for example, lead), work area (for example, labs), or work activity (for example, soldering) (Paul, Daniels, and Rosofsky 1989, 272–73). In only one case did a company restrict male employees (272). In 1991 OTA undertook a survey of medical monitoring and screening practices at 1,500 companies and the 50 largest utilities. The survey did not specifically address fetal protection policies, but it found that 8 percent of companies reporting that medical criteria could affect employment eligibility listed pregnancy as a condition excluding employment (OTA 1991, 12–13). Respondents also indicated that in 53 percent of cases, the corporate personnel office rather than the health office decided which tests to include in pre-employment screening (5).

Heavy industries such as automotive, chemical, steel, and rubber manufacturers are especially likely to have implemented fetal protection policies (Petchesky 1979, 238). The following companies have all excluded women in some way: Allied Chemicals, American Cyanamid, ASARCO, B. F. Goodrich, Bunker Hill Smelting, Delco-Remy, Dow, DuPont, Eastman Kodak, Firestone Tire and Rubber, General Motors, Gulf Oil, Johnson Controls, Monsanto, Olin, St. Joe's Minerals, Sun Oil, and Union Carbide (OTA 1985).

Production jobs in these industries have long been male strongholds. Women who gained access to these jobs in the 1970s, often because of gov-

---

cinogenic gas used in the plastics industry, or cadmium, a poisonous heavy metal used as a substitute for zinc to prevent iron from corroding, and in control rods and shielding for nuclear reactors (Scott 1984, 184). Lead is perhaps the best-understood workplace toxin and one that figures prominently in corporate policies that exclude fertile women from jobs. Lead is a component in batteries, pigments, and insecticides, as well as steel production. Lead can adversely affect neurological development in fetuses or young children and increase the risk of strokes and heart attacks in adults. Major sources of lead poisoning in children include lead paint in older housing, as well as lead pollution in tap water from plumbing and in the soil from gasoline (Holloway 1990, 228). Among rural and urban children alike, poverty, old housing, and poor nutrition are all associated with lead poisoning (*Science News* 1994). The damage caused by lead has been called the most serious pediatric problem for African American children (Herbert Needleman, quoted in *Essence* 1991, 80). The widespread nature of lead-related harm in daily environments suggests that fetal protection policies are an inadequate remedy at best.

ernment pressure to hire them, could easily be replaced with male workers. Federal investigators targeted the American Cyanamid plant at Willow
Island, West Virginia, which employed no women in production work until 1974. By 1978, when the plant had about twenty-five women in production jobs, it implemented a fetal protection policy (Bertin 1989, 277;
Faludi 1991, 441). Bunker Hill hired its first women production workers
under pressure from the Equal Employment Opportunity Commission
(EEOC) in 1972 and adopted a policy to exclude them in 1976 (Stellman
and Henifin 1982, 123). Up through the late 1960s, the Olin Corporation
had official job descriptions reserving many craft maintenance jobs for
men. Its practice during the 1970s was to fill certain job categories exclusively with women (*Wright v. Olin Corporation* 1982, 1181).

Many women entering traditionally male jobs encounter resistance and
hostility from male co-workers and supervisors, ranging from questions
about why they are "taking away a man's job" to sexual harassment and
physical assault. Resistance is not always confined to the workplace: One
Kentucky coal miner found herself the subject of a church sermon about
the sins of women "stepping out of their place" (Moore 1990, 209). At the
same time that discriminatory policies were being implemented during
the 1970s, so were major cuts in public funding of abortion services for
low-income women. Rosalind Petchesky argues that these dual conditions
put pressure on women to depend on men or on sterilization for their
livelihood (1979, 237). This was precisely the case for Betty Riggs. Her job
at American Cyanamid paid six times more than her previous job at a
market, allowing her to leave a violent husband and still support her son
and her two parents (Faludi 1991, 441–44). Women's need for these jobs
made them stay on, despite the significant costs.

Lower-paid jobs held primarily by women, in contrast, are not regulated
with fetal protection policies. Both nursing and elementary school teaching, almost exclusively female occupations, are quite hazardous, exposing
workers to chemicals and infections known to cause reproductive damage
on a daily basis, and yet no one suggests that women should leave these
jobs (Coleman and Dickinson 1984; Scott 1984, 182). Operating room
nurses are exposed to anesthetic gases that may triple their rates of miscarriage and birth defects (Coleman and Dickinson 1984, 46). Women
who work in day care centers with children under the age of two face a
fivefold risk of contracting cytomegalovirus, which can cause severe mental retardation in a developing fetus (Adler 1989). Since child care is the
epitome of "women's work"—low-paying, low-prestige, and emotionally
demanding—no one proposes closing this job to women.

Perhaps the most incriminating example of the fetal protection double standard is that fertile women have been banned from jobs manufacturing pesticides but not from farm work that exposes them to the same chemicals, even though these products have been associated with birth defects. Clearly the production jobs are more economically desirable and less dangerous than the agricultural ones (Jasso and Mazzora 1984). In this case racism and nativism may also play a role, as many farm laborers are people of color and undocumented workers. The case of DBCP further exposes the double standard when it comes to "fetal protection." The families of men working with the pesticide DBCP at a chemical plant experienced low birth rates, and fourteen of twenty-five men tested were found to be sterile or have extremely low sperm counts (Bertin 1989, 280). The Environmental Protection Agency (EPA) banned most uses of this pesticide as a hazard to men's reproductive health rather than force men to choose between their jobs and their fertility (OTA 1985, 75–76).

Because of the cultural predisposition to view reproduction as a female matter, the vast majority of reproductive health research has been conducted on women. According to the Office of Technology Assessment, "Most suspected hazards have not been thoroughly researched for their reproductive effects in both males and females," and what research has been done "generally fails to confirm or disconfirm a need for differential exposure standards for men and women" (OTA 1985, 26). People tend to believe that fetuses are more susceptible to certain toxins than adults because they are developing so rapidly, but there is no consensus among scientists about whether or to what extent this is true.[9] Based on the available evidence, the Occupational Safety and Health Administration (OSHA) set one acceptable level for exposure to lead for both sexes (*Federal Register* 1978). Currently some 250,000 babies are born with birth defects each year in the United States, and the cause of 60 to 80 percent of them is unknown (Blakeslee 1991). Epidemiological research indicates that exposure to a wide range of occupational and environmental substances including lead, nuclear radiation, herbicides and pesticides, paints, solvents, and anesthesia may damage men's sperm. Sperm damage in turn may lead to male workers' sterility; their partners' miscarriages; or leukemia, kidney tumors, heart abnormalities, mental retardation, and learning disabilities in their children.[10]

[9] For instance, one appellate judge cites expert affidavits testifying that lead is not more risky to fetuses than it is to adults (*UAW v. Johnson Controls, Inc.* 1989, 915).

[10] See Blakeslee 1991; Davis 1991; Purvis 1990; and Wright 1979. Wright's essay indicates that at least some evidence on reproductive damage to men dates back as far as 1860.

Corporations have been selective in their concerns about whose health to "protect" as well as in their review of the empirical evidence. Just as they ignored risks to men, they drafted policies out of fear of liability for women's children, even though as of 1984, a decade into the fetal protection era, the OTA found "no records of any lawsuits brought by the children of exposed women workers" (OTA Summary 1985, 27). According to Mary Becker, the conflict employers face between upholding Title VII and avoiding tort liability "is entirely theoretical" (1994, 89). Ten years after the OTA study, there were still no known cases "in which substances or activities regarded as fetal hazards . . . have led to employer liability as a result of maternal or paternal exposure," largely because of difficulties in proving that occupational exposure caused a birth defect (Becker 1994, 89).[11]

As the cases discussed later show, courts have often gone along with corporations' sex-biased reasoning. They have upheld restrictions on women's employment on the basis of skewed information, while dismissing evidence on men as inconclusive and inadequate.

Fighting Fetal Protection Policies

Workers subjected to fetal protection policies have challenged them through arbitration, complaints with state commissions, collective bargaining, government lobbying, and litigation in state and federal courts. Unions have engaged in a number of these strategies on behalf of the workers they represent. In one of the earliest union efforts, the United Auto Workers (UAW) went to arbitration against General Motors' policy excluding fertile women from lead-exposed jobs in their plants. The union lost in Ohio in 1978, because the arbitrator was not able to assess the risk to potential fathers and said "it would be unrealistic to deal with women on an individual basis with respect to their childbearing intentions" (quoted in Scott 1984, 185; see also Kenney 1992, 245–50). After the union lost its arbitration in Ontario, Canada, the next year over the same policy, other unions may have been discouraged from using this traditional means to resolve grievances.

---

[11] See also House Ed. and Labor Comm. 1990, 10n28. *Security National Bank v. Chloride* (1985) concerned a girl who allegedly suffered injuries as a result of her mother's employment. She lost in a jury trial. The difficulty that exposed workers have in proving causation when their children are disabled suggests the need for other avenues for redress and assistance besides tort suits. The section on "Policy Alternatives" at the end of Chapter 4 reviews some possibilities.

Workers have not fared much better by appealing to state commissions. In 1975 and 1976 the Bunker Hill Company in Kellogg, Idaho, implemented a series of policies to regulate the toxic exposure of its female workforce at its lead smelter and zinc plant. The company began by requiring women to undergo pregnancy testing. When eleven of thirty-one employees refused to submit to this violation of privacy, they were fired. The women's union, the United Steelworkers of America (USWA), filed a grievance on their behalf and won reinstatement to their jobs (Stellman and Henifin 1982, 123). At this point the company adopted a policy to exclude fertile women from lead-exposure jobs unless they underwent surgical sterilization (Kenney 1992, 303–306). At least three women did so. This time the union did not fight the policy. The benign explanations for the USWA's failure to help include both inadequate resources and expertise at the local level and fear of limiting women's opportunities even further by protesting at the national level. On their own, the women filed charges with the Idaho Human Rights Commission and the EEOC. The commission suggested that the company transfer women to other positions at the same rate of pay. The company refused, and the EEOC stepped in. The EEOC essentially negotiated the same deal that the state commission had failed to seal, one that protected the current group of women's economic benefits but that closed the better-paying production jobs to all future groups of women. In another case, a forty-eight-year-old woman involuntarily transferred from her job working with vinyl chloride at a B. F. Goodrich plant filed a discrimination complaint with the Illinois Human Rights Commission. An administrative law judge ruled in favor of the company in 1982 (Scott 1984, 190).

Unions have also used less conventional tactics to oppose fetal protection policies. Both the International Chemical Workers Union (ICWU) and the USWA, for instance, challenged implementation of American Cyanamid's policy at plants in Pearl River, New York, and Linden, New Jersey, respectively. Many ICWU members at the New York plant, a pharmaceutical factory, had bought into a company stock ownership plan, and in 1980 they drafted a stockholder resolution calling on the company to study and disclose to shareholders all reproductive health hazards, and to add to the board of directors a new member concerned with these hazards. Worried by the resolution, the company offered to conduct a study and to appoint three of its current board members to a special committee on reproductive health policies if the workers would drop their proposal (Scott 1984, 185–86). (Scott's account does not make it clear whether the policy was actually dropped while the company conducted the study or what impact it had on other facilities.) When managers in New Jersey informed women that they had six months to transfer out of their jobs in sixteen of the plant's twenty-one departments, the union demanded a full accounting of the chemicals in question and their health effects on men and women who were not pregnant as well as on pregnant women. Unlike the USWA local at Bunker Hill, this one insisted that the company reduce the level of exposure for all workers by improving engineering controls. In response, management postponed the policy, and the next year it dropped it altogether because the hazardous materials were not even in use in the factory (Scott 1984, 186). Had the union not responded so swiftly and assertively, the company might well have forced women out of most of the plant's departments or into unwanted sterilizations on the basis of a completely nonexistent risk.

Canadian unions appear to have been more successful in resolving reproductive health issues at the bargaining table. In 1982 the Ontario Public Service Employees Union won the right for its 29,000 women members to transfer out of jobs working with video display terminals during pregnancy, as did the UAW representing workers at DeHavilland Aircraft and Northern Telecom (Scott 1984, 188).

For the most part, women's employment advocates have fought these battles without assistance from the government. Although Congress passed the PDA in 1978, it did not take any further action when it became clear that employers were discriminating against women despite the PDA, and when courts bemoaned the lack of specific guidance on fetal protection policies. In 1990, as part of its oversight activities, the majority staff of the House Committee on Education and Labor prepared a report investigating the EEOC's handling of fetal protection cases. The report found that the commission "entombed" approximately one hundred discrimination charges filed by fertile and pregnant women. Many charges were considered "pending" a decade after they were filed, although no action had ever been taken to resolve them. Throughout the 1980s, EEOC policy was simply to ignore them, utterly abdicating its responsibility to enforce federal anti-discrimination laws (House Ed. and Labor Comm. 1990, esp. 16–20).

As these stories show, individual workers and their unions tried a variety of approaches to prevent companies from implementing fetal protection policies. Most of them failed. It is perhaps inevitable that the federal courts became the primary forum for resolving this issue during the 1980s. Plaintiffs challenged fetal protection policies primarily under Title VII of the Civil Rights Act. Before examining those cases, I discuss the one case brought under occupational safety and health law—the case of the women workers at American Cyanamid with which this chapter begins.

The Occupational Safety and Health Model

Congress passed the Occupational Safety and Health (OSH) Act in 1970 to "assure so far as possible every working man and woman in the Nation safe and healthful working conditions" (quoted in *OCAW v. American Cyanamid Co.* 1984, 447). The act created OSHA within the Department of Labor to set standards and monitor workplaces. From the outset, however, OSHA faced difficulties that hampered its ability to function effectively, including a cumbersome standard-setting process. On average, OSHA has only issued one permanent standard per year to regulate the use of potentially harmful substances. Hundreds of other substances await regulation (Samuels 1995, 111). Industry interest groups have vigorously opposed even this modest amount of regulatory activity. Another problem is that authority is fragmented between OSHA and the National Institute for Occupational Safety and Health (NIOSH), located within the Department of Health and Human Services, and between OSHA and the Occupational Safety and Health Review Commission, an independent body that hears appeals of citations (Samuels 1995, chap. 6). At least equally important has been the agency's lack of executive support to carry out its mandate— President Richard Nixon never intended to give OSHA very much power, and Ronald Reagan slashed its budget and appointed officials who were not interested in the agency's mission. This legacy persists. Currently there is only one OSHA inspector for every six thousand businesses (Cook 1996). In North Carolina, for instance, this means it would take fifty-five years to inspect every workplace just once (Anderson 1995).

The first fetal protection policy to gain widespread attention was challenged under the OSH Act. That policy was the one implemented by the American Cyanamid Company at its Willow Island plant in West Virginia. Early in 1978 the director of the Willow Island plant conducted a series of meetings with women workers. He explained that the company would be implementing a "fetus protection policy," one that he claimed had government backing and that would regulate women's exposure to a broad array of chemicals in use in American Cyanamid's operations. No woman under age fifty could continue to work in areas that exposed her to the chemicals unless she could prove that she was infertile. A company doctor and nurse who attended these meetings described tubal ligation surgery and explained that the workers' health insurance plan would cover the costs of the operation. The policy, which would bar fertile women from all but seven of the plant's jobs, was to go into effect on May 1.

The corporate medical director at the company's headquarters initiated the policy, but the local management at Willow Island implemented it with particular zeal. Before headquarters even distributed the official version, the plant director had already called meetings with female employees. Over the coming months, the deadline was delayed to October 2, and the scope of the policy was narrowed from twenty-nine substances to cover only lead in the inorganic pigments department. Five women underwent sterilization operations in order to keep their jobs in this department; two women who decided not to be sterilized were transferred into the janitorial pool, where their salary was lowered after a ninety-day grace period. Even women who simply had to walk through the pigments department to reach the lunchroom or restroom were considered exposed to lead and had to be sterilized or transfer to another area of the plant. At least one woman was so transferred, with loss of pay (Kenney 1992, 297).

In its study of reproductive hazards at work, the Office of Technology Assessment concluded that "the chronology of events suggests that [American Cyanamid] initiated its exclusionary policy with little scientific justification and little sensitivity to the needs of its workers" (OTA 1985, 251). The company did not develop the policy in response to workers' complaints of birth defects; it apparently had no such history of complaints. The company conducted no independent research—neither surveys of workers to assess reproductive problems nor laboratory studies of suspected hazards. It did not even conduct a review of the relevant literature. Finally, it did not consider the impact of suspected toxins on men's reproductive health.

A company memo about the policy used moral language, declaring, "We recognize that this [policy] may infringe on the scope of jobs available to the individual woman, but in our judgment this is certainly the lesser of the two evils" (quoted in Faludi 1991, 445). The company tried to position itself as an arbiter of competing moral concerns, and ultimately as the champion of the correct ethical position—that of protecting potential future children from harm. This degree of concern for safety was new, at least at the Willow Island plant, which was dirty and prone to explosions (Faludi 1991, 444–45; *Secretary of Labor v. American Cyanamid*, OSHRC Docket No. 79-2438, 1980).

At the same time that the company's medical director was developing its fetal protection policy, OSHA was formulating its safety standard for workers' exposure to lead. The Willow Island plant manager told women that the company was "getting the jump on OSHA" (quoted in Faludi 1991, 446). But OSHA's final standard, published in the *Federal Register* in November 1978, did not resemble American Cyanamid's. In fact, it ex-

If this standard applied broadly, then women could be excluded from all kinds of jobs.

plicitly refuted it, by establishing a single permissible exposure level for male and female workers alike, including male and female workers planning pregnancies.[12]

The Occupational Safety and Health Administration investigated the Willow Island plant early in 1979, in response to a complaint from the Oil, Chemical, and Atomic Workers Union (OCAW), which represented the workers there. The secretary of labor issued two citations against American Cyanamid. One citation alleged that the company had violated numerous regulations governing the exposure of employees to toxins. The citation alleged that employees were illegally exposed to lead in a contaminated lunchroom, where the walls, tables, benches, water fountain, and candy machine were covered with the yellow, orange, and blue pigments that the workers made. It further alleged that workers were exposed to levels of lead and chromates above the legal limit in their work areas. The inspector also cited shortcomings in safety training regarding the proper fit and use of respirators.

American Cyanamid contested the citation and closed its pigments department, putting out of work the women who had sacrificed their fertility for their paychecks. Administrative law judge Cecil Cutler ruled in favor of the company on most counts, finding the evidence presented by the OSHA inspector inadequate. The inspector had taken samples of the pigment found in the lunch area but had not sampled the level of lead in the air or demonstrated that any workers had ingested excessive amounts of lead. In the work areas, the inspector had sampled the air in the room, finding levels of lead and chromate above the legal limit, but had not sampled the air from inside the respirators that workers wore on the job. The judge did find the company "completely indifferent as to whether its employees checked their respirators for a proper fit" and imposed a fine of one thousand dollars (*Secretary of Labor v. American Cyanamid*, OSHRC Docket No. 79-2438, 1980, 32, 37).

The inspector had also charged American Cyanamid with failing to implement "feasible administrative or engineering controls" to reduce employee exposure to lead and chromates (14).[13] Judge Cutler, however, vacated this charge on the basis that the controls were costly, and "eco-

---

[12] Proposed federal regulations are submitted for public review, and industry groups actively opposed the lead standard, so it is reasonable to assume that American Cyanamid officials were aware of OSHA's intentions. See Oren 1996, 343–49, for a summary of the lead industry's actions against OSHA's proposed standard.

[13] OSHA favors a hierarchy of controls approach to managing hazards, preferring engineering controls over work practice controls or reliance on personal protective equipment (OTA 1985, 198).

nomics must be considered a component of the word feasibility, and the cost to the employer of implementing technically feasible controls must be weighted against the benefits that would accrue to the employees" (21).[14]

The second citation concerned the fetus protection policy, which the labor secretary said should be ended immediately. The secretary charged the company with a willful violation of the general duty clause of the OSH Act, which requires employers to furnish "employment and a place of employment which are free from recognized hazards that are causing or are likely to cause death or serious physical harm" to employees. The citation alleged that American Cyanamid violated this clause by "adopt[ing] and implement[ing] a policy which required women employees to be sterilized in order to be eligible to work in areas of the plant where they would be exposed to certain toxic substances," and proposed a fine of ten thousand dollars (quoted in *Secretary of Labor v. American Cyanamid*, OSHRC Docket No. 79-5762, 1980, 2).

But the company prevailed on this charge as well. The Occupational Safety and Health Review Commission affirmed the decision two to one on the ground that the citation did not specify a violation that was cognizable under the act.[15] This finding, that American Cyanamid's policy did not constitute the kind of hazard that Congress had intended the OSH Act to prevent, formed the crux of the final appeal.

The women's union initiated the appeal of the Review Commission's decision. The labor secretary who had issued the citation was a member of the Carter administration, and his successor under Ronald Reagan did not assist the union in its fight with the company. In a unanimous, three-judge ruling, Judge Robert Bork of the District of Columbia Circuit Court upheld the earlier rulings against the women.

At the heart of these disagreements between the parties lie a number of different definitions of the hazard being addressed. Is the problem that OSHA and the affected workers seek to resolve best understood as one of excessive exposure to toxins? Is it a policy requiring the exclusion of fertile women? A policy requiring the sterilization of women? Is it the sterilization operations themselves, or is it a "choice" between fertility and

[14] Judge Cutler elaborates the role of cost in determining feasibility at *Secretary of Labor v. American Cyanamid*, OSHRC Docket No. 79-2438, 1980, 17–22; see also Samuels 1995, 110–11.

[15] In his dissenting opinion, Commissioner Bertram Cottine argued that the purpose of the general duty clause is to allow OSHA to intervene in precisely those situations that pose a risk to health and safety but have not been regulated by specific standards. Accordingly, he held that the charge should be remanded for further development (*Secretary of Labor v. American Cyanamid* 1981, 1603).

employment? All of these understandings appear in the string of opinions the case generated.

The District of Columbia Circuit Court began by explaining that its task was to interpret what Congress meant by the word *hazard,* because the OSH Act itself does not define the term. The court accepted the Review Commission's interpretation: "It is clear that Congress conceived of occupational hazards in terms of processes and materials which cause injury or disease by operating directly upon employees as they engage in work or work-related activities. The fetus protection policy is of a different character altogether. It is neither a work process nor a work material" (quoted in *OCAW v. American Cyanamid Co.* 1984, 447). Although the fetal protection policy "operates directly upon employees" and thus might be considered a condition of work, the court relied on cases throughout the 1970s that interpreted working conditions to mean physical attributes of the workplace, not policies (448).

The court accepted as matters of fact that lead poses a severe danger to developing fetuses, that American Cyanamid could not lower the ambient lead levels in the plant to be safe for fetuses, and that the company "had to prevent exposure to lead of women of childbearing age" (and only women of childbearing age) (449). Therefore, the court reasoned, the company faced "unattractive" alternatives—firing women or letting them be sterilized. The women, too, faced a "distressing" and "most unhappy" choice (445, 450). The court's language suggested that the "choices" open to the company and open to the women were somehow equivalent, and also that the company lacked other choices, such as investing in improved containment and ventilation technology. The court asserted that "it requires some stretching to call the offering of a choice a 'hazard' to the person who is offered the choice" (448). Quoting again from the Review Commission, the court declared that "an employee's decision to undergo sterilization in order to gain or retain employment grows out of economic and social factors which operate primarily outside the workplace. The employer neither controls nor creates these factors [as he creates or controls work processes and materials]" (447). The court concluded that

> the case might be different if American Cyanamid had offered the choice of sterilization in an attempt to pass on to its employees the cost of maintaining a circumambient lead concentration higher than that permitted by law. But that is not the case. The company could not reduce lead concentrations to a level that posed an acceptable risk to fetuses. *The sterilization exception to the requirement of removal from the Inorganic Pigments Department was an attempt not to pass on costs of unlawful conduct but to permit*

the employees to mitigate costs to them imposed by unavoidable physiological facts.
(450; my emphasis)

The view of the world that emerges from the court's opinion is one of omnipotent natural forces, with little room for human intervention. "Unavoidable physiological facts" construct an inevitable chain between fertile women in the workplace, pregnancy, and fetuses carried to term. Another unavoidable physiological fact is the threat from workplace hazards, whose impact should be mitigated by removing fertile women rather than by lowering lead levels through engineering controls, job rotation, improved protective equipment, or other means. The invisible hand of the market shapes the economic and social conditions that constrain workers' choices, and individual corporations and government bear no responsibility to counteract harmful forces. This view, as much as the reasons the court itself cites ("precedent, congressional intent, and the unforeseeable consequences" of treating policies as "hazards"), accounts for the outcome in this case (450).

A further conceptual problem underlies the company's policy and the court's decision. Employers such as American Cyanamid frame the problem as one of preventing risk of harm to a fetus, not to their employees. To prove a violation of the general duty clause, OSHA must demonstrate that the employer has failed to eliminate a hazard that poses substantial risk of serious bodily harm or death to employees. If companies acknowledged that the risk was one of reproductive harm to the employee, then the requirements of the OSH Act would clearly apply. It is only by conceiving of a fetus as a free-floating individual, instead of as a developing being formed by male and female genetic contributions and embedded in a woman's body, that corporations and courts can so easily separate the effects of industrial materials and processes from those of policies.

In this case occupational health and safety law failed to provide a remedy for discriminatory policies. The combination of the court's decision and the Reagan administration's ongoing hostility to the needs of working people effectively foreclosed further litigation under the occupational safety and health framework. Although many opponents of fetal protection policies prefer to cast them as work-related health problems, the current status of the law makes it difficult to sustain a challenge outside of the sex discrimination paradigm.[16] Sally Kenney argues that this fact of Amer-

---

[16] Even under this paradigm, as Chapter 4 demonstrates, women are not always successful. In the American Cyanamid case, while the union's fight to enforce OSHA's fine against the company wound its way through the review process, a group of thirteen women also filed

ican law "is what creates the false impression that, in bringing cases on exclusionary policies, women seek the right to poison themselves and their children" (Kenney 1992, 211).

---

a sex discrimination lawsuit under Title VII. The company, which did not want to pay for engineering controls or even a $10,000 fine, spent enough money to wear the women down in three years of pretrial proceedings, and they eventually settled for $200,000 to be divided among the eleven remaining plaintiffs (Faludi 1991, 449).

4

Overcoming Discrimination

Women and Corporate Risk Management II

G iven organized labor's unsuccessful experience trying to change the workplace through occupational safety and health law, it is not surprising that workers have focused instead on Title VII as a way to challenge fetal protection policies. Litigation under sex discrimination statutes began early in the 1970s and culminated with the Supreme Court's unanimous decision to invalidate a fetal protection policy in 1991.

One of the most striking features of these cases is the courts' refusal to address the stated issue, sex discrimination, and to focus instead on harm to fetuses. This pattern means that these cases often subordinated discussion of gender equality to allow fetal rights. In almost all the decisions, the image of helpless fetuses and damaged children swayed the judges to answer the question "How can this [potential] tragedy be avoided?" instead of the question put before them: "Does excluding only women from certain jobs violate Title VII?" The very names of the policies, "fetal protection" and "fetal vulnerability" programs, conjure these images. One court concluded its opinion by declaring that "stillbirths, reduced birth weight and gestational age, and retarded cognitive development are abnormalities too serious for this Court to find unimportant" (*United Auto Workers v. Johnson Controls* 1988, 317). Certainly these possible effects of exposure to lead are important, and to no one more than the employees themselves. But their importance does not relieve courts of the responsibility to determine whether excluding women from working with lead is illegal sex discrimination. Nor does it relieve employers of the responsibility to determine the best legally permissible strategy to ensure fetal health. Ultimately, most courts' desire to reach a certain outcome led them on a circuitous route, one that ignored the plain letter of the law and created new meanings for everyday terms, in a series of gender-biased and business-friendly decisions that upheld blatant employment discrimination. The controversy generated by these cases led to the Supreme Court's review in *United Auto Workers v. Johnson Controls*, in which it ruled that fetal protection policies are illegal sex discrimination.

The Sex Discrimination Model

Under Title VII of the Civil Rights Act, workers can challenge a discriminatory policy in two ways. They can claim *disparate treatment* when a policy explicitly treats one group differently from another. In cases of disparate treatment, employers must prove that the trait by which they discriminate is a BFOQ: a "bona fide occupational qualification reasonably necessary to the normal operation of that particular business or enterprise" (42 U.S.C.A. 2000e-2[e]). This standard may not sound very demanding, but courts have interpreted the phrase "reasonably necessary" quite narrowly, requiring an employer to prove that the discrimination is very important to the proper functioning of the business, going to its essence or central mission, and that less restrictive alternatives have been exhausted.

Workers can also claim to suffer from *disparate impact* when a neutral-sounding policy has a discriminatory effect on an identifiable group. An example of disparate impact is when minimum height and weight requirements for a job operate to exclude a disproportionate number of women. In these cases employers can justify neutral policies that have a disparate impact on one sex with a less stringent defense known as "business necessity," a defense that places a greater burden on the plaintiff to prove that she has suffered discrimination.

Over the years, Congress and the Supreme Court have gone back and forth over these defenses. At times Congress has passed new clarifying legislation in response to decisions that undermine workers' rights. The crucial point in sex discrimination cases is that the Pregnancy Discrimination Act (PDA) always requires employers to justify pregnancy- or fertility-based discrimination by meeting the exacting BFOQ standard.[1]

---

[1] See Kenney 1992, chap. 4, for an overview of Title VII doctrine and Congress's responses to court decisions. Whether plaintiffs' experience of discrimination falls under the

Court Cases

The Olin Corporation banned fertile women from many jobs at its Pisgah Forest plant in North Carolina, which produces cellophane, belts, and papers for the tobacco and printing industries. In *Wright v. Olin*, Theresa Wright represented the class of women hourly employees since 1976 claiming to have suffered sex discrimination, including subjection to the "fetal vulnerability" program (*Wright v. Olin Corp.* 1982, 1179). Under that program, women under age sixty-three were restricted from certain jobs unless they could prove they were incapable of bearing children. Women who were not pregnant could work in a second set of restricted jobs only if they signed a form stating their awareness that the job presented some risk. Pregnant women were barred from these jobs unless given permission to work after an individual evaluation. Men were warned verbally about the risks of exposure to lead at the plant, as the Occupational Safety and Health (OSH) Act requires, but these warnings were less formal, and men were not restricted from any jobs on the basis of fertility.[2] This program was implemented in early 1978, after several years of planning, to "protect the unborn fetuses of pregnant women employees" (1182). The record does not indicate that any female employees had given birth to children with birth defects related to chemicals used at the plant (toluene, carbon disulfide, and lead). The company had apparently reviewed medical literature and considered other options, such as improving ventilation or protective equipment to lower workers' exposure to toxins, and decided that only excluding women would protect potential fetuses from lead exposure. The district court found that the fetal vulnerability policy was based on "sound medical and humane reasons" and did not constitute sex discrimination against women (1182–83). Wright appealed.

Acknowledging its role as the first appellate court to rule in such a case, the three-judge panel of the Court of Appeals for the Fourth Circuit struggled anxiously to formulate the proper analytical framework for evaluating fetal protection policies. The court began with the premise that Olin's discrimination against women under the guise of its fetal vulnerability program "does not fit with absolute precision" into any of the devel-

---

disparate treatment or disparate impact rubric, they must first file a complaint with the EEOC before suing in federal court.

[2] The appellate court opinion revealed a further discrepancy in the treatment of male and female workers. The opinion stated that women could be placed in restricted jobs "only after consulting with Olin's medical doctors to confirm the woman cannot bear children *and will sustain no other adverse physiological effects from the environment*" (1182; my emphasis). How does this requirement relate to fetal safety, industrial safety, or consumer safety? Protecting men from adverse effects nowhere appears to be a concern of the company.

oped theories of Title VII litigation (1184). Hence "the proper course is to seek guidance in the general principles underlying Title VII" and "to stay as near as may be within a developed doctrine" (1185). This approach sounds conservative, yet after this statement the court departed from all settled doctrine. Tellingly, the court rejected Wright's claim that the PDA provides the one appropriate framework: Overt discrimination—excluding only women from certain jobs—must be justified as a bona fide occupational qualification (BFOQ) related to the duties of the job (1183–84n17). Relying on pre-PDA precedent, the court chose instead the doctrine of disparate impact/business necessity, because it saw as the closest parallel to the fetal vulnerability program those cases involving a facially neutral employer practice that falls more harshly on one group. "While the 'facial neutrality' of Olin's [sex-specific] fetal vulnerability program might be subject to logical dispute," the court maintained, "the dispute would involve mere semantic quibbling" (1186).

The court soon ran into semantic difficulty again. It began the opinion by referring to the "unborn fetuses" of "pregnant women" or "women workers." When it reached the question of whether the safety of potential offspring can legitimate a discriminatory employment policy, however, its language shifted. The court compared "unborn children"—that is, fetuses —to a "special category" of invitees and licensees and to personal service customers of a business exposed to hazards while on the premises (1189). By making this analogy between fetuses and "third parties," the court implicitly granted fetuses the same rights as business customers and others to a safe visit to the plant, as later courts have noted.[3]

The court emphasized "the need to adapt the business necessity defense to some of [the fetal vulnerability program's] unique and previously unencountered aspects" (1187). The court repeatedly used the word *unique*, invoking the notion of reproduction as women's unique sphere. The court found that a company can rest its business necessity defense of limiting women's employment on a "general societal interest" in businesses operating "in ways protective of the health of workers and their families, consumers, and environmental neighbors," even as it acknowledged that a defense resting on the need to avoid liability would clearly violate Title VII (that is, refusing to hire women workers because they cost more) (1190n26).

The court set out a multipronged test for employers restricting women's access to jobs in order to protect the health of unborn fetuses. An employer must show that women, but not men, expose their "unborn chil-

---

[3] See, for example, *Hayes v. Shelby Memorial Hospital* 1984, 1552n14, which is discussed next.

dren" to significant risks of harm from workplace hazards. To do this, an employer need not demonstrate a general consensus in the scientific community but can show that "within that community there is so considerable a body of opinion that significant risk exists, and that it is substantially confined to women workers, that an informed employer could not responsibly fail to act on the assumption that this opinion might be the accurate one" (1191). The employees then have the burden of rebutting the employer's defense by demonstrating the existence of equally effective but less discriminatory means to accomplish the goal of protecting fetal health.

Despite its recognition that an employer's good intentions do not justify discrimination, that Title VII was designed to eliminate barriers to women based on stereotypical assumptions about their "special" societal role (1188), and that Olin's policy did indeed adversely affect women's opportunities, the court did not strike down the company's policy. It went out of its way—and out of the law—to help the company prevail. First, the court disagreed with Wright that because the fetal vulnerability program was an overt act of discrimination against women, the employer should be "confined to a b.f.o.q. defense," a defense "that obviously cannot be established" (1185n21). Second, the court decided the case as one of disparate impact, because otherwise the employer is prevented "from asserting a justification defense which under developed Title VII doctrine it is entitled to present" (1186). That defense is the lesser business necessity defense, a defense Olin did not even assert. The court decided to remand the case for further proceedings in order to give Olin another chance to do so, despite the "minor procedural awkwardness" this entailed (1187n23). Procedural "awkwardness" aside, the employer is still not entitled to present a business necessity defense if it actually engages in overt discrimination.

When the case was remanded to the district court for further proceedings, Olin won. The company presented expert witnesses whose testimony on the risks of chemical exposure to workers satisfied the appellate court's tests. The opinion did not mention whether Wright presented any expert witnesses to make the opposite case. In addition to upholding the fetal vulnerability program as a legitimate business necessity, Judge Woodrow Wilson Jones stated, "An employer such as Olin can justifiably choose a policy of fetal protection as a moral obligation to protect the next generation from injury, and it is a social good that should be encouraged and not penalized. Women in general should applaud the effort" (*Wright v. Olin Corp.* 1984, 1453). Here the court not only condoned Olin's practice of sex discrimination (burdening women with the costs of fetal rights) but also venerated it. This logic recalls *Muller v. Oregon*, suggesting women should be grateful for paternalism and portraying women as primarily responsible for reproduction and safeguarding children.

Around the same time, two related cases were making their way through the courts in Texas and Alabama. The Texas case was initiated before Congress enacted the PDA. Rita Zuniga was hired in 1971 as the first female X-ray technician at the county hospital in Kingsville, a small community in the southern part of the state. When she became pregnant in 1973, the hospital administrator told her to resign or be fired. The district court upheld the hospital's action, and Zuniga appealed to the Fifth Circuit. The courts treated the policy of firing pregnant technicians as facially neutral and so evaluated the case under the disparate impact/business necessity model. But the court of appeals ruled that it need not reach the question of whether concern for fetal safety or future liability are valid business needs because the hospital could have taken action that would have had a less discriminatory impact on Zuniga. It failed to give her leave under the hospital's policy, which grants employees sick leave, insurance benefits, and job reinstatement and can be taken for reasons including personal and family health. The administrator who forced Zuniga to resign had never denied such a leave of absence to any other employee during his tenure. (Apparently, staying on the job was never the question.) The court concluded that "it is difficult to conceive of a more straightforward prima facie case of sex discrimination" (*Zuniga v. Kleberg County Hospital* 1982, 991n8). This ruling in Zuniga's favor without benefit of the PDA's guidance makes the decisions in other courts upholding fetal protection policies all the more remarkable.

Sylvia Hayes was also fired from her job as an X-ray technician at Shelby Memorial Hospital in the Birmingham area when she informed her supervisor that she was two months pregnant. A district court found that the hospital violated Hayes's rights under Title VII and could not justify its action by either the BFOQ or business necessity defenses: Hayes's pregnancy did not interfere with her ability to do her job or the hospital's ability to do its job of providing safe and efficient medical services to its patients. To expand the concept of business necessity to include "the avoidance of possible future liability to the fetus" would "shift the focus of the business necessity defense from a focus of concern for the safety of hospital patients to a focus of concern for hospital finances" (*Hayes v. Shelby Memorial Hospital* 1982, 264).

The court held that even if it were inclined to expand the defense in this way, the hospital would still have failed in its obligation to seek a less discriminatory way to achieve its goal of protecting Hayes's fetus. The hospital made no attempt to determine whether Hayes's job was likely to expose her to doses of radiation in excess of those recommended for pregnant women by the National Council on Radiation Protection. The hospital did not attempt to modify her radiology duties, or to find her other work within the hospital.

It appears that Hayes may have had the basis for a race discrimination claim as well as sex discrimination. The court does not identify Hayes's race, but it noted that the hospital had previously accommodated two white X-ray technicians during their pregnancies, by allowing one to restrict her duties to reading X-ray films and permitting the other to take greater safety precautions in her usual duties. The Eleventh Circuit Court of Appeals would later explain in its opinion that under the PDA, firing Hayes because she was pregnant is just as facially discriminatory "as it would be to fire her solely because she was black" (*Hayes* 1984, 1548).

The district court concluded that the hospital's concern for Hayes's fetus did not warrant its "paternalistic and extreme" treatment of her (266). It awarded her modest back pay and, because she had sued under Section 1983 of the Civil Rights Act of 1871 for deprivation of civil rights as well, $6,000 in compensatory damages for emotional distress.[4]

The hospital appealed to the Eleventh Circuit, which agreed with the earlier ruling but modified it in certain ways. Instead of simply affirming the lower court's decision, the court made it easier to justify fetal protection policies.

The court explained that "the Pregnancy Discrimination Act mandates that a pregnancy-based rule can never be 'neutral'" (*Hayes v. Shelby Memorial Hospital* 1984, 1547). And yet four sentences later the court said that "to ensure complete fairness to the Hospital, we will also analyze this case under the disparate impact/business necessity theory." It went on to say that a policy applying only to women or to pregnant women created a "*presumption*" of facial discrimination. An employer could rebut this presumption by proving "that although its policy applies only to women, the policy is neutral in the sense that it effectively and equally protects the offspring of all employees" because only women's offspring are at risk (1548; emphasis in original). With this formulation, the court turned a policy that singles out members of one sex for different treatment into a gender-neutral and hence presumptively legal policy. The court's language di-

---

[4] Because Hayes had not sought other employment after being fired, thinking that her pregnancy made a job search pointless, the court found that she had not made a good-faith effort to mitigate damages and limited her back pay. Hayes's instincts were probably right. Another woman, fired from her job as a bookkeeper in Massachusetts when she became pregnant, reports that "as I got larger, the interviews got shorter. . . . I knew they weren't hiring me because I was pregnant, but I couldn't do anything about it" (quoted in Shellenbarger 1993, B2).

rected attention to only one impact of fetal protection policies: "The policy is neutral in the sense that it effectively and equally protects the offspring of all employees." Nowhere does the court justify why this is the only sense that matters, and *not* the impact on women workers that Title VII expressly concerns.

Unlike the Fourth Circuit Court of Appeals in *Wright v. Olin*, the court here recognized the existence of "a certain amount of subtle bias" in the preponderance of reproductive health research on women, but did not find this bias sufficient to restrain employers from adopting sex-specific fetal protection policies (1548–49). The court also distanced itself from the Fourth Circuit's comparison of fetuses to business visitors while accepting fetal safety as a self-evident, legitimate business necessity needing no explanation.

The court simplified the Fourth Circuit's test for the legality of a fetal protection policy: A policy applying only to members of one sex violates Title VII unless the employer can show "(1) that a substantial risk of harm exists and (2) that the risk is borne only by members of one sex; and (3) the employee fails to show that there are acceptable alternative policies that would have a lesser impact on the affected sex" (1554). "To add any more requirements," it said, "would be to render it nearly impossible to have a fetal protection program under any circumstances" (1553).

Because the hospital had failed to consider any less restrictive alternative to firing Hayes, the court of appeals upheld the lower court's ruling in her favor. But it put important new constructions into the legal landscape, such as the notion that a policy applying only to women could be considered neutral with respect to gender. This new landscape would influence the *Johnson Controls* case.

More than any other, the reasoning of the Seventh Circuit Court of Appeals opinion in *Johnson Controls* epitomizes the kind of biased jurisprudence that shapes judicial outcomes on the basis of gendered ideology. The majority's decision turned on several key factors: how to define the legal question, the company's mission, and, ultimately, what it means to be a woman in the workplace. The case was first argued before a three-judge panel, but when the panel's opinion was circulated the judges voted to have a rehearing before the entire appellate court. The court upheld Johnson Controls' policy in a seven-to-four decision, with majority and dissenting opinions reflecting sharp differences on how to define the critical terms of the case. Those dissenting views helped pave the way for the Supreme Court to strike down the policy.

Based in Milwaukee, Johnson Controls is the nation's biggest manufacturer of automobile batteries. In 1977 Johnson Controls started a program to warn employees of the reproductive risks associated with exposure to lead, an essential ingredient in batteries, and required women to sign a form indicating that they had been informed. Five years later the company switched from a policy of informing women to a policy of excluding them.

The policy excluded all women up to age seventy who could not prove they were infertile, regardless of their intentions to become parents or to have more children, and was put into effect at plants in nine states.[5] The policy was especially broad, because it denied women jobs working with lead *and* all jobs in a line of progression to positions working with lead. The workers who sued the company included a woman who had been sterilized in order to keep her job, a man who was refused a temporary transfer in order to reduce the level of lead in his blood so that he and his wife could plan a pregnancy, and a woman who had been transferred out of her production job to one washing other workers' protective equipment. Most of the female plaintiffs were over fifty years old. Johnson Controls justified its policy by noting that during a five-year period (1979–83) a total of eight employees nationwide became pregnant while their blood lead levels exceeded the threshold recommended by OSHA for male and female workers planning children. There was no proof of birth defects or other abnormalities among the children. The district court granted Johnson Controls' motion for summary judgment, and the United Auto Workers appealed to the Seventh Circuit.

The circuit court begins its opinion by stating that, "since 1982, Johnson Controls has maintained a fetal protection policy designed to prevent *unborn children and their mothers* from suffering the adverse effects of lead exposure" (*UAW v. Johnson Controls, Inc.* 1989, 874; my emphasis). The court repeats this assertion about mothers and children throughout its lengthy discussions of the company's history, the history of the policy, and the health effects of lead.[6] The court takes its time before addressing the legal issues, claiming that "proper analysis of the Title VII issues this case presents requires a thorough understanding of the following fundamental question: Does lead pose a health risk to the offspring of Johnson's *female* employees?" (879; my emphasis). The court understands the fundamental question, the first question, as one of scientific risk assessment, not sex discrimination.

Following *Wright v. Olin* and *Hayes v. Shelby Memorial Hospital*, the Seventh Circuit Court of Appeals saw this case as a question of disparate im-

---

[5] The locations are Garland, Texas; Louisville, Kentucky; Texarkana, Arkansas; Atlanta, Georgia; Fullerton, California; Holland, Ohio; Owosso, Michigan; Bennington, Vermont; and Middletown, Delaware.

[6] See, for example, pp. 876n7, 879, 883, and 884.

pact rather than of disparate treatment. It interpreted the fetal protection policy as facially neutral, arguing that even though it applied only to women, it "effectively and equally" protected the offspring of male as well as female employees, and was therefore not illegal sex discrimination. Again like the *Hayes* case, the court failed to explain why this is the only impact that matters.

The court did implicitly consider the impact that Johnson Controls' fetal protection policy had on women's economic opportunity, but it situated that impact within its overriding concern for fetal health. The court attributed women's labor force participation solely to "their desire to better the family's station in life" (897). Because of this desire, "it would not be improbable that a female employee might somehow rationally discount this clear risk in her hope and belief that her infant would not be adversely affected from lead exposure" (897). The court repeatedly described the adverse effects of lead on a fetus.[7]

The court saw this case as one where "the interest in financial reward is balanced against a medically established risk of the birth of a medically or physically deprived baby" (883). The court did not specify whose interest in financial reward needed to be thus balanced, but given its arguments about the reasons why women work, it likely had women in mind. This construction casts all the trade-offs as between women and fetuses. But wouldn't it make at least as much sense to say that the problem is between women who want to earn a living without sacrificing their health and the company's interest in its own financial reward?

When answering the scientific question it had set for itself, the court dismissed the union's evidence of fetal risk through paternal exposure as "speculative and unconvincing," because the primary evidence was from animal studies (889). The scientific evidence of risk through maternal exposure "overwhelmingly" justified a fetal protection policy that excludes only fertile women (883).[8]

The *Wright* court spoke of women workers' potential fetuses as if they actually existed, but the Seventh Circuit went even further. In its majority opinion, the court also transformed the potential fetuses that women working at the factory might someday conceive into "unborn children." It then attributed compelling interests to these unborn children, on which they cannot act on their own behalf. These interests must be balanced

[7] In addition to Section II, devoted entirely to this topic, see especially comments on pp. 896, 897, 898, and 899.

[8] The majority's dismissal of evidence from animal studies has been widely criticized, by, for example, dissenting Judges Easterbrook and Flaum (915, 918–19, 920) and groups such as the Natural Resources Defense Council (discussed in Daniels 1993, 79–81).

against the employer's and employees', but ultimately everyone's interests are fulfilled except women's. The employer continues operating the business without fear of tort liability, the fetus can be conceived in a body free from lead contamination, and the woman loses her well-paying union job. Johnson Controls assumes, and the court allowed, that female employees have only maternal interests, and that these interests are equivalent to those of their born or unborn children. The court did not stop there, approving of "Johnson's interest in protecting the health of the unborn *through* the female employee" (899; my emphasis). Here the court allowed the company to turn women into vehicles for the interests of others, even the interests of nonexistent beings.

How did the court's majority see women? It frequently made remarks like "[Johnson's] primary interest in this case is protecting the development and health of female employees and their unborn children," yet the policy does nothing to promote the health of infertile female employees (884). Furthermore, the unborn children in question have not yet been conceived, may never be conceived, and may not even be anticipated, insofar as not all fertile female employees *want* children. The policy emphasizes that many pregnancies are unplanned but discounts those that are planned; these include, among others, most lesbians' pregnancies. None of these women—infertile, childless by choice, or lesbian—count as female in the court's construction of what it means to be a woman.

The court understood the problem of preventing injury to fetal health as resting with women, not as resting with the dangerous substance of lead itself. It quoted an expert affidavit stating that, because lead accumulates in the body and takes time to be eliminated, "a woman with a significant blood lead burden would pose a potential hazard to any conceptus *for many years after exposure*" (882; emphasis in original). It also described Johnson Controls' need to adopt a policy that "would address the health/safety problems related to its female employees" (986). Both these statements construct women as the locus of the problem: The woman poses a hazard, not the lead; the health/safety problems in the factory are related to women, not to lead.

The court approvingly quoted *Wright*'s "cogent observation" that the business necessity defense legitimately extends to general societal interests. By broadening the defense to include general ethical or moral concerns in the health of future unborn children, courts held women exclusively responsible for producing healthy children who will not be economic burdens on society. Insofar as pregnancy is grounds for constraining women, pregnancy is considered of general social interest. More often, when pregnancy might be grounds for providing aid to women, as in the case of poverty, pregnancy is considered a woman's "private" affair, carrying no social entitlement to adequate wages or health care. If companies that manufacture hazardous products really cared about the health of future generations, not to mention the health of their workforces, then they would take steps to make the workplace as safe as possible for everyone. Once again, the ghost of *Muller* haunts the court's logic, burdening women with reproductive responsibility.

All of the judges seemed to assume that women who become pregnant always carry their pregnancies to term. But women's reproductive experiences are not dichotomous—either sterility or mandatory childbearing. Women can and do control their fertility, through birth control and abortion. Women who want to work in battery production and postpone childbearing can decide whether they want to exercise their legal right to have an abortion if they get pregnant while working in a high-lead environment, a fact that neither the majority nor the dissenting opinions mentions. The omission of this possibility is consistent with the majority's implicit view that women are incapable of deciding for themselves what job they want, what level of risk is acceptable, and what childbearing plans to make.

Ordinarily, once a court has explained its judgment, its opinion is finished. But in this case, after establishing that Johnson Controls' business necessity defense shielded it from liability under Title VII, the court went on to discuss how the company would also be able to satisfy the more stringent BFOQ defense. That discussion relied heavily on *Dothard v. Rawlinson*, a 1977 Supreme Court case brought by women against two Alabama policies for hiring prison guards: (1) that they be at least five feet two inches in height and weigh at least 120 pounds, and (2) that only men can be prison guards in "contact" positions in men's facilities, closing to women 75 percent of the total jobs in the system. The majority opinion argued that the BFOQ exception is "extremely narrow" and struck down the height and weight requirements as not sufficiently related to the stated job qualification, strength. The Court, however, upheld the sex requirement. It argued that the policy was not an exercise in "romantic paternalism" but was necessary because the Alabama prisons were "peculiarly inhospitable," "violent," and "disorganized," and women's presence might incite men to sexually assault them (*Dothard v. Rawlinson* 1977, 2729–30). The Court said that inmates might assault women guards "because they [are] women," and that their "very womanhood would thus directly undermine" their capacity to perform the essence of the job, which is maintaining prison security (2730). The Court also declared that while Title VII ordinarily allows a woman to choose for herself whether to take a dangerous job, in this case "more is at stake" than "an individual woman's decision to weigh and accept the risks of employment" (2730; quoted by the Seventh Circuit on p. 897).

Only Justices Thurgood Marshall and William Brennan dissented, warning that "expansion of today's decision beyond its narrow factual basis would erect a serious roadblock to economic equality for women" (2735). Their warning came true when the Seventh Circuit took the *Dothard* decision as a basis to uphold sex as a BFOQ for battery production jobs, on the theory that "industrial safety" is critical to Johnson Controls' business mission (the way that security is critical to a prison), that women's very womanhood means they cannot perform the job of making batteries "safely" because they might injure a fetus they might be carrying or someday conceive, and so "more is at stake" than women's right to decide their own fate (897–98). Although irrelevant to how the court approached the case at hand, *Dothard*'s influence permeates the opinion's conclusion that working women are the real danger to be controlled at Johnson Controls plants.

The Seventh Circuit's expansive notion of industrial safety as part of the essence of Johnson Controls' business may stem from its deference to businesses in designing their own employment practices. The court repeatedly stated that judges should be wary of mandating employment policy, because they are generally less competent than employers at structuring business practices (892, 893, 897, 901).

Finally, the court found it especially easy to nullify women's rights under Title VII to make their own employment decisions because it had granted fetuses rights of their own. Earlier I showed the way the court personified and attributed interests to fetuses. The court also bestowed rights on fetuses by image and analogy. One typical comment warned of the risk of giving birth to a "medically or physically deprived baby" (883). The word *deprived* evokes notions of child neglect and abridged rights. Following up with the neglect analogy, the court compared the situation of a fetus exposed to lead to that of a minor child whose parents refuse to allow doctors to administer a needed blood transfusion (897). In the transfusion instance, the state *may* override the parents' right to direct their children's medical care because of its interest in the child's survival.[9] Next, the court compared the costs to society of caring for children born impaired by lead exposure to the costs of caring for injured motorcyclists who did not wear helmets (898). Just as the state can limit the motorcyclists' freedom, so can

---

[9] Chapter 5 examines the practice of granting fetuses rights through the analogy to minors' rights to medical care.

a company limit women's freedom. The unifying theme in these analogies is that the court personifies potential fetuses by comparing them to the situations of real, living children and adults instead of to hypothetical beings. For all these reasons, the Seventh Circuit upheld the district court's decision in favor of the company.

Four judges dissented, filing three opinions between them. All dissented because of a simple, central point: Fetal protection policies constitute disparate treatment—"intentional discrimination against a protected group"—and must be justified according to the stringent BFOQ defense (Posner, 903). Picking up on the majority's deference to business, Judge Frank Easterbrook, joined by Joel Flaum, noted that the majority had to analyze the case as disparate impact, because the company couldn't win otherwise (910). He also undermined the majority's industrial safety argument, contending that concern for the next generation is not an objective related to making batteries (912). Easterbrook firmly maintained that an employer's fear of liability (understood as "extra" costs associated with hiring women) is not a legitimate reason to discriminate under Title VII.[10] Easterbrook's analysis is all the more notable because he took risks to fetal health seriously and referred to fetuses as "children." Yet this personification and concern did not impair his legal analysis, the way they did for so many of his colleagues.

One important thing that distinguishes *Johnson Controls* from the other cases is that all the other cases went to trial or were remanded to the lower court for further factual development. The *Johnson Controls* case is different in that the appellate court upheld the district court's decision to grant the company summary judgment—that is, to rule on the legitimacy of the policy without a trial. Judges Richard Cudahy and Richard Posner both found fault with this, saying that although they thought it would be difficult to sustain a BFOQ defense, the employer ought to be given the opportunity to try (901, 908).

After the Seventh Circuit ruling, the tide began to turn on the legitimacy of fetal protection policies. In 1990 a California court invalidated Johnson Controls' fetal protection policy at its subsidiary Globe Battery. The court found that the policy violated state fair employment laws (*Johnson Controls, Inc. v. CFEHC*). That same year a three-judge panel of the Sixth Circuit Court of Appeals ruled on a General Motors fetal protection policy. Taking its cue from the Seventh Circuit dissenters in *Johnson Con-*

---

[10] In his own opinion, Judge Posner disagreed, at least as far as potentially ruinous tort costs are concerned, such as those that bankrupted the asbestos industry. He also asserted that the "normal operation" of a business encompasses ethical concerns about the impact on third parties.

trols, the court recognized GM's fetal protection policy as facial discrimination and sent the case back to lower court for further proceedings (*Grant v. GM Corp.* 1990, 1311).

When the Supreme Court finally ruled in the *Johnson Controls* case in the spring of 1991, it unanimously struck down the company's fetal protection policy. All nine justices concurred in the judgment, but they filed three separate opinions disputing the scope of the precedent they wanted to set.[11] Justice Harry Blackmun's majority opinion held that a fetal protection policy excluding women cannot be upheld, because it singles out some workers on the basis of their ability to become pregnant, and that clearly violates the PDA.

The Supreme Court correctly saw the case as a question of disparate treatment. Under this framework, to justify requiring sterility of women, an employer must prove that pregnancy or the potential to become pregnant interferes materially with a woman's ability to do her job. In this case, the Court rejected the claim that childbearing capacity impairs women's ability to make batteries. The majority considered its ruling neither remarkable nor unprecedented; it did "no more than hold that the Pregnancy Discrimination Act means what it says" (*UAW v. Johnson Controls, Inc.* 1991, 1210).[12]

The biggest discrepancy between the justices' opinions concerned a cluster of issues linking the BFOQ defense and employers' liability for harm should a worker's child suffer because of prenatal lead exposure. The majority believed that the basis for employer liability was "remote at best" if "the employer fully informs a woman of the risk, and the employer has not acted negligently"—in other words, if the employer has complied with OSHA standards (1208). In his concurring opinion, Justice Byron White, however, indicated that a company's concerns about the cost of tort liability might be "reasonably necessary to the normal operation" of the business and, if so, could legitimate an exclusionary policy. According to precedent, even a company that complies with OSHA standards can be held liable. Children can sue their parents' employers, and even though state tort liability for prenatal injuries generally requires proof of negligence, how is an employer to determine in advance what counts as negli-

[11] Justice Harry Blackmun, joined by Justices Thurgood Marshall, Sandra Day O'Connor, David Souter, and John Paul Stevens, wrote the majority opinion. Justice Byron White, joined by Justices Anthony Kennedy and William Rehnquist, and Justice Antonin Scalia wrote concurring opinions.

[12] In his opinion, Justice Scalia concurred that evidence about harm to men's reproductive systems is "entirely irrelevant": "By reason of the Pregnancy Discrimination Act, it would not matter if all pregnant women placed their children at risk in taking these jobs, just as it does not matter if no men do so" (1216).

gence (1211)? White also suggested that employers might be held "strictly liable," in which case proof of negligence is not required, but this is only if the work can be defined as "abnormally dangerous."

A related discrepancy concerned understandings of the terms *safety* and *third party* and their proper relation to the BFOQ standard. The majority maintained that a company must show that safety to third parties is essential to its business in order to claim a BFOQ defense, and that Johnson Controls cannot do so. White again disagreed, finding the analogy to *Dothard* compelling, and also invoking another case involving airlines and passenger safety. It should not be surprising that White considered potential fetuses third parties entitled to protection; he considered fetuses to be future citizens in need of protection from abortion (*Thornburgh v. ACOG* 1986, 2196). All nine justices concurred in the judgment because they agreed that Johnson Controls was not entitled to summary judgment on so sparse a record, especially when the policy's reach was so broad and the lower courts had applied the wrong tests.

Fetal Protection Policies and Women's Employment Choices

Many of the opinions that led up to the Supreme Court's decision assume that women are incapable of making important decisions. In fact, women make important decisions all the time, and they do so under real material constraints, such as job availability and income. In West Virginia, where unemployment is high, women took jobs at American Cyanamid because they offered the only living wage in the area (Faludi 1991, 441). Queen Foster sued Globe Battery in Fullerton, California, because she wanted to double her income by becoming a machine operator instead of a clerical worker (Glanton 1988). At fifteen to twenty dollars per hour, Johnson Controls' battery production jobs are among the highest paying in Bennington, Vermont (Kilborn 1991). These factories are often the biggest employer in town, and they exist alongside primarily low-paying service-sector jobs that do not provide health benefits or opportunity for advancement.

The rhetoric of "free choice" simply doesn't measure up to economic reality. The "choice" women are supposed to make is untenable when they have families they must support, or when they need money now but want children later. Questioned at his confirmation hearings about his decision in the American Cyanamid case, Judge Robert Bork replied, "I suppose the five women who chose to stay on the job and chose sterilization, I suppose they were glad to have the choice" (quoted in Faludi 1991, 449). Stunned, former employee Betty Riggs sent a telegram to Congress: "I cannot believe that Judge Bork thinks we were glad to have the choice of getting sterilized or getting fired. Only a judge who knows nothing about women who need to work could say that. I was only twenty-six years old, but I had to work, so I had no choice. . . . This was the most awful thing that ever happened to me" (quoted in Faludi 1991, 450).

When Johnson Controls issued its original warning policy in 1977, the company recognized that trying to assume prospective parents' responsibility to protect future children would infringe on employees' rights "as persons" (1199). But fear of having to pay damages to employees' children made the company change its moral stance. Dropping its concern for women as persons, the company shifted its concern to children only, announcing, "To knowingly poison unborn children is morally reprehensible. Johnson Controls will do everything in its power to avoid having that happen at our manufacturing plants" (cited in Daniels 1993, 64).

Why, then, did Johnson Controls refuse to allow male workers concerned about harming their future children to transfer temporarily out of production jobs involving lead? This refusal belies any full commitment to fetal welfare, or to cost control, since the children of male workers might sue the company. Instead, it reveals a false construction of the problem of workplace safety as one resting entirely with women, which led to a "solution" of discrimination instead of other possible arrangements the company could have made.

Compared with men, women have borne the full moral costs, the blame, for imperfect children. Both scientific research and employment restrictions have singled them out. Industrial managers do not talk about excluding men from the workplace, because they don't take seriously the possibility that they could harm their children prior to conception. As Johnson Controls' expert witness put it, "If you don't look for a problem, you don't find it" (*Johnson Controls, Inc. v. CFEHC* 1990, 537). After all, if companies excluded both fertile men and women from their factories, they would have to close down.

Future litigation on more narrowly tailored fetal protection policies will have to determine the ultimate scope of women's right to work. As things now stand, the Supreme Court will not permit employers to allay their concerns about fetal vulnerability by externalizing all the costs of fetal protection onto women. Because of this decision, women should not be closed out of some twenty million jobs involving exposure to toxins (Greenhouse 1991). However, sharp disagreements divide the Court. For instance, Justices William Rehnquist and Anthony Kennedy believe that a policy excluding only pregnant women could meet the BFOQ defense. The changing composition of the Court leaves open the question of women's equality in employment and signals the need for ongoing political organization to ensure women's access to industrial jobs.

State Legislation

Despite the incredible controversy generated by such cases as *Johnson Controls* and the attention that scholars, the media, and courts have paid to fetal protection policies in the workplace, very few legislatures have regulated these policies. States have been known to innovate in the area of employment rights; six states, for instance, had passed their own pregnancy discrimination laws by the time Congress enacted the PDA.[13] In general, though, states tend to follow, not lead the federal government. Individual states are especially sensitive to the impact that legislation may have on their "business climate," and so tend to be reluctant to enact regulations that might drive away businesses.

Congress itself has entertained such legislation only once. In 1990, on the heels of the Seventh Circuit's decision upholding the policy at Johnson Controls, Representative Pat Williams of Montana introduced the Employee Protection Act to prohibit employers from making sterilization, fertility testing, or a promise not to have children a condition of employment, promotion, or transfer. Williams and others decided to wait for the Supreme Court's decision before sending the bill from the House Committee on Education and Labor to the floor, and after the decision, no further action was taken (Samuels 1995, 77–78).

Between 1977 and 1989, only five states passed relevant laws: California, Connecticut, Louisiana, Minnesota, and Oregon. The laws vary in their scope, covering workplaces employing as few as three people to those employing twenty-five or more. Until 1992 California's law applied only to employers of between five and fourteen people. The legislature enacted its law at the same time that Congress was drafting the PDA, and it feared its own provisions would be pre-empted by the federal law, so it exempted those employers subject to Title VII (employers of fifteen or more people) (Norton 1990). As it turned out, California's law contains specific provisions that the federal act does not, but even so, it took well over a decade before the legislature amended the law to apply to Title VII employers as well.

The strongest and clearest of these laws prohibit sterilization as a condition of employment, effectively outlawing the kinds of fetal protection

[13] The six states are Alaska, Connecticut, Maryland, Minnesota, Montana, and Oregon (Maschke 1989, 52).

policies challenged in court. Both California and Connecticut have enacted this law (in 1980 and in 1981, likely in response to the events at American Cyanamid). No one has ever filed a claim under this law in Connecticut, but it played a role in the case against Johnson Controls in California.

The remaining statutes aim to protect women's employment rights but tend to be vaguely worded and defer to employers' needs. To varying degrees, all five states provide that pregnant women in hazardous or strenuous jobs should be transferred temporarily to alternative assignments, as long as the transfer can be "reasonably accommodated" without forcing the employer to create any new jobs. In some cases the law directs employers with a policy, practice, or collective-bargaining agreement providing transfer to temporarily disabled employees to make sure to include pregnant women; in others, pregnant women appear to be covered regardless. Such vague wording may have been the result of political compromises, purposely deferring questions of intent and scope to other state agents. For instance, a 1977 Minnesota statute simply says that it is *not* an unfair labor practice "to provide special safety considerations for pregnant women involved in tasks which are potentially hazardous to the health of the unborn child, as determined by medical criteria" (Minn. Human Rights Act).

There is no reported case law in two of the states, and only one case each brought in California, Connecticut, and Minnesota.[14] Even though some of these laws give women more explicit rights than Title VII, it may be that they pursue claims under Title VII anyway for other reasons. Louisiana, for instance, created a Commission on Human Rights in 1988 but did not appropriate any funding (LeBlanc 1991). In addition, there is so little precedent from state law that courts look to Title VII principles for guidance in cases brought under state law. A woman in Louisiana may therefore prefer to bring her claim to the EEOC for either resolution with her employer or the right to sue in federal court.

The two cases brought in Minnesota and Connecticut show how employers fail to accommodate women's own concerns about their fetus's health. Tammy Englund worked as a full-time stylist at a Minneapolis Great Expectations hair salon. She became pregnant in 1983 and began to suffer headaches when she gave permanents. She averaged only two

---

[14] Laura Schlichtmann's research on accommodating pregnant workers on the job confirms the limited extent of legislative protection and case law in the states (Schlichtmann 1994, 394–97). Most research does not address the possibility of combating fetal protection policies through state measures at all (for example, Blank 1993; Daniels 1993; Kenney 1992; and to a lesser extent Samuels 1995, who looks only at state OSH plans but not anti-discrimination laws).

permanents per week, and asked to be relieved of giving them for the duration of her pregnancy. Meanwhile, Englund's husband apparently called her boss to express concern with Englund's "permanent giving because of a family history of birth defects" (*Khalifa v. G.X. Corporation* 1987, 223). When her boss denied her request and placed her on involuntary medical leave of absence instead, she turned to the state Department of Human Rights, which represented her in an action against her employer.

Englund alleged that her employer had discriminated against her on the basis of her pregnancy-related disability. Neither the administrative law judge nor the court of appeals was satisfied that she had substantiated this claim. State law defines a disabled employee as one who "can perform the essential functions" of the job with reasonable accommodation. The judges held that Englund did not meet the definition because she was asking to be relieved of an "essential" function of her job, giving permanents.

In the final part of its decision, the court of appeals asserted that even if Englund had successfully established a case of discrimination, her employer could justify his action by raising the "serious threat" defense. This defense allows "an employer to refuse employment to a person when the individual has a disability which poses a serious threat of harm to the disabled person or *others*" (225; my emphasis). The court took Englund's headaches, her doctor's note advising her to stop giving permanents, and her husband's concern with a family history of unspecified birth defects as sufficient evidence that Englund's continued employment constituted a serious threat to an "other." This conclusion seems even less warranted than the finding of no discrimination, demanding only the lowest level of evidence to bar a woman from employment.

Janeen Rose eventually fared better in her case against Fenn Manufacturing, where she worked as a stockroom coordinator at a plant producing parts for airplanes and military equipment in West Hartford, Connecticut. Her workstation was in the corner of a big open space, and she was exposed to fumes when co-workers spray-painted parts with zinc chromate primer nearby. These fumes became the source of a protracted struggle between Rose and the plant's management. Rose had been informed by her doctor to avoid contact with aerosols and hydrocarbons during her pregnancy, and obtained temporary permission from her immediate supervisor to leave her work area to avoid the primer, bringing paperwork to another part of the plant for the fifteen or so minutes it took for the fumes to clear. Rose's workstation was slated to be moved to another part of the plant, and so she settled on this as a temporary course of action. When she learned that her stockroom was not going to be moved after all, and that the spray-painting was scheduled to continue, she undertook a con-

certed research campaign, reviewing the material safety data sheet for the
primer, contacting the state's commission on the status of women to determine her legal rights, and filing a grievance through her union to obtain formal permission to work in another area when her co-workers were
painting. Denied permission, Rose left work out of concern for her fetus,
and filed a complaint with the state Commission on Human Rights and
Opportunities.

The hearing officer found that Fenn had discriminated against Rose by
failing to accommodate her, and awarded back pay and five thousand dollars for emotional distress. The company appealed to the superior court,
arguing that Rose's fears were not "reasonable." The trial judge agreed
with the company that the hearing officer lacked the authority to award
damages but upheld the finding of discrimination. The company's recal-
citrance clearly influenced this finding:

> Having come to the firm view that Ms. Rose's belief in the possible exis-
> tence of workplace danger was baseless, it devoted considerable energy
> to disabusing her of that belief, but never once gave ground on its basic
> position, most clearly voiced by [safety officer] Mr. Brooks in his last
> meeting with her: "If you can't work in your department, you can't work
> at Fenn." . . . [B]y committing itself to resisting her every effort to seek a
> safe alternative to working in her existing position, it took the calculated
> risk that its unyielding resistance would later be treated as a total failure
> to make any effort, much less a reasonable effort, to transfer her to any
> suitable temporary position which may then have been available for
> her. . . . Had Fenn relented by simply granting her the continuing right
> to work away from her desk a short 10–15 minutes each day, it would not
> only have alleviated her legitimate concerns for the health and safety
> of herself and her fetus, but in the bargain would have retained the com-
> petent services of a competent, qualified employee for at least three
> months. (*Fenn Manufacturing v. Commission on Human Rights and Opportu-
> nities* 1994)

The Connecticut Supreme Court affirmed the decision a year later.

As Rose's case shows, these state laws represent a positive step toward increased job security for women that should be improved upon, enacted,
and enforced in other states. These provisions at least open the possibility
of shifting the cost of fetal safety from women alone to the employer, and
hence to society at large through consumers of the company's goods and
services. Legislatures seem most willing to shift the costs in response to
women's pregnancies—that is, to the presence of actual fetuses—but not

in response to more general concerns about occupational threats to all workers' fertility.

As Rose's case also shows, it can take more than a decade to bring a case all the way through the administrative review and court systems. Some women, like Rose, are fortunate to be represented by a government agency like the state Commission on Human Rights and Opportunities, limiting the costs of pursuing justice. Even so, after eleven years of meetings, investigations, and trials, she recovered less than $7,500 in back pay and work time lost to attend hearings. It seems plausible that one reason there are so few cases on record is that most women decide it is not worth pursuing a remedy in the courts that takes so long and results in so little material compensation.[15]

Expanding the Inquiry: Other Pregnancy Discrimination Cases

Problems of fertility-based discrimination are not confined to unusually hazardous or toxic workplaces. Pregnant women who are temporarily disabled from performing some or all of their normal job duties routinely experience discrimination, and federal courts have not required employers to accommodate the needs of temporarily disabled pregnant workers so that they can remain on the job (Becker 1994, 81–86). Some scholars believe that the question of how to accommodate pregnant workers when toxic exposure is not an issue is simpler than resolving the fetal protection debate. Laura Schlichtmann argues persuasively that the problem nevertheless remains unsolved (1994, 340). Her discussion of the difficulties pregnant workers face when trying to modify their jobs in even quite minimal ways shows how far from being concerned about healthy pregnancies most employers really are. Two cases illustrate this problem.

Denise Dunning worked in a factory making wire harnesses for electrical systems in Montgomery County, Alabama. About midway through her pregnancy, she was transferred to a workstation in a different part of the plant, doing the same work but near molding machines that made the room considerably warmer. The heat was especially uncomfortable because Dunning was pregnant. She asked for ice but was not allowed to have any at her work area. Like all pregnant women, she found herself having

---

[15] The federal Civil Rights Act of 1991 may encourage more women to file suit. Passed by Congress in response to a series of Supreme Court decisions making it harder for employees to win discrimination suits, the law gives workers the right to compensatory and punitive damages in addition to back pay and job reinstatement; it also gives them the right to a jury trial.

to leave her work to go the bathroom more often (and even more so because she drank extra water to compensate for the heat). She asked to be moved to a cooler work area. The supervisor who denied her request commented that it wasn't his fault that she was pregnant and uncomfortable, and warned her to keep up her production quota. He did, however, promise to transfer her if she brought in a doctor's note. The firm's president overruled the promise, and told Dunning to keep working, quit, accept a layoff, or take early maternity leave, the last of which she did. After her baby was born, Dunning filed a complaint with the EEOC, and in retaliation was denied her old job back. She then sued in federal court for race and sex discrimination and retaliation under Title VII. The court did not understand the "exact nature" of Dunning's claim that her treatment involved sex discrimination, "inasmuch as Dunning offered no evidence on [the company's] policy with respect to men experiencing difficulty at work because of medical problems" (*Dunning v. National Industries* 1989, 930n9). The judge did find, however, that she had suffered from race discrimination, because the record showed that the factory had accommodated white women with light duty assignments in the past, whereas Dunning, who is Black, had in effect been forced to leave. Dunning won job reinstatement with full back pay (see also Schlichtmann 1994).

Eva Gutierrez worked as a part-time bakery/deli clerk at a Save Mart supermarket in Porterville, California. A few months into her pregnancy, Gutierrez experienced some abdominal pain and her doctor instructed her not to lift more than ten pounds. Some of the bakery clerk's tasks included lifting heavy trays and cleaning the mixing bowl, which weighed more than ten pounds. The store had a rule that prohibited workers from other departments from helping out in the bakery area, and as a part-time employee, Gutierrez had to work whatever shifts she was given, including some when she was the only person on duty. She asked that she either be relieved of heavy lifting or allowed assistance from another employee, but the store had a policy not to accommodate any temporarily disabling conditions and instead placed her on unpaid leave, costing her $4,500 in wages and benefits. She complained to the state Fair Employment department, but, as discussed earlier, the state provisions on accommodating pregnancy-related disabilities exempted Save Mart and other employers subject to Title VII. In the end the only thing that saved Gutierrez's job was a union contract guaranteeing workers' right to return to work after up to six months of leave (see Schlichtmann 1994 and *Department of Fair Employment and Housing v. Save Mart* 1992).

These two cases hint at the range of difficulties pregnant women routinely encounter in their jobs. Wendy Chavkin explains how "inflexible work rules that don't allow snacking, easy access to the bathroom, changes in position, or rest breaks" create real hardship for pregnant women (Chavkin 1984). In both Dunning's and Gutierrez's cases, the employer could have made minor modifications in order to keep the women on the job, and productively so.

Employers' failure to accommodate pregnant workers in jobs that are not unusually hazardous, along with the loss of income, job security, and health insurance this can entail, undermines arguments that corporate America is morally compelled to protect fetuses. True, most employers outside of heavy industry are not making fetal rights arguments. If anything, their arguments are more baldly about liability, such as fearing a pregnant waitress will slip and fall (see, for example, *EEOC v. Corinth, Inc.* 1993). But taking their actions together with those of Olin, Johnson Controls, and American Cyanamid, and compounded by the failure of Congress and the states to act, it is clear that the United States lacks any effective national pregnancy policy to benefit fetuses, women, children, or families.

Policy Alternatives

What might corporations and the government do instead of excluding women to promote health among working people and their families?

The single best thing is cleaning up the workplace. In many cases, this will eliminate the need to provide specific accommodation for pregnant workers. It is the surest way to protect employees, communities in which businesses operate, future generations, and corporations themselves. Money invested in research and development to identify alternatives to toxic substances used in production and engineering controls to minimize pollutants and by-products is well spent, whether measured by increased human health and well-being, environmental protection, or corporate protection from liability and bad publicity. If humane reasons ever did inspire corporations to implement fetal protection policies, then that moral concern can be redirected in productive directions like these. As the Supreme Court made clear in *Johnson Controls*, "Title VII does not prevent the employer from having a conscience." It does, however, prevent the employer from discriminating against women: "These two aspects of Title VII do not conflict" (1991, 1208).

In other instances, even after implementing a serious program of hazard reduction, there will still be hazards that cannot be eliminated or lowered sufficiently so as not to pose a reproductive health risk. An example from this chapter is battery production. Workers' exposure to lead can be limited, but there is yet no substitute for lead in batteries. Committing resources to create a national public transportation infrastructure, common in other industrialized countries, is one way to reduce demand by decreasing individuals' reliance on cars to transport only one person (Matthews 1996). But as long as people continue to depend on batteries for cars, they must share in the costs of making those products. Companies will certainly pass on some of their costs to consumers in the form of higher prices, and people should be prepared to accept this. Yet the corporations that derive the highest profit from the manufacture and sale of these products—and the officials, such as CEOs and shareholders, who incur the least risk from actual exposure to the toxins used in the process—must also share the burden.

In a unanimous decision, the California Supreme Court recently upheld a policy designed to redistribute the costs of lead pollution. A 1991 law imposes fees on industries engaged "in the stream of commerce of lead or products containing lead" (quoted in McElroy 1997, 7). These fees—up to $16 million each year—go to prevention, early detection, and treatment of childhood lead poisoning. The court endorsed both the legislature's power to shift some of the costs of these services to the industries responsible for inflicting the harm and its hope that the fees might encourage research on safer alternatives.

Along these lines, Yvonne Sor proposes the establishment of a national compensation fund for children born with birth defects that can be attributed conclusively to their parents' exposure to hazards at work. Industries using hazardous materials would be required to contribute to the fund. The reason for pooling funds is that it may be impossible to determine which exposure caused the harm if the parent(s) have worked at more than one job involving toxins. A national fund spreads the burden across the industry instead of leaving it to the individual worker to negotiate with an employer (Sor 1986–87, 227).

A more progressive and preventive policy would be to transfer affected workers temporarily, with guaranteed paid leave if no other assignment could be found, when there is indisputable evidence that exposure to an occupational hazard causes birth defects. This policy would give employers strong incentive to accommodate the pregnant employee or the employee, male or female, who wants to plan a pregnancy. The idea of reproductive leave for workers of both sexes is not new. Union activists have been advocating it for at least twenty years (for example, Wright 1979). Robert Blank advocates paid leave, but his example of its cost-efficacy is of a ten-week leave, which by his own account is not adequate because of harm incurred during the first trimester (Blank 1993). A more expansive leave could be financed jointly by the company, the industry as a whole, or the government. The study of Massachusetts electronics and chemical companies described in Chapter 3 found that a number of companies make arrangements for women who are pregnant or are planning to become pregnant, testifying to the feasibility of accommodation (Paul, Daniels, and Rosofsky 1989).

The Canadian province of Quebec mandates alternative employment or some form of compensation for women who are pregnant, breast-feeding, or planning to conceive (Taub 1996, 452). In addition, the European Union issued a "Pregnancy Directive" in 1992 to ensure that women who are pregnant or breast-feeding cannot be fired from occupations considered hazardous; nor can they be required to do work that exposes them to risks. Instead, employers must adjust these women's working conditions or hours, transfer them to other jobs, or suspend them without loss of pay for as long as necessary to protect against health risks. The directive applies to potentially hazardous agents like lead, and also more broadly to "movements and postures," travel, and work-induced "mental and physical fatigue." Two British writers point out that the directive does not allow pregnant workers to make their own choices (Morris and Nott 1995, 63). (The directive also requires paid time off for prenatal appointments and at least fourteen weeks subsidized maternity leave; countries with more generous benefits must retain them.) [16] None of these policies, from the ones adopted in Massachusetts to those adopted in other countries, is a perfect model because almost all exclude men, but they provide excellent starting points.

In 1985, the National Institute for Occupational Safety and Health included reproductive injuries in a list of the ten leading work-related illnesses and injuries in the United States (House Ed. and Labor Comm. 1990, 11n34). These injuries include infertility, miscarriages, and birth defects. Workers have very little recourse when they suffer from job-induced reproductive or sexual impairment. Workers' compensation laws in most states provide an inadequate remedy or no remedy at all for these harms. To make matters worse, workers generally cannot sue their employers for conditions covered by workers' compensation laws, even if they are unable to collect benefits under those laws (OTA 1985, 20–23). What this bind makes clear is that, to the extent that reproductive harm is recognized at all, it is the fetus that matters, not the adult worker whose own health is at risk.

---

[16] Council Directive 92/85, in *Official Journal of the European Communities* No. L 348.

Joan Bertin proposes bringing these injuries explicitly under OSHA's ambit, amending the OSH Act to overturn the ruling in the American Cyanamid case. The changes would include defining "serious physical harm" or "material impairment of health or functional capacity" to include any loss of reproductive or sexual function, and prohibiting discrimination against fertile workers. She suggests creating a private right of action for workers to bring their complaints directly to court instead of to the secretary of labor (Bertin 1989, 288–89). In addition, Bertin suggests federal legislation to prohibit discrimination on the basis of reproductive capacity. Given the likely difficulty of amending Title VII—and the possibility that any attempt to do so could result in diluting current protections—she argues that a freestanding statute might be the most politically feasible course of action.

In her assessment of where workers and employers stand after *Johnson Controls*, Mary Becker identifies several outstanding issues, such as OSHA's failure to enforce workers' rights to know about reproductive hazards (1994, 79–96). Because federal courts have not ruled that Title VII requires employers to accommodate pregnant workers or those planning pregnancy, Becker looks elsewhere for solutions to these problems. She examines both the Americans with Disabilities Act (ADA) and the Family and Medical Leave Act (FMLA) for solutions. She argues that the ADA provides the right remedy—accommodation—but excludes pregnancy. The FMLA covers pregnancy but provides the wrong remedy—a short, unpaid leave. Becker suggests that Congress could amend the ADA to include reasonable accommodation of workers trying to become parents in the face of reproductive risks (Becker 1994, 86).

This amendment would need to be carefully drafted to maintain an important conceptual distinction. In its current form, the ADA distinguishes pregnancy from permanent physical or mental impairments. This is appropriate, as pregnancy is a temporary condition and not necessarily disabling. Although activists have often found it expedient to compare pregnancy to temporary disabilities for the purpose of securing benefits, feminists have long debated whether pregnancy should really be classified as a disability. As Laura Schlichtmann argues, "The meaning of the term pregnancy-related disability is not entirely intuitive" in the employment context (1994, 358). It may be the job that is disabling rather than the pregnancy. As the cases of Janeen Rose and Denise Dunning show, disability arises in interaction between a woman's physical experience, the rules of the job, and the attitudes of management.

In September 1998, California Governor Pete Wilson vetoed an omnibus civil rights bill that would have required employers to give pregnant women reasonable accommodation to stay on the job. Current state law requires that employers move pregnant women to a less strenuous or hazardous position when such a transfer is reasonable. The bill's advocates argued that accommodation would help more women stay on the job and can be less disruptive than transferring to a new post. In other words, if a woman could continue working simply by putting her feet up to ease the pressure of varicose veins or eating crackers at her desk to help with morning sickness, the new law would have required employers to let them do so, even if employees are not generally allowed to eat at their desks. The fact that such a bill succeeded in making it through the country's biggest state legislature shows that these strategies are getting a serious public hearing and are politically possible.[17]

The number of proposals just presented illustrates that our policy choices are neither limited nor inevitable. A variety of avenues to pursue greater workplace opportunity and protection already exist, such as the Occupational Safety and Health Act, Title VII, and others like the Toxic Substances Control Act (Buss 1986).[18] Strengthening regulatory action is largely a matter of political will. Even if the existing mechanisms are not perfect, workers and their advocates can use them to accomplish important gains, if elected and appointed officials feel the pressure to be accountable. Indeed, the handling of related policy issues provides a striking contrast. In 1996 President Clinton proposed giving benefits to children of Vietnam veterans who suffer from spina bifida, even though research has not definitively concluded that soldiers' exposure to Agent Orange actually caused the defect (Purdum 1996). Despite the scientific uncertainty, the Clinton administration (and Congress, in earlier laws) weights the evidence in favor of the veterans when determining policy.

Preventing reproductive harm in the first place is clearly the best course of action and the reason why cleaning up the workplace is a first priority. But compensating employees and their children for work-induced injuries remains an important component of any comprehensive policy. Even without a perfectly detailed blueprint, it is still clear that a range of choices exists, and that the decision to focus on one set of choices over another is

[17] See AB 310 Senate Judiciary Committee bill analysis. The provision was previously introduced in the 1995–96 session as part of AB 658, which failed by two votes.

[18] One such avenue is the medical removal protection clause of the OSHA lead standard. Both Judith Scott and Laura Oren describe this provision as a powerful element of the lead standard, guaranteeing workers of either sex the right to transfer out of their jobs in order to lower their blood lead level, with no loss of pay or seniority, for up to eighteen months. Most of the literature, however, is silent on this provision, and neither Scott, writing in 1984, nor Oren, writing in 1996, recounts any history of successful enforcement of it by unions or OSHA.

a product of more than simple technology and economic calculation. Ingrained cultural and structural biases against seeing women as economic actors and against seeing men as reproductive beings, combined with free-market biases against regulating business, shaped corporations' choice of policies and many courts' legitimation of them.

The Supreme Court decision to strike down Johnson Controls' fetal protection policy did not settle for all time all questions of employment opportunity or employee health. Victories in court rarely settle a controversial issue definitively (consider the ongoing struggles over school desegregation, affirmative action, and abortion). Vigilance is needed to ensure that the parties comply with the ruling and to identify other companies using loopholes to defy it. This is the case with all political action, not something unique to the politics of fetal rights or a reason to turn away from the courts as an avenue (in the matter of fetal protection policies, the most promising and successful avenue) for creating change.

The precise impact of the decision on employment practices may take some time to gauge. Most comments appear to be speculative, rather than the result of empirical research. Susan Faludi argues, for instance, that the Supreme Court ruling did not discourage companies from imposing fetal protection policies. Instead, she says, "they simply shifted to subtler and more sophisticated tactics, 'counseling' women in new, required-training sessions about fetal threats on the job, or demanding that women get letters from their doctors permitting them to work, or requiring them to sign legal waivers" (Faludi 1991, 440). In contrast, Mary Becker reports that a number of speakers at a symposium on new challenges in occupational health indicated that many employers have responded by making their workplaces safer (1994, 81). Both of these statements may be true, with respect to different companies or industries. The first signals a need for continued action, and the second indicates that safety and opportunity need not be mutually exclusive.

Some feminists have warned against celebrating *Johnson Controls*, arguing that it legitimates the false choices women are supposed to make between parenthood and work, and between health and work (see, for instance, Rosen 1991). The fact that there is more work to do to secure full opportunity and safety is not a reason to diminish the positive meaning the Supreme Court's decision holds for women. In addition to the material costs, fetal protection policies exacted a heavy ideological price from women. The policies helped to reinscribe an ideology of "separate spheres" for men and women and exacerbated the socially fostered tension between women's economic and reproductive labor. One thing the victory against Johnson Controls means is that corporations and courts cannot create a new set of fetal rights and elevate them over women's statutory rights. This is important on its own terms and when compared with the battles over fetal rights in the medical care and substance abuse arenas, where there is no decision of national scope articulating women's autonomy.

The use of fetal protection policies to discriminate against women workers illustrates how fetal rights become mechanisms for distributing costs. When corporations, and many courts, asserted a fetus's right to be conceived and born without exposure to potentially harmful industrial substances, they burdened women with the costs of ensuring those rights. When it came to the possibility that women workers might bear injured children, corporations tolerated zero risk.[19] Rather than cleaning up the workplace to the maximum extent possible, fully informing workers of the risks of each job, providing job rotations to workers to plan pregnancies, and insuring against the costs of raising an injured child, the companies chose simply to exclude women. That exclusion located the problem of workplace hazards with fertile women, rather than with the workplace and its management. It cost women employment opportunity, wages and benefits, and the ability to make their own decisions about jobs and parenthood.

Whatever their particular strengths and weaknesses, the range of policy proposals presented in this chapter demonstrates one important conclusion: There is no single way that problems of fetal and worker safety must inevitably be addressed. Rather, there is a range of options that corporate officials and government representatives can choose from, and that unions and women's groups can organize their members and allies to fight for. As the next two chapters show, the pattern of fetal rights imposing costs on women recurs.

[19] Judge Easterbrook repeatedly criticizes this policy of zero tolerance in his dissenting opinion in *Johnson Controls* (1989, 913, 916–21).

5

"No Less than Ravishment"

Forcing Medical Interventions

on Pregnant Women

In 1986 Ayesha Madyun, a nineteen-year-old college student, was pregnant with her first child. She was admitted to the District of Columbia General Hospital in the middle of the night, two days after her water broke. Predicting a 50 to 75 percent chance that the fetus would develop a potentially fatal infection if Madyun did not soon deliver, Dr. John Cummings recommended a cesarean. When Madyun refused to have the operation, the doctor sought and gained a court order to perform the operation over her objections. After the baby was delivered without signs of infection, the doctor did not seem troubled: "You don't know that until it's done" (quoted in Gorney 1988).[1]

Ayesha Madyun's experience, while troubling, is not unique. During the 1980s reports surfaced of doctors seeking judicial sanction to compel pregnant women to submit to unwanted medical procedures on behalf of the fetus. This chapter shows how medical interventions forced on pregnant women reinforce women's subordination. The example most commonly discussed in the literature is to force women to undergo cesareans against their will, but women have been forcibly detained in hospitals and forcibly medicated as well, and they may be required to undergo fetal surgery and therapy when these medical practices become standard.

---

[1] The account of Madyun's case draws on *In re Madyun*, appended to *In re A.C.* 1990; Irwin and Jordan 1987; and Gorney 1988.

In these instances, competent adult women lose jurisdiction over their bodies and are subjected to physical violation that is almost never otherwise perpetrated in civil society or in the criminal justice system. As I argue, the state's interest in protecting potential life and prohibiting late-term abortions does not justify these intrusions into pregnant women's lives.

The expression "maternal-fetal conflict" commonly used to describe these situations is a misnomer, but these cases certainly are about conflict—between women and medical authority and between women and state authority. Conflicts emerge because there is a difference of opinion between the pregnant woman and the physician, one based on different priorities and on different interpretations of medical uncertainty. There is of course also a power differential between the woman and her physician that allows the physician to name their difference of opinion a conflict between woman and fetus instead of one between doctor and patient, and that gives the physician's opinion greater weight. No longer are women subjected solely to a cultural mandate to do their best for the fetus. Thanks to the successful assertion of fetal rights by doctors, legislatures, and courts, pregnant women increasingly find themselves subject to a political mandate to conduct themselves in ways that other people deem best.

The creation of these newfound fetal rights carries within it profound costs to women. A woman's ability to protect her body from violation and to make her own decisions is integral to self-determination. The implications for a woman's autonomy do not stop at the bounds of her flesh; rather, they radiate out from her body to encompass many facets of her life—the outcome of the contested pregnancy, her health, her spirituality, and her sense of order in the world. Pregnant women are not a monolithic group sharing the exact same identity or priorities. How a woman defines herself and understands her place in the world as well as the place of pregnancy and childbearing in her life are important elements of her identity. One woman may willingly sacrifice her preferences or even her life for her fetus. Another may value her life over the outcome of any given pregnancy. Some pregnant women may trust their own insight and experience more than doctors' predictions. Or the commitment women feel to their religion may be greater than what they feel for one particular fetus or even their own lives (such a distinction may not even make sense to these women, because they do not understand their lives as separable from their religious context and worldview). The point is that women's particular priorities shape their decisions when doctors diagnose a "conflict" between them and their fetuses. Regardless of what decision ultimately reigns, it is women who will live with its consequences in the most intimate and enduring ways, not the doctors or judges who pass through women's lives and pass judgment on them.

To some doctors and judges, the most important thing—indeed, sometimes the only important thing—is to "rescue" the fetus. Women, especially when ill or deemed unreasonable, cease to matter at all. They become means to an end, their bodies unfortunate obstacles to reaching the fetus. When third parties can make fundamental decisions for pregnant women—decisions that reduce them from people to mere bodies and then use those bodies as vehicles for the interests of others—women's identity, autonomy, and very personhood are jeopardized. Imagine the sense of betrayal that pregnant women must feel when they go to a hospital for help and are overruled and injured instead. Such actions create a climate of fear and distrust that can drive women away from seeking medical care at all.

Medical coercion carries important political implications for the status of women. Estimates suggest that around 90 percent of women in the United States give birth at some point during their lifetimes (May 1995, 12). All women therefore live under the threat that doctors or state agents can wrest away control over what happens to their bodies and their lives. Regardless of whether it is actually carried out, that threat helps to shape the conditions in which women live. Each year scientists continue to identify more and more possible ways to lower health risks to fetuses in the beginning of pregnancy or even before conception. Without concerted opposition, political conservatives can take these new findings as a basis for restricting women's lives, and thus make the sphere of regulation and intervention even wider.

Intervention forces women to understand in the most tangible way that they are not entitled to the same respect and security as other members of society, that their status as potential childbearers reduces them to a kind of second-class citizenship. As Chapters 3 and 4 demonstrate, all women are defined in terms of their childbearing potential and are assigned primary responsibility for fetal welfare. Yet enforcement of that responsibility is often selective. Those women most likely to experience unwanted medical treatment are women whose social standing is already vulnerable in some way: They are poor, members of religious minorities, members of ethnic or racial minorities, immigrants, or speakers of a primary language other than English. These women are more likely to give birth at large public institutions in which they have not developed ongoing personal relationships with a health care provider. They are more likely to be perceived as an incomprehensible "other" by the medical staff, for not only are they female and thereby automatically different most obstetricians, but they are also "foreign" by virtue of culture (George Annas, quoted in Lewin 1987; Irwin and Jordan 1987). Those characteristics that set pregnant women apart from their doctors are often the very ones that make middle-class professionals suspicious of their capacities as mothers in the first place (Ikemoto 1992a, 1992b). While the dominant pattern of enforcement exempts professional white women, they, too, have found it difficult to resist doctors' pressures to enforce treatment (Irwin and Jordan 1987, 328).

Let us return now to the case of Ayesha Madyun. Her story illustrates the ways in which court-ordered interventions on pregnant women rely on flawed legal reasoning and on stereotypical assumptions about women. Because this case also exposes more general problems characterizing women's experiences of pregnancy and childbirth, it is worth examining in some detail.

Throughout his opinion, the judge interchangeably uses the terms *fetus*, *unborn infant*, *infant*, and *baby* to describe Madyun's fetus. He also refers to her as the "mother" rather than as a pregnant woman. This assumes that she is already a mother and not an expectant mother, and it suggests that all other aspects of her identity cease to be relevant at the moment her doctor perceives a conflict. This failure to distinguish between a fetus and a child, and between a pregnant woman and a mother, is extremely common in authoritative legal and medical texts.

The judge that Dr. Cummings contacted held a late-night hearing at Madyun's bedside. He appointed a lawyer for Madyun and a separate lawyer for her fetus. Madyun's lawyer questioned whether the state's ability to order medical treatment of a child over parents' objections applied equally to a fetus, but the court found the answer to be yes, and it authorized the cesarean. Madyun appealed the decision, but her appeal—conducted by telephone between 1 and 2 A.M.—was denied.

The judge devotes an entire paragraph of his opinion to Dr. Cummings's credentials. He does not do justice to Madyun's own credentials, as a human being with self-knowledge and religious convictions: "Neither parent, however, is a trained physician. To ignore the undisputed opinion of a skilled and trained physician to indulge the desires of the parents, where, as here, there is a substantial risk to the unborn infant, is something the Court cannot do" (*In re Madyun*, appended to *In re A.C.* 1990, 1263). Madyun has two reasons for refusing to consent to a cesarean, a refusal her husband fully supported her in making. One involves her desire for a vaginal birth and her belief that such a birth is possible, given the proper time and conditions. The other involves her religion. The opinion reports that Madyun is a Muslim. The opinion first reports that Madyun believes that a Muslim woman has "the right to decide whether or not to risk her own health to eliminate a possible risk to the life of her undelivered fetus," and later describes a Muslim woman as having the choice to "decide between her health and body and that of the fetus" (1260, 1263). These two statements differ, and one does not apply very clearly to the situation at hand. Unfortunately, Madyun's beliefs—whatever their precise nature—are filtered through the judge's presentation, and it appears that he does not understand them. He ultimately decides that Madyun's refusal has less to do with religious conviction and more to do with personal preference, and so it does not trigger First Amendment protection of her right to freedom of religion. (Although in his view even that right would give way to the fetus [1262–63].) Neither does the seriousness of the operation, which the judge says poses only "minimal risks to the mother" even though a cesarean is major abdominal surgery exposing women to significantly higher risks of morbidity and mortality than vaginal delivery (1264). The judge finds that "all that stood between the Madyun fetus and its independent existence, separate from its mother, was, put simply, a doctor's scalpel" (1262).

The body of law the judge draws on to legitimate his decision is questionable. He draws on the state's enforceable interest in overriding parents' religious refusals to consent to medical treatment of their children, thereby equating a fetus with a born child. He draws on *Roe v. Wade* and on other court-ordered treatment cases, and with them all the flawed legal reasoning they represent (I develop these points more fully throughout the chapter). Although the judge claims never to doubt Madyun's mental competency to make decisions, he is very dismissive of her, deferring completely to the doctor's medical authority.

In addition to these serious problems of jurisprudence, Madyun's case also demonstrates problems with the contemporary treatment of pregnancy and birth. Many medical professionals and the culture at large regard pregnancy and childbirth more as problems to be managed than as ordinary biological and social experiences. Madyun's doctor did not think her labor was progressing normally; almost one-third of cesareans are performed for this reason (Guillemin 1993). Yet average labors are simply that—averages of the full range of experiences women have, not a standard every woman is supposed to meet. Madyun's cesarean is part of a broad trend of increased surgical births. Between 1968 and 1988 cesarean births in the United States rose from 4.5 percent to 24.7 percent (Shearer 1993). Madyun was prevented from standing and walking around, activities she thought would facilitate her labor and delivery. The hospital staff had attached her to an electronic fetal monitor, which forced her to remain in bed, lying on her side; the staff also informed Madyun that hospital regulations and city statutes required her to remain in bed with the monitor. The fetal monitor in turn incorrectly indicated fetal distress, or was misinterpreted by the person reading it. The use of monitoring has also increased in the last two decades, and its safety and efficacy remain controversial (Malnory 1993; see also Irwin and Jordan 1987, 325–26). These practices coincide with the fetus's emerging status as a "second patient" with its own rights. Finally, Madyun was repeatedly examined at D.C. General—she had ten vaginal exams in less than twenty-four hours, each of which increased her risk of infection. By relying on aggressive and controversial medical surveillance techniques, the staff themselves may have created, or at least contributed to, the conditions that led to the decision to perform the cesarean that Madyun did not want and ultimately did not need.

The experiences Madyun was subjected to, the physical violation of her body and will, are painful reminders that women's position in the social and political community remains insecure. In this chapter I argue that forced medical interventions operate to deny women equal membership. I examine instances of perceived conflict between pregnant women and their fetuses that led to the attempted or successful use of state authority to intervene in pregnant women's medical care against their will. The analysis draws from court decisions and other reported instances of forced medical intervention between 1973 and 1992 and from state legislation concerning pregnant women's power to make their own medical decisions. First I provide an overview of the scope of forced medical intervention against pregnant women. Next I situate women's treatment refusals in the context of their lives in order to show how refusing treatment makes sense to women but not to doctors and other authorities who have the power to override their decisions. Then I summarize the historical development of relevant legal principles of bodily integrity and of the notion of the fetus as a distinct medical patient. After analyzing court opinions, state laws, and public opinion in this area, I discuss implications for the future of pregnant women's autonomy in the medical realm.

The Scope of Forced Medical Intervention on Pregnant Women

It is impossible to determine the full extent of court-ordered medical intervention in the lives of pregnant women. Applications for court orders may be made to juvenile or family courts, whose proceedings are private and decisions unpublished or sealed. Some judges do not put their orders in writing at all. If the cases are not appealed and the media do not somehow learn of them, there will be no discernible record. Reports in newspapers and scholarly journals are often sketchy and partial and do not necessarily say where or when the incident took place. Law professor Lori Andrews describes being on a panel with a California obstetrician who claimed to have obtained forty-nine of fifty court orders he sought for cesareans on unwilling patients (Andrews 1993, 1994). This doctor's record alone exceeds all the published accounts of forced cesareans that I have culled from court opinions, medical journals, and other sources. What his record indicates is that we should regard those incidents that have come to light as only the tip of the iceberg. They reflect the powerful effect of introducing the assertion of fetal rights into the already unequal obstetrician-patient relationship, an unequal relationship that hospital administrators support.[2]

According to a variety of sources, between 1973 and 1992 courts in at least twenty-five states and the District of Columbia granted orders to doctors seeking to overrule their pregnant patients' refusal to consent to medical treatment. Many of these states have been the site of more than one such conflict.[3] Most court orders go into effect when the woman presents herself for care at the hospital, but courts in at least two states (Colorado and Michigan) have authorized the police to find the pregnant woman and bring her to the hospital (Irwin and Jordan 1987; Rhoden 1986). In one of these instances a pregnant woman in Michigan evaded the police and found another medical facility that would honor her wishes (Rhoden 1986). At least one New York woman ordered to submit to a cesarean is known to have given birth at home instead (Rhoden 1986).

To bring to light conflicts between pregnant women and medical authority, Veronika Kolder, Janet Gallagher, and Michael Parsons surveyed directors of maternal-fetal medicine programs about the use of court orders to obtain compliance from pregnant women. They identified twenty-one attempts to override a pregnant patient's refusal of therapy in eleven

[2] In addition, two doctors published an account of how they performed a cesarean without the woman's consent *or* a court order (Jurow and Paul 1984). Irwin and Jordan report knowledge of other such instances (Irwin and Jordan 1987, 332n15).

In a related context, Sue Fisher studied how doctors persuaded women to have hysterectomies for cervical dysplasia or cancer, when less invasive alternatives were available. Doctors successfully deployed the power of medical authority over their less powerful and less rhetorically resourceful patients to convince them to have major surgery they did not need (Fisher 1986).

[3] The states are Alabama, California, Colorado, Florida, Georgia, Hawaii, Illinois, Kentucky, Louisiana, Maryland, Massachusetts, Michigan, Minnesota, Missouri, Nebraska, New Jersey, New Mexico, New York, Ohio, Oregon, Pennsylvania, South Carolina, Tennessee, Texas, and Wisconsin, and the District of Columbia.

states during a five-year period (1981–85) (Kolder, Gallagher, and Parsons 1987).

Kolder's study found that courts granted 86 percent of applications for permission to perform involuntary cesarean sections or intrauterine transfusions or to detain a woman who refused therapy, making the vast majority of decisions within six hours. Hospital psychiatrists and courts investigated the woman's competency to make her own decisions in only 15 percent of the cases, finding each of those women competent; in the vast majority of cases, the question was never investigated. Eighty-one percent of the women involved were Black, Asian, or Hispanic, and 24 percent did not speak English as their primary language. When awarding temporary custody of the fetus, courts never designated a relative of the pregnant woman but usually a hospital employee. In concrete terms, these orders mean that medical personnel can forcibly restrain struggling women, anesthetize them, and cut them open, all against their will. Cesarean sections are major surgery, as one court opinion *authorizing* the procedure recognizes: "The surgery presents a number of common complications, including infection, hemorrhage, gastric aspiration of the stomach contents, and postoperative embolism. It also produces considerable discomfort. In some cases, the surgery will result in the mother's death" (*In re A.C.* 1987, 617).

The survey also assessed physicians' opinions about pregnant women's rights to make medical decisions. Forty-six percent of respondents agreed with the statement that women who refuse medical advice and thereby endanger the fetus should be detained in hospitals or other facilities to enforce compliance (Kolder, Gallagher, and Parsons 1987, 1193). Only 24 percent consistently supported competent women's right to refuse medical advice (1194).

The medical literature is the most likely to report instances in which a woman who refused intervention gave birth to a stillborn infant, or instances in which a woman who underwent an unwanted cesarean gave birth to an infant whose condition confirmed the doctor's predictions of infection or distress. This literature suffers from sample bias. The accounts published in medical journals are submitted by doctors describing their own experiences, not by independent researchers who have conducted randomized surveys. (Kolder's study is the only one of its kind, surveying doctors directly to identify instances of conflict.) Doctors have no incentive to publish accounts of how they needlessly forced women to have major surgery.

Even here the numbers are small. A team of Israeli doctors report two instances in which women who refused to have cesareans delivered stillborn infants (Leiberman et al. 1979). In instances when U.S. courts have refused to grant doctors the authority to override women's wishes and information on birth outcomes is available, I know of only one outcome that may have been compromised by the woman's refusal—a 1975 case of a woman thirty to thirty-four weeks pregnant with symptoms "suggestive of severe preeclampsia" who refused a cesarean and delivered a stillborn infant (Elkins et al. 1989).

Doctors express surprise, though not regret, at the fallibility of the medical technology on which they rely. A Colorado physician-lawyer team that obtained a court order to force a woman to undergo a cesarean remarked, "That a more asphyxiated infant with poor neonatal outcome did not result after so long a duration of apparent fetal distress simply underscores the limitations of continuous fetal heart monitoring as a means of predicting neonatal outcome" (Bowes and Selgestad 1981, 211).

Taken together, Kolder's study and the other reports and published court decisions demonstrate that judicial intervention is sought and granted in many states, not just one geographic area with particularly conservative political attitudes. The number of conflicts on the public record cannot reflect how often the threat of intervention compels a woman to "agree" to treatment she does not want. The available evidence represents a dangerous and significant trend, because these cases serve to redefine the boundaries of acceptable treatment of pregnant women.

Understanding Treatment Refusals in the Context of Women's Lives

In almost every case for which information is available, the women on whom doctors sought to force unwanted procedures were mentally competent adults.[4] Judges, doctors, and hospital psychiatrists did not dispute these women's mental clarity or their religious sincerity when the women invoked it. But they did not always respect the women's choices. When doctors and judges interpreted the women's actions as compromising their commitment to motherhood and the health of their future child, they came to see the women as irrational, incompetent, and bad, as the cases to

[4] In California a possibly incompetent woman was detained in a hospital by order of the juvenile court for the last six weeks of her pregnancy. An appellate court later ruled that the juvenile court had erred by declaring the fetus a child within the meaning of the dependency statute and violated the woman's due process rights by wrongfully detaining her under that provision when the district attorney's office indicated that the medical evidence against her was insufficient to proceed with an involuntary commitment under the mental health statute. See *In re Steven S.* (1981).

follow show. Sometimes these social judgments became legal ones, backed by the coercive power of the state.

A 1979 article published in the journal *Obstetrics & Gynecology* argues that if a woman continues to refuse medical advice after such factors as fear and ignorance are overcome, "a suspicion of an occult reason arises. It is probable that the patient hopes to be freed in this way of an undesired pregnancy and in no case will the patient share her secret thoughts with the physician. . . . The patient may conceal her *mens rea* (guilty mind) in different ways" (Liebermann et al. 1979, 515, 516). The authors conclude that women who refuse to have recommended surgery should be guilty of a felony. As one of the earliest publications on this subject, this article helped to shape medical discourse about pregnant women's refusals to consent to unwanted procedures.

The article's echoes can be heard in another article published in the same journal. The authors describe the unconsenting woman as unsympathetically as possible: She is "angry and uncooperative," the progress of her labor is "desultory," and she displays "unreasonable insensitivity to the welfare of her infant." The hospital staff, in contrast, feel "a devastating sense of helplessness" at the "ominous" situation, and yet continue to care for the patient with "sympathy and compassion." They are described as having legitimate "frustrations and anxieties," while the woman's fear of surgery—more risky for her because she is very overweight—is not accorded the same respect (Bowes and Selgestad 1981).

Hospital personnel seek court orders to compel women to undergo treatment in a wide variety of circumstances. Although most of the well-documented conflicts involve a woman's refusal based on religious grounds, that is not always the case, as the following three incidents show. These cases illustrate the range of situations in which disputes arise, as well as illuminating important themes explored throughout this chapter.

In 1981 a pregnant woman with terminal cancer instructed her doctors to resuscitate her first if she went into cardiac arrest from the chemotherapy, before trying to save the fetus. She was one of the almost 3,500 women with cancer who are pregnant each year (Mullholland 1987, 859). The obstetrical staff wanted the woman to undergo a cesarean, but her other doctors said that the operation would kill her (she was six months pregnant at the time). Undaunted, the obstetrical staff contacted the Los Angeles Department of Social Services, which filed a petition with the juvenile court charging that the woman was a neglectful and unfit parent, and asking the court to take jurisdiction of the fetus and veto the woman's medical instructions. An appellate court ultimately ruled in the woman's favor, but accounts of the case do not make clear what happened to her before then.

The incident is still instructive. Several doctors and a state agency were willing to force a woman to undergo a fatal operation in order to retrieve a very premature fetus. Their callous disregard for the woman's life, health, and priorities reflects both the devaluation of women as independent human beings and the consequences of treating the fetus as a second patient. In this instance, the obstetricians treated the fetus as an autonomous individual with distinct and compelling needs, but the same treatment was not accorded the pregnant woman carrying it. These doctors' mission, to preserve life, only applied to the fetus, and could not be expanded to include the pregnant woman even in the face of contrary medical opinion from their peers (see Gallagher 1984, 1987).

In 1984 a Nigerian woman living in Chicago was pregnant with triplets. She was hospitalized for the last six weeks of her pregnancy. The hospital staff decided that a cesarean delivery would be needed for this multiple birth, but the woman refused to consent to one, a decision her husband supported. Unbeknownst to her, the hospital obtained a court order awarding temporary custody of the three fetuses to the hospital administrator and authorizing a cesarean once the woman went into labor. Although many of the medical staff knew of the plan, the woman was not informed until she began labor and it was time to put the plan into action. She was therefore deprived of the opportunity to find another doctor at a different hospital or to appeal the decision (that the court would grant such an order without ever hearing her side of the story is remarkable). It took seven security guards to remove her husband from her room, and the woman resisted and screamed as she was tied down and prepped for surgery (see Gallagher 1987).

Had she been able to represent her own views, the woman, whose name we never learn, might have indicated that she believed a vaginal delivery was possible, and also that she and her husband planned to return to a region of Nigeria where medical facilities for future cesarean surgeries might not be available should she have more children. As Lisa Ikemoto explains, "She understood pregnancy and childbirth in the context of her future" (1992a, 515). The effects of the court's decision, Ikemoto continues, "include not only three healthy babies but also the physical violation of this woman and the forcible recharacterization of her understanding of pregnancy—a personal experience implicating health and future —to that of the medical profession—a pathology meriting physician control" (516).

The third case arose in Rockville, Maryland, in early 1990.[5] In that case Tawanda Walters arrived around 10 P.M. at her local hospital in premature labor. The on-call obstetrician wanted to transfer her to a facility better equipped to care for premature newborns. Walters was willing to go to another hospital, but not to the one the doctor chose. He wanted to send her to the University of Maryland hospital in Baltimore, and she wanted to go to Fairfax Hospital in Virginia, where she had given birth to her first child. The doctor and the hospital's attorney mistakenly assumed that because Walters was a Maryland resident receiving public medical assistance, the Virginia hospital would not admit her. Walters wanted to go to Fairfax because she had no car and, unlike Baltimore, Fairfax is easily accessible by public transportation, so she would be able to visit the baby in the hospital after she was released. She was also responsible for her nineteen-month-old son. Both these factors made giving birth in Baltimore unacceptable. Walters asked to be released so that her mother could drive her to Fairfax, but apparently she was prevented from leaving. The hospital's attorney contacted a judge by telephone, who shortly after midnight appointed the hospital administrator the temporary emergency guardian of Walters. The judge ordered Walters to "receive all such medical care as is ordered by her attending obstetricians to treat her premature labor and deliver her child," and to be transported to Baltimore as soon as possible (Order Granting Emergency Protective Services). The judge did not speak with Walters or appoint counsel for her, although he did order the hospital to provide her with an attorney the following morning. Walters gave birth the next day in Baltimore.

The hospital withheld critical information from the judge. First, the lawyer did not even inform the judge that Walters wanted to go to Fairfax; he merely said she refused to go to Baltimore. Had the judge spoken with Walters, of course, he would have learned this. Second, the lawyer did not tell the judge all that motivated the petition. Although seven months pregnant, Walters had only recently become aware of her pregnancy. She had gone to a clinic seeking an abortion, only to learn that her pregnancy was too far along. She then accepted the fact that she was going to have a baby. The doctor interpreted Walters's refusal to follow his instructions in light of this information, claiming that "she did not care about this baby at all," that it was up to him to save the baby, and, echoing Ayesha Madyun's doctor, that "the outcome justifies all of this" (Nurmi and Leclair 1990, A16).

Walters's case raises similar issues to that of the Nigerian woman dis-

---

[5] This account draws from Nurmi and Leclair 1990 and from the *Shady Grove Adventist Hospital v. Tawanda Walters* docket.

cussed earlier. Although an involuntary transfer and an involuntary cesarean represent different degrees of coercion, both women were dismissed as reasonable decision makers. In both cases women made decisions according to different criteria than those used by doctors and judges—that is, according to the material realities of their lives, be that lack of hospital facilities for future births, responsibilities to existing children, or lack of transportation to visit the hospitalized newborn. In both cases these conditions were ignored or denied. And although Walters had no conflict about her course of medical treatment with the obstetricians at the hospital where she gave birth, if one had arisen, the doctors would have had it within their power to compel her to submit to anything, thanks to the court order.

Three themes from these cases emerge again and again in instances of coerced medical intervention. First, the doctors and judges successfully depict pregnant women who are unwilling to follow doctors' orders as unfit to be mothers. These officials construct pregnant women by turns as irrational, incompetent, and immoral. Even when they recognize pregnant women as being mentally competent and not necessarily evil, they still often depict the women as unreasonable for making what they consider to be the wrong decisions.

Second, the courts defer to medical authority over women's judgments. Medicine is not a perfect science, and doctors' predictions of fetal distress and harm have very often proved to be wrong in hindsight.[6] Given the limitations of the data, this finding may be somewhat arbitrary. As I mentioned earlier, of all sources, the reports from doctors in medical journals are the most likely to describe incidents in which the doctor's prediction was right, but there is probably a selection bias operating here; doctors who force women to have cesareans for no reason are probably less likely to publish accounts of their actions for their peers to read. The crucial point is that medical uncertainty is typically calculated to the doctors' advantage because medical authority counts for a great deal in this society, and pregnant women have no culturally recognized counterclaim to an authority of their own.

Third, implicit in the first two cases and explicit in Walters's, the only one for which court documents are available, is a balancing of the pregnant woman's interests against those attributed to the unborn fetus. The judge's order granting emergency protective services concluded that,

[6] For instance, Veronika Kolder and her colleagues report that doctors' predictions of harm were wrong in twelve of fourteen forced cesarean cases (Kolder, Gallagher, and Parsons 1987, 1193).

"while Tawanda Walters is an adult capable of decision-making, compelling public interests concerning protection of her unborn fetus entitle the Court to enter an order under these circumstances," that "these emergency protective services are the least restrictive alternatives available under the circumstances," and that "balancing the consent rights of Tawanda Walters with the medical care needs of her unborn fetus compels this decision." The judge reached this decision even though the hospital's emergency petition for protective services clearly stated that "Walters does not lack the capacity to make a decision" but only that "she is exercising that capacity arguably to the detriment of the unborn fetus" (Nurmi and Leclair 1990, A16).

Given this and other similar outcomes, it is tempting to say that trying to strike a balance between competing interests in the first place is the problem. But because constitutional interpretation is virtually synonymous with balancing, critics of fetal rights cannot hope to influence actual judicial processes and outcomes by arguing simply that judges should abandon balancing. It is possible, however, to have an impact by exposing the ways that current balancing practices stack the interests against women. Lisa Ikemoto points out that the balancing formula courts most often use in these cases "ignores the process through which interests become important enough to be weighed" in the first place. That process is not neutral, she argues, but political, and it is one that devalues women before they ever find themselves in these situations (1992b, 1301). Because women caught in these conflicts usually lack meaningful legal representation, opposing counsel and judges have the power to determine what interests to balance. Moreover, Ikemoto shows that judges tend to assume that harm can be quantified and that it is finite, affecting women only at the time of intervention and not after they leave the hospital; this assumption of limited harm further weighs against women (Ikemoto 1992a, 492–96).

Bodily Integrity and Patients' Rights

As feminist scholars have shown, court decisions forcing pregnant women to submit to unwanted medical procedures go against an important tradition of legally guaranteed bodily integrity. The legal right to refuse medical treatment has both common-law and constitutional foundations. Common-law recognition and protection of human autonomy and self-determination, with roots in eighteenth-century English law, informed pivotal American court decisions in the area of informed consent (Hoefler and Kamoie 1992, 342–43). In 1891 the U.S. Supreme Court asserted that "no right is held more sacred, or is more carefully guarded, by the common law, than the right of every individual to the possession and control of his own person" (*Union Pacific Railway Company v. Botsford*, 251). In 1914 New York's highest court declared that "every human being of adult years and sound mind has a right to determine what shall be done with his own body," and that a surgeon operating without consent was guilty of "trespass" (*Schloendorff v. Society of New York Hospital*, 93).

The Constitution also protects people's right to refuse medical treatment. The right to bodily integrity, derived from the right to privacy guaranteed by the Ninth and Fourteenth Amendments, includes the right to accept or to refuse medical treatment, even if refusing leads to death. For some people, the decision to refuse medical treatment has a religious dimension that is further protected by the First Amendment's guarantee of religious freedom. The Thirteenth Amendment's protection against subordination and the Fourth Amendment's protection of the right to be secure in one's person from unreasonable searches and seizures might also be applied to medical decision-making (Gallagher 1987). In 1985 the Supreme Court reaffirmed the principle of bodily integrity, finding it constitutionally impermissible to perform surgery to remove a bullet wanted for evidence from a robbery suspect's chest without his consent.[7]

It is this body of law that grounds the doctrine of informed consent. As Rosalind Ladd observes, informed consent is both a legal and a moral principle (1989). The doctrine of informed consent requires that patients understand that they can refuse any advised treatment. They must be told, in a language they can understand, the risks and benefits of proposed treatment, any alternatives that may exist, and the likely consequences of refusing. Informed consent ensures that patients have the knowledge they need to make a meaningful decision, and it embodies the principle that patients have a choice, which doctors must then respect. This doctrine applies to mentally competent adults. Parents must give their consent for the medical treatment of their minor children, unless state statutes specify exceptions, such as pregnant minors' right to consent to prenatal care. When parents refuse to consent to their children's treatment because it

[7] According to the Court in *Winston v. Lee* (1985), the state of Virginia had proposed to "take control of respondent's body, to 'drug this citizen—not yet convicted of a criminal offense—with narcotics and barbiturates into a state of unconsciousness,' and then to search beneath his skin for evidence of a crime." The Court also noted that "the medical risks of the operation . . . are a subject of considerable dispute; the very uncertainty militates against finding the operation to be 'reasonable'" (1619; quoting in part from the Fourth Circuit Court of Appeals). See also *Cruzan v. Missouri Department of Health* (1990).

violates their religious beliefs, the state can often establish a compelling interest in protecting children and thereby intervene to enforce the treatment. Legislatures and courts have taken steps in recent years to protect the rights and well-being of those people who are not legally competent to make their own decisions from the capricious or harmful decisions of others in their name (Gallagher 1987, 17–21). Anyone subjected to treatment without his or her consent may be able to press a tort claim for negligence, malpractice, or battery against the doctor and other hospital authorities. If the doctor or hospital can be said to be a state actor, then the patient might also have a cause of action under federal civil rights laws (Gallagher 1987, 52n221).

Yet it would be a mistake simply to recount this history as if it has always included women to the same extent as men. As we saw in Chapter 3, early in the century the Supreme Court declared women's bodies to be objects of public interest in the case *Muller v. Oregon*. This public interest justified the government in making important life decisions for women by regulating their labor force participation. Although women came to have a firmer grasp on many of the rights of citizenship as the century progressed, the historical precariousness of women's legal position is one force at work to tilt the balance against them in the adjudication of medical disputes.

Courts frequently circumvent pregnant women's right to refuse medical treatment in three related ways. One is to assert a countervailing state interest in "innocent third parties" who may be affected by the patient's decision. In these cases the innocent party is the patient's unborn child or newborn. It is telling that courts making this assertion frequently follow it up with examples of decisions to override a parent's refusal of medical treatment for a child because of religious beliefs. These cases do *not* compromise the parent's bodily integrity, and so are dubious precedents.

Another way is to impose on pregnant women unique obligations to assist others. This judicial strategy rests on a prior assumption that the fetus is distinguishable from the pregnant woman as "another" person. Yet even if courts were right to assume that a fetus is an independent other, it still wouldn't have a right to the woman's body, because the law does not recognize an affirmative duty to rescue. Laurence Tribe observes that "the law nowhere forces *men* to devote their bodies" to help others (1988, 1354; emphasis in original). This is true "even in those tragic situations (such as organ transplant) where nothing less will permit their children to survive" (Tribe 1988, 1354).

Under our legal system, people have no claim to the resources of someone else's body. When faced with the question of whether a person can be compelled to donate blood, bone marrow, or organs against his or her will, courts have consistently answered no, even in cases of close relatives, and even in cases of imminent death. Perhaps the clearest expression of this principle comes from a 1978 Pennsylvania case concerning a person who refused to donate bone marrow to a dying cousin. The decision asserts that "for our law to *compel* the Defendant to submit to an intrusion of his body would change every concept and principle upon which our society is founded." The court declined to embark on such a course, because "one could not imagine where the line would be drawn."[8]

The third way that courts circumvent pregnant women's medical rights is to ascribe rights directly to the fetus, rather than assert a state interest in the potential life of the fetus or the life of the pregnant woman. This final strategy relates to the way the institution of medicine has transformed the fetus into a second patient. In 1971 the standard textbook *Williams Obstetrics* said that "the fetus has acquired status as a patient" because of "increased knowledge of the fetus and his environment"; the 1980 edition of the textbook hailed the fetus's "rightful achievement" of the status of second patient, "a patient who usually faces much greater risks of serious morbidity and mortality than does the mother" (quoted in Bowes and Selgestad 1981, 213). This language represents a significant departure from earlier editions, which emphasized the health risks to the pregnant woman and spoke of her baby (see the 13th [1966] edition). The American College of Obstetricians and Gynecologists also describes the pregnant woman and the fetus as "two patients" (ACOG 1987). By constructing the fetus as a distinct, independent entity, even though it is still inside the pregnant woman, the medical profession has created an adversarial

---

[8] *McFall v. Shimp* 1978, 91; emphasis in original. The court made it clear that it found the cousin's refusal to donate his bone marrow morally indefensible; however, it emphasized in lurid detail that such moral decisions properly rest with the individual and not the state: "For a society which respects the rights of *one* individual, to sink its teeth into the jugular vein or neck of one of its members and suck from it sustenance for *another* member, is revolting to our hard-wrought concepts of jurisprudence. Forcible extraction of living body tissue causes revulsion to the judicial mind. Such would raise the spectre of the swastika and the Inquisition, reminiscent of the horrors this portends" (92; emphasis in original).

Cases of this kind are extremely rare. In my review of the literature I have not come across a single case besides *McFall* that challenged a competent person's refusal to donate an organ or bone marrow. Nancy Rhoden discusses five cases involving potential donors who are not legally competent to give consent (Rhoden 1986, 1978, 1981–82). In addition, in 1990 the Illinois Supreme Court upheld a woman's right to withhold consent for her minor children, three-year-old twins, to undergo blood testing and possible bone marrow extraction as requested by the children's noncustodial father for the twins' half-brother (*Curran v. Bosze* 1990).

Finally, Rhoden observes that the state cannot remove organs from a dead person without that individual's prior consent or the consent of the family (Rhoden 1986, 1982). Why should pregnant women have less self-determination than the deceased?

relationship between women and their fetuses and between women and their doctors. A review of medical literature reveals obstetricians' tendency to treat the fetus as an autonomous patient, and ultimately as the more important patient, dropping women out of their discussion altogether at many points (Bowes and Selgestad 1981; Elkins et al. 1989; Liebermann et al. 1979; Jurow and Paul 1984).

In addition to embracing these three strategies, proponents of rights for fetuses cast their arguments in a fourth troubling way. When balancing the rights of the pregnant woman against her fetus, writers such as John Robertson misidentify the rights at stake. In his treatise on procreative freedom, Robertson argues that freedom encompasses the right to choose whether to procreate but does not encompass women's decisions about how to manage their pregnancy. He speculates that the Supreme Court is unlikely to find a right to direct pregnancy-related care and choose a method of giving birth in a claim of "familial or procreative autonomy" or "personal choice" (Robertson 1983, 450–58). Yet women do not need such a ruling, because of the rights to choose and refuse medical treatment discussed in this section. Robertson never mentions these rights, nor the principle of informed consent. This omission helps him build his argument that the state may subordinate pregnant women's "preferences" in favor of fetal rights.

Finally, court-ordered interventions must be understood in terms of the bittersweet legacy of *Roe v. Wade*, which remained the touchstone for legal conceptions of the fetus throughout the 1973–92 period. The Supreme Court's *Roe v. Wade* decision did not do all that women had hoped it would—it did not secure women's absolute right to control their bodies, nor did it secure equal access to abortion regardless of age or ability to pay. One thing *Roe* did secure, however, was governmental protection of a woman's interest in her health and life throughout her pregnancy.

As explained in Chapter 2, the *Roe* decision legalizing abortion established a three-part framework of "separate and distinct" competing interests and set up a particular formula for balancing those interests. This framework is all too frequently misinterpreted by legal scholars and courts to impose duties on pregnant women to their fetuses (see, for instance, Balisy 1987; Parness 1992; Robertson 1983). During the first trimester of pregnancy, a woman's fundamental privacy right encompasses her decision to terminate a pregnancy without state interference. During the second trimester, the state may regulate abortion in ways reasonably related to its compelling interest in protecting women's health. The court found that a woman's privacy right is not absolute, and so after viability, during the final trimester, the state may regulate and even prohibit abortion to further its compelling interest in "the potentiality of human life," *except* where abortion is necessary to preserve a woman's life or health. Fetal rights advocates consistently misconstrue this part of the framework as allowing state intervention into the lives of pregnant women who are not seeking abortions. What it says is that attaching any weight to the fetus is constitutionally optional but attaching weight to the woman is not; that is required. Indeed, Janet Gallagher argues that *Roe* actually paved the way for greater patient autonomy in other medical decision-making situations (1987).

Court Opinions

Two cases of forced intervention before 1973 influenced the later rulings. The first case arose in September 1963, when Jessie Jones sought emergency medical treatment for a ruptured ulcer. The physicians at Georgetown Hospital believed that without a series of blood transfusions Jones would bleed to death, but she refused to consent to any blood transfusion, as did her husband, both Jehovah's Witnesses. The hospital then sought court approval to force Jones to submit to the transfusions. When the first judge denied the order, the hospital attorney appeared at the chambers of an appellate judge, who accompanied the attorney to the hospital and granted permission. Jones was given the blood transfusions. The whole process took one hour and twenty minutes.

After the involuntary treatment, Jones asked the entire appellate court to rehear the case and determine her rights. Although the appellate court denied her a (re)hearing, the judge who ordered her transfusions wrote an opinion, and several other judges wrote dissenting opinions.

When the judge met Jones, her condition looked serious. He advised her of the doctors' opinions: "The only audible reply I could hear was 'Against my will.' It was obvious that the woman was not in a mental condition to make a decision" (*Application of the President and Directors of Georgetown College* 1964, 1007). Declaring Jones incompetent and comparing her to a child, the judge says that he can assume guardianship of her.

Jones was not pregnant, but she was the mother of a seven-month-old baby. The judge reasoned that "the state, as *parens patriae*, will not allow a parent to abandon a child, and so it should not allow this most ultimate of voluntary abandonments" (1008). The judge added that "the patient had a responsibility" not to her child but "to the community to care for her infant. Thus the people had an interest in preserving the life of this mother" (1008).

The judge also gives a great deal of consideration to the doctors' and hospital's position. He repeatedly sympathizes with the hospital staff who find themselves caught in this dilemma, which he stresses is not of their own making (1007). He suggests the hospital would be exposed to civil and criminal liability for failing to treat Jones and letting her "die in the hospital bed" (1009). Perhaps more significantly, he questions "just where a patient would derive her authority to command her doctor to treat her under limitations which would produce death," not finding it easily in constitutionally protected liberty as Jones's lawyer suggests in her motion for rehearing (1009). The dissenting judges feared, rightly, that this decision would be used as precedent.[9]

The following year in New Jersey, a hospital sought permission to administer a blood transfusion to a pregnant Jehovah's Witness over her religious objection. The hospital claimed that Willimina Anderson was likely to hemorrhage at some point during the pregnancy, endangering her life and that of her fetus. The lower court denied the hospital's request, and the woman left, against medical advice. On appeal, the state supreme court reversed the decision, finding that "the unborn child is entitled to the law's protection" and thereafter referring to it as "the infant child" (*Raleigh Fitkin-Paul Morgan Memorial Hospital v. Anderson* 1964, 538). The final outcome of Anderson's pregnancy is unknown.

Given such precedents on bodily integrity as *Botsford* and *Schloendorff*, *Georgetown* and *Raleigh-Fitkin* were bad decisions when they were handed down. But later courts still tend to cite them as authority without reconsidering their merits in the current legal era of better-developed patient rights, including the right to abortion. Laurence Tribe and Janet Gallagher both explain that, beginning in 1978, courts became increasingly receptive to arguments that competent adults have the right to refuse any kind of medical treatment, including treatment that could significantly prolong the person's life (Tribe 1988; Gallagher 1987). Their analyses reinforce the extent to which interventions on pregnant women go against the grain. Moreover, if Jones truly was incompetent (and the record leaves this question open to interpretation), then her case is not valid as a precedent in the cases of women who are alert and capable of making decisions.

---

[9] The opinion is noteworthy in another respect. The first judge also raised the state's interest in preventing suicide. Because Jones was not suicidal and did not want to die, he assumes that if a court orders treatment, then no harm has been done: "If the law undertook the responsibility of authorizing the transfusion without her consent, no problem would be raised with respect to her religious practice. Thus, the effect of the order was to preserve for Mrs. Jones the life she wanted without sacrifice of her religious beliefs" (1009). But of course the court's action has injured her religious beliefs: Her faith does not merely prevent her from agreeing to a blood transfusion; it dictates that she not ever have one.

Bearing this history in mind, I now turn to the cases arising between 1973 and 1992. I first discuss four cases involving conflict over a woman's refusal to have blood transfusions, and then four cases concerning a woman's refusal to have surgery or other treatment.

Forced Blood Transfusions

In 1976 a New York judge refused to order Kathleen Melideo to submit to a blood transfusion over her religious objections because "she is fully competent, *is not pregnant*, and has no children" (*In re Melideo*, 524; my emphasis). This logic underscores the significance of "innocent children" in judicial determinations of women's rights to refuse potentially life-saving blood transfusions and is relied on as precedent in some of the court decisions analyzed in this chapter.

Four instances of conflict between pregnant women and hospitals over blood transfusions resulted in published opinions; two of these cases reached courts of appeal. In all these cases the women were Jehovah's Witnesses (one opinion does not identify the woman's religion, but the nature of her objection strongly suggests that she is a Jehovah's Witness). Members of that faith take literally the biblical injunction to "abstain from blood," lest they be denied eternal salvation. They do, however, accept many other forms of medical and surgical intervention. These four cases demonstrate a significant willingness on the part of doctors, hospital administrators, and judges to suspend ordinary procedures in order to intervene in the lives of pregnant women.

The 1985 case *In re Jamaica Hospital* illustrates the problems for women subjected to one-sided judicial balancing. In this case a woman experienced internal bleeding during her eighteenth week of pregnancy. The fetus was in "mortal danger," a doctor maintained, and without a blood transfusion the woman and her fetus would die (899). The unnamed woman was a single mother of ten children, and her next of kin, a sister, could not be reached.

The opinion in this case is notable for the personal quality of its reasoning. The judge narrates much of the opinion in the first person, an unusual rhetorical device, explaining how the hospital contacted him at home, and how he came to be involved in the case. He reports that, given the facts, and "because I consider the fetus as a potentially viable human being in a life-threatening situation," he ordered a hearing at the patient's bedside (899). "In so doing," he continues, "I felt that the usual formalities of the assignment of counsel [and] notice to her family . . . must be dispensed with because of the danger of imminent death" (899).

At the hearing, one doctor testified that the patient would die without a blood transfusion, and a second that the fetus would die, too. The hospital's attorney, who had escorted the judge to the patient's room, was also presumably present. It was left to the judge, then, to address the woman and to elicit and represent her views, which he does in a single sentence.

The judge initially identifies the fetus as a potentially viable human being. After the hearing he designates the fetus, "for the purposes of this proceeding," as "a human being, to whom the court stands in *parens patriae*, and whom the court has an obligation to protect" (900). He maintains that "the court must consider the life of the unborn fetus," even while recognizing that *Roe v. Wade* does not consider the state's interest in potential life compelling prior to viability. He cites as precedent the 1964 *Raleigh Fitkin* forced transfusion case and a forced cesarean case, although both of those cases concerned women pregnant with viable fetuses, unlike this woman's eighteen-week pregnancy. He also states that if the patient were not pregnant, she could not be forced to have medical treatment over her religious objections. Because the woman has no attorney to help her make a case, it is the judge's prerogative to identify all the interests at stake as well as to balance them. He articulates only one interest for her, that in her religious beliefs. Concluding that "the decisive nature of the interests of the unborn fetus" outweigh the woman's "important and protected interest in the exercise of her religious beliefs," he therefore appoints the doctor as special guardian of the unborn child, with "discretion to do all that in his medical judgment [is] necessary to save its life, including the transfusion of blood into the mother" (899, 900).

Given that his own action runs counter to his understanding of *Roe v. Wade*, it is not clear why the judge invokes that decision. Although he does not spell it out, he appears to embrace the philosophy that a woman who has not terminated a pregnancy can be subjected to unusual requirements in the name of her fetus. Apparently the judge does not "feel" he has to spell out his reasoning, just as he does not feel he has to observe other standards of fair judicial conduct, such as determining a person's competence and assuring that the aggrieved party has legal representation. His use of the first person suggests that he took personal responsibility for rescuing the fetus (Ikemoto 1992a, 505). But when it comes time to render a decision, the judge cloaks himself in the official language of "the court."

In another case arising in New York the same year, Stacey Paddock's pregnancy was complicated by anemia, Rh-negative blood type, and the position of the placenta. Paddock's doctor determined that these conditions called for a premature cesarean delivery, to which Paddock agreed. She refused, however, to agree to the blood transfusions the doctor deemed necessary to safeguard her life and that of her fetus. The hospital contacted a judge from an appellate court, who held an emergency hearing and granted the hospital authority to intervene. In his opinion, the judge asserts the state's "vital interests in the welfare of children" and makes no distinction between an unborn fetus and a child, nor between a patient's refusal to consent to treatment of herself and a parent's refusal to consent to treatment of a child (*Crouse Irving Memorial Hospital, Inc. v. Paddock*, 444). It is not clear from the opinion whether the hospital sought authority to transfuse the baby after birth. The opinion describes the case as a hospital petition "for an order authorizing necessary blood transfusions to a mother and child during surgical procedures" (443). This certainly sounds like an order to authorize blood transfusions to a pregnant woman during cesarean delivery. The court next turns to the question of "Blood Transfusions to Safeguard the Mother's Welfare" (445). The analysis begins with "the premise that every adult of sound mind has the right to determine what happens to his [*sic*] own body" and finds that "Mrs. Paddock is an adult obviously of sound mind and deep religious conviction" (445).

The tone of the opinion then shifts abruptly, as does the articulation of the interests at stake. It moves quickly to the claim that Paddock has put "the hospital and her doctors in an untenable position" by agreeing to only some of their recommendations (445). Instead of acknowledging the difficulty of the situation for all the parties, the court portrays Paddock's attempt to control the birth process as rude and demanding, as well as irrational: "A hospital is not the patient's servant," the judge intones, "subject to his orders" (445; he is quoting from a 1968 law review article). Recognizing the hospital's desire to preserve life, as well as its exposure to civil and criminal liability for failing to treat (although the opposite is more likely in this case), the court grants the hospital authority to administer blood transfusions during the cesarean operation *and afterwards*, as necessary to stabilize Paddock's condition. By this point the court has stopped casting the determining interests as state interests, even when taking the extraordinary step of authorizing treatment of Paddock herself after the birth. In the rest of the analysis the judge chastises Paddock about patients' obligation to give the hospital complete authority to carry out its work, as articulated in *Georgetown*.

A third New York case reached the state's highest court in the beginning of 1990. In this case Denise Nicoleau established a relationship with a prenatal care provider and made it clear that she would not consent to a blood transfusion during the anticipated cesarean delivery. When she was admitted to the hospital in premature labor, she specifically refused transfusions of blood on the hospital's general consent form. Nicoleau's baby was successfully delivered through a cesarean operation, but afterwards she began to hemorrhage and had to undergo further surgery. At this point her doctor informed her that she would likely die without a transfusion, but still she refused to consent to one.

Unbeknownst to Nicoleau or her husband, the hospital sought and gained a court order to administer transfusions necessary to save her life. At 9 A.M., the hospital attorney contacted a judge, who granted the order by noon without arranging for Nicoleau to be served with the order. The hospital carried out the order at six o'clock that evening, transfusing Nicoleau against her will. Nicoleau was deprived of any semblance of due process—she had no knowledge of the hospital's intentions to override her decision, no opportunity to represent her position to the judge, and no opportunity to appeal the court's decision. As the preceding cases show, in most other emergency situations, some form of hearing was held; in this case nine hours seems sufficient to have conducted one. The hospital administered a second transfusion on New Year's Day, before Nicoleau successfully petitioned the Appellate Division to nullify the hospital's authority to do so. The hospital appealed.

The New York court accepted the appeal because the case presented "significant and novel issues of state-wide importance which are likely to recur" (*Fosmire v. Nicoleau* 1990, 78n1). All of the judges affirmed the appellate court's action to vacate the hospital's order to give Nicoleau blood transfusions, but they did so for different reasons. The majority opinion emphasizes Nicoleau's common-law and statutory rights as a competent adult to determine the course of her own medical care, arguing that the constitutional questions of religious freedom or bodily integrity need not be reached because of these other legal protections (80). Judge Stewart Hancock's opinion indicates that he might well have ordered the blood transfusions, but that the lower court's violation of Nicoleau's due process could not be tolerated. In his concurring opinion, Judge Richard Simons rests his decision on Nicoleau's constitutional right to freely exercise her religion: "The use of her body, without her consent and contrary to her religious beliefs, is to her no less than ravishment" (86).

The timing of this case makes it unusual. It would probably never have arisen if Nicoleau had not been pregnant.[10] In other words, if Nicoleau had been admitted to the hospital under other circumstances, such as a

---

[10] Neither the majority nor the concurring opinions cite the lower New York court cases of *Paddock* and *In re Jamaica Hospital* or the Maryland case of *Mercy Hospital v. Jackson*, discussed next.

car accident resulting in blood loss, it is extremely unlikely that a court would have authorized the hospital to administer a transfusion over her objections. It is unlikely that the hospital would have sought an order in the first place. But Nicoleau had just given birth to a baby and was suffering complications as a result, and her status as a new mother was foremost in the hospital's mind. As the court opinion shows, the hospital argued that the state should make value judgments about which people can exercise their right to refuse medical treatment, limiting the right to patients with terminal or degenerative diseases (79). The state ought to weigh an (otherwise) healthy mother's parental duties more heavily than all the interests and rights she is recognized as holding, preserving her life for the benefit of her child (83). This argument appears to have been at least somewhat compelling to both concurring judges, even though other arguments settled the question for them in Nicoleau's favor.[11]

Ernestine Jackson's refusal to consent to blood transfusions during a premature, emergency cesarean delivery underscores the importance of due process and also the primary role of fetal welfare. In 1985 a Maryland hospital petitioned the circuit court to appoint a guardian for Jackson, who could consent to the recommended transfusions on her behalf. Instead the circuit judge appointed a lawyer for Jackson, convened a hearing at the hospital, and then denied the hospital's petition. Jackson delivered her child by cesarean, without transfusions, and both survived the operation.

This case turns on three issues. First, courts rarely appoint guardians for competent adults. Jackson is recognized at all times as a "competent, conscious, rational adult" (*Mercy Hospital v. Jackson* 1985, 1130–31). Even if Jackson were deemed incompetent, her husband would be the next in line to make decisions for her. Next, the court took Jackson's First Amendment right to freedom of religion seriously. It appeared particularly unsympathetic to what it perceived as the Catholic hospital's efforts to substitute its own religious principles for Jackson's. Finally, and perhaps most important, the fetus was not at risk from Jackson's decision. While her doctors predicted a 40 to 50 percent chance that she would die during or after the cesarean (presumably by bleeding to death or from a heart attack), the fetus's chances of survival did not depend on the administration of blood to Jackson.

---

[11] An intermediate opinion vacated the hospital's order to give Nicoleau a blood transfusion but made it clear that in the case of a pregnant woman, the fetus's welfare is "paramount" (*Fosmire v. Nicoleau* 1989, 498). One of the concurring opinions picks up on the mandate in *Georgetown* to save mothers for the sake of their children, not feeling satisfied with a father and extended family to nurture and support the child.

The facts are not entirely clear. Jackson prematurely went into labor at twenty-five or twenty-six weeks gestation and sought care at the University of Maryland hospital in Baltimore. It appears that the university refused to perform a cesarean without blood transfusions, and so Jackson then went to Mercy Hospital, which admitted her but sought permission from the court to administer the transfusions against her will.

After the judge denied its petition and Jackson delivered her child, Mercy Hospital asked an appellate court to determine whether that judge had improperly balanced Jackson's right to religious freedom against competing state interests in preserving life, protecting such innocent third parties as minors and unborn children from losing a parent, and maintaining the ethical integrity of the medical profession.[12] A three-judge court of special appeals heard the case because it thought the situation was likely to arise again. It identified the crux of the issue as whether Jackson or Mercy Hospital "should be allowed to make the final decision regarding what medical invasions would be made to her body" (1133n7). That court ends its opinion by saying that Jackson's "baby was never at risk," quoting from the circuit judge that a pregnant woman can refuse a transfusion, where her decision "will not endanger the delivery, survival, or support of the fetus" (1134). This conclusion strongly suggests that the court would have balanced the interests differently if the fetus's life or health had ever been at risk.

More than a year later, the full court of appeals vacated the special appeals court's decision, finding that the case was moot (*Mercy Hospital v. Jackson* 1986). According to this opinion, courts should not rule on moot questions, because future conflicts would depend on unique fact situations that could easily be distinguished from the case at hand. The entire appellate court may have had legitimate reasons for declining to use this particular case as a platform to articulate a set of guiding principles. But the effect of the court's decision not to do so, especially given the fetus's favorable medical circumstances in this case, is to leave the door open to further interventions against pregnant women in Maryland. The cases in New York, especially that of Nicoleau, in which the life or health of her fetus was never at stake, also leave open that possibility.

Forced Detention, Treatment, and Surgery

In 1982 a Massachusetts man sought permission of the court to force his wife to have a cerclage operation to help hold her pregnancy. At the time

[12] Whether a private hospital may assert these state interests as its own is another question; Connecticut's supreme court said no in *Stamford Hospital v. Vega* (1996).

Susan Taft was four months pregnant, and Lawrence Taft wanted her to have her cervix sutured in order to keep her from miscarrying. Taft had had the operation in the past, when pregnant with three of her four children, and had miscarried once without it. Like her husband, she wanted the child to be born. But she had since become a born-again Christian and believed that Jesus Christ would protect her fetus.

Although the family court judge found Taft to be sincere in her religious beliefs, he found that the state could burden her right to religious freedom because of its "fundamental and traditional interest in the physical and mental health of all parents, their children already born and their unborn children," and so ordered that the husband "be granted the authority to force [the wife] to undergo the surgical procedure" (quoted in *Taft v. Taft* 1983, 396). When Susan Taft appealed this decision, an appellate court judge prevented the order from going into effect, and then the state's highest court decided to take over the appeal.

The Supreme Judicial Court overturned the lower court's decision, arguing that the judge had not taken seriously Susan Taft's constitutional rights to privacy or religious freedom, or her mental competence to refuse medical treatment. The court found the judge's construction of the state's interest in family health overly broad, observing that Taft's refusal posed no apparent threat to the physical or mental health of the father or existing children. It also found the state's reach too broad, identifying no prior case where a court ordered a woman to undergo an operation against her will for the benefit of a fetus that was not yet viable. The court did not rule on whether a husband has the right to make his wife have surgery against her will to assist in completing a pregnancy, assuming for this case only that the question was properly before the court.

The Supreme Judicial Court did not definitively foreclose the possibility that "the State's interest, in some circumstances, might be sufficiently compelling" to order a pregnant woman to have surgery over her objections (397). The court seemed particularly troubled that the family court judge had granted Taft's husband authority over her on such a factually sparse record. In particular, the court noted the absence of expert medical testimony about the risks of the operation to Taft and the probability that she would miscarry without it, underscoring the importance of medical authority. Although the court consistently refers to Susan Taft as "the wife," it does not subordinate her to her husband's authority.

A later conflict turned the possibility of subordination into reality, muting the promise of this ruling for women in Massachusetts. In 1986 twenty-three-year-old Dolores Britto came to Brigham and Women's Hospital in Boston at thirty-two weeks pregnancy experiencing severe abdominal pain. She was diagnosed with partial placenta abruptio, meaning that the placenta was detaching from the uterus, a condition that could result in fetal death and in Britto's suffering cardiac collapse or hemorrhaging to death. To prevent this from happening, the physician proposed amniocentesis to determine fetal lung maturity, continuous fetal heart monitoring, drawing blood for tests, and administering intravenous medications.

Despite the danger, Britto wanted to leave the hospital. The hospital initiated a hearing, and a judge appointed counsel for Britto and heard testimony from four people. The only testimony the judge reports in the opinion, though, is that of the chief ob/gyn resident (with degrees from Stanford and Cornell), who testified about Britto's condition and stated that the proposed treatment would pose minimal short-term risks. The judge's opinion never explains why Britto objects, only that she is mentally competent to do so. Casting the conflict as one between an individual's right to privacy and the state's interest in preserving life and protecting innocent third parties, the judge concluded that the state's "compelling interest in preserving the viability of the fetus" was "established before the court by expert medical testimony" and justified forcing detention and treatment necessary to preserve viability (fetal monitoring, blood tests, and intravenous drug therapy).

Three things about this case stand out: the weight of medical authority, the weight of fetal viability, and the flimsiness of privacy. The judge described Britto's right to refuse treatment as arising from the constitutional right to privacy, specifically "the freedom to be left alone." But Britto could not be left alone, because she carried a viable fetus, and the judge recognized no other more affirmative rights to fortify her position—such as common-law rights to bodily integrity and informed consent (*Brigham and Women's Hospital v. Britto*).

Only two appellate courts have published opinions specifically on the question of forced cesareans. To a woman opposed on religious grounds to certain kinds of medical intervention, a cesarean may not represent a worse violation than a blood transfusion or cerclage operation. In many ways, however, it represents an even greater infliction of costs on pregnant women. Because it is major surgery, a cesarean poses significant risks of infection and complications from anesthesia; it costs more money than a vaginal delivery; and it takes the longest to recover from, compromising the woman's health, comfort, and ability to care for her newborn.

The only state supreme court decision comes from Georgia, in 1981. A few days before she was due to give birth, Jessie Mae Jefferson had a disagreement with the hospital staff. They informed her that the ultrasound showed the placenta was blocking the fetus from passing through her cervix, that it was virtually impossible that the condition would correct itself, that the fetus would have only a 1 percent chance of surviving vaginal birth, and that she herself faced a 50 percent chance of dying. Jefferson refused to consent to the advised cesarean delivery on religious grounds. A Baptist, Jefferson stated that the Lord had healed her body, and whatever happened to the child would be the Lord's will. The hospital sought permission from the superior court to "administer" medical treatment to save the life of both fetus and woman. The court saw "the issue [as] whether this unborn child has any legal right to the protection of the court," and decided yes, invoking *Roe v. Wade* but departing from that opinion's holding by declaring that "a viable unborn child has the right under the Constitution" not to be terminated arbitrarily (*Jefferson v. Griffin Spalding County Hospital Authority*, 458). This statement seriously misconstrues the Supreme Court's decision by turning the state's interest in the potentiality of human life into actual constitutional rights for fetuses.

The superior court granted the hospital's request for authority to administer medical treatment necessary to save the life of Jefferson's fetus, but not its request to administer treatment to save *her* life, in keeping with typical judicial reluctance to interfere with competent patients' right to refuse treatment. The court also denied the hospital's request that Jefferson submit to surgery before going into labor. Instead, it extended an invitation to state agencies to intervene, and the next day it granted the Department of Human Resources temporary custody of Jefferson's "unborn child" and the authority to consent to surgical delivery on its behalf. "The temporary custody of the Department shall terminate," the court decided, "when the child has been successfully brought from its mother's body into the world or until the child dies, whichever shall happen" (459). The state supreme court denied Jefferson's motion for a stay.

How did the court reach its decision? It found that the "intrusion" involved in Jefferson's life "is outweighed by the duty of the State to protect a living unborn human being from meeting his or her death before being given the opportunity to live" (460). Two concurring opinions balance more elaborately, with one naming the rights at stake and discussing their relative weights. Very little weight is given to Jefferson's rights to bodily integrity, medical decision-making, or religious freedom. Remarkably, no weight was given to the fact that the decision effectively awarded temporary custody of Jefferson herself to the state. The court erred again by turning the state power upheld in *Roe v. Wade*—to stop an invasive medical procedure by banning abortions of viable fetuses—into the power to compel an invasive medical procedure. The Georgia Supreme Court adopted the lower court's opinion, reprinting it in full and adding little of its own. In its closing two-sentence paragraph denying the motion for a stay and making the trial court's orders immediately effective, the court cites without analysis three cases as precedent. They are, of course, *Roe v. Wade, Raleigh Fitkin* (cited without regard for the different level of intrusion and risk between a blood transfusion and a cesarean), and *Strunk v. Strunk* (a 1969 case in which a Kentucky court consented on behalf of an incompetent individual to a kidney donation to a sibling).

In the end, when Jefferson arrived at the hospital in labor, the court-ordered sonogram showed that the "impossible" had happened—the placenta had moved. (More likely, the first ultrasound had been misinterpreted.) [13] Jefferson gave birth vaginally to a healthy infant.

The second case arose six years later in the District of Columbia regarding a twenty-seven-year-old woman named Angela Carder who had been fighting leukemia for half of her life. Twenty-five weeks into her pregnancy, when she complained of back pain and shortness of breath, doctors discovered an inoperable tumor in her right lung and admitted her to the hospital. Carder and her doctors decided that she would undergo a cesarean at twenty-eight weeks, at which point the fetus would have a reasonably good chance to survive, even though she might not. Meanwhile, she consented to a course of treatment to make her as comfortable as possible, one including therapy that may have posed some risk of harm to the fetus.

Despite the fact that patient and doctors had chosen a treatment plan, hospital administrators went over their heads and sought the guidance of the trial court when Carder's condition worsened prior to twenty-eight weeks, asking whether to intervene to (try to) "save" the fetus. A judge appointed counsel for Carder and for her fetus, as well as allowing the District of Columbia to act as *parens patriae* for the fetus, and then held a three-hour hearing in the hospital—though neither he nor Carder's attorney ever met Carder, who was going in and out of consciousness from sedation. When her doctor consulted her, she initially agreed to the surgery recommended by the judge, but later, when she was more alert, insisted that she didn't want the surgery done. Carder's husband was too distressed to offer an opinion, but Carder's parents opposed the surgery, as did her personal physician. In fact, the entire obstetrics department refused to operate without Carder or her family's consent. When the judge authorized the hospital to operate, Carder's attorney appealed, but three judges from the appellate court upheld the decision over the telephone. The hospital administrator contacted six outside obstetricians before find-

---

[13] See Angier 1996 for a thoughtful and poignant discussion of the limits of ultrasound technology.

ing one to perform the surgery. On June 16, 1987, Carder underwent the court-ordered operation to deliver her 26.5-week-old fetus. The infant died in two hours, and she died in two days. Carder's death certificate lists the operation as a contributing factor.[14]

Carder's estate asked the full appellate court to rehear the case on its merits, and in the spring of 1990 the full court decided seven to one that the previous decisions were wrong. The trial judge and the three appellate judges had all treated the issue as one of balancing the interests of two parties, as in the *Jefferson* case, and they all explicitly subordinated Carder's interests to those they ascribed to the fetus (*In re A.C.* 1987, 617).

The opinion of the entire court goes in a different direction, attempting to chart a clear course to resolve future disputes. It does not focus on competing interests but on the right to make medical decisions. The court explains,

> In virtually all cases the question of what is to be done is to be decided by the patient—the pregnant woman—on behalf of herself and the fetus. If the patient is incompetent or otherwise unable to give an informed consent to a proposed course of medical treatment, then her decision is to be ascertained through the procedure known as substituted judgment [which is designed to determine what the patient would consent to were she able, based on her past actions and statements]. . . . We do not quite foreclose the possibility that a conflicting state interest may be so compelling that the patient's wishes must yield, but we anticipate that such cases will be extremely rare and truly exceptional. This is not such a case. (*In re A.C.* 1990, 1237, 1252)

The opinion does not clearly indicate what an exceptional case of conflict would look like. It declines to comment on whether Ayesha Madyun's case was one (1252n23). The opinion may appear to beg the question of how much weight to attribute to the fetus, but in essence it gives the fetus virtually no weight of its own, leaving that determination to the pregnant woman herself.

In contrast, the sole dissenting opinion by Judge James Belson holds to the original balancing framework that authorized the surgery as the appropriate one. (Belson was one of the three judges involved in the telephone appeal.) His reasoning is important because it makes explicit many of the assumptions that undergird the creation of fetal rights. He asserts that both the "viable unborn child's interest in survival" and the "state's

[14] For accounts of Carder's life and of the hearing and its aftermath, see Alderman and Kennedy 1995; Gorney 1988; and Remnick 1988.

parallel interest in protecting human life" deserve "substantial weight" (*In re A.C.*, 1254). All of the many interests Belson identifies Carder as having in "her own life, health, bodily integrity, privacy, and religious beliefs" merit "correspondingly great weight" (1257–58). Rhetorically, the fetus is presented as the standard; the woman's interests merely correspond to those the court attributes to the fetus. With the fetus assigned an interest and the state assigned an interest in it, the balance of forces is weighted two to one against the woman. Moreover, Belson identifies the most important factor on the fetus's side of the scale as "life itself, because the viable unborn child that dies because of the mother's refusal to have a cesarean delivery is deprived, entirely and irrevocably, of the life on which the child was about to embark" (1258).

Belson gives no actual credence to the state's professed compelling interest in women. He invokes *Beal v. Doe* and *Roe v. Wade* as authority for interfering with a woman's constitutionally protected privacy interest. Yet *Roe*'s trimester framework and *Beal*'s denial of publicly funded abortions foreclose certain options to women; they do not authorize forcing treatment on them. In addition, the passage Belson quotes as support for state authority to regulate and proscribe abortion in the third trimester unequivocally asserts the state's interest in "preservation of the life or health of the mother" (quoted on pp. 1254–55).

Belson disagrees with the "narrow view" his colleagues take of the "state's interest in preserving life" (1253). Yet why shouldn't the state have any interest in preserving Angela Carder's life? In the earlier opinion, the court declared that "the Caesarean section would not significantly affect A.C.'s condition because she had, at best, two days left of sedated life" (*In re A.C.* 1987, 617). But Carder's father says, "For 14 years our daughter was considered terminally ill and what right did the court have to decide that her life was over?" (quoted in Field 1989, 117). Judge Belson treated Carder as if she were already dead.

Despite Supreme Court opinion to the contrary, Belson says that the fetus is a person. He calls the fetus a "person" held "captive" within the woman's body (1256). In order to liberate the fetus, Belson disregards the dangers of surgery for Carder, designating pregnant women carrying possibly viable fetuses as a unique category of persons on whom the state may impose unusual burdens, without granting them unusual entitlements in return.

The court's final ruling in this case resembles Janet Gallagher's conclusion that the applicable constitutional balancing test is not of fetal versus women's rights but of patient's rights to make medical decisions versus the state's interest in overriding them. Gallagher argues that state-sanctioned coerced treatment must meet three standards: "clear necessity, procedural regularity, and minimal pain" (Gallagher 1987, 54–55). As the cases discussed show, these standards can almost never be met. But Gallagher's formula is problematic because it leaves open the possibility that some intervention could be approved, and because it fails to weigh what is most important to the woman. A blood transfusion that doctors can predict might be needed in advance of a woman's due date, leaving time for court proceedings, is the sort of procedure that may gain approval. But the criteria of pain and invasiveness are not always the most salient to women who refuse treatment; after all, women have refused blood transfusions while consenting to cesareans. Despite these weaknesses, the underlying message of Gallagher's proposal is clear: Pregnant women are to be treated with the same legal respect as all other patients; that is, they are not to be viewed as "different" because they carry fetuses and hence deserving of second-class citizenship.[15]

These cases raise the question of who has the right to be wrong. Judges insist that they don't want the responsibility for adjudicating these disputes, yet they don't all trust women to make decisions for themselves. Neither do doctors. The Kolder survey discussed earlier found that only 24 percent of maternal-fetal medicine program directors consistently upheld competent women's right to refuse medical advice, despite the official positions of the American Medical Association and the American College of Obstetricians and Gynecologists against court-ordered medical treatment of pregnant women (AMA 1990; ACOG 1987). As the cases described here show, doctors and judges make mistakes, but only pregnant women are denied the right to exercise their judgment because they might make one, too. Hence women must bear the costs of everyone else's mistakes—whether intimidation and the emotional distress of a court challenge or actual bodily invasion.

State Legislation

In the legislative arena, a similar pattern of forcing medical care on pregnant women emerges. As discussed earlier in this chapter, common-law principles of informed consent and constitutional protection of bodily integrity generally govern patients' rights to determine the course of their medical care, and they appear to account for the small number of statutes

---

[15] The distinction between constitutional and common-law foundations of the right to refuse may have important implications here. Laurence Tribe explains that as courts have moved toward broader recognition of the right to refuse, some have also shifted to a common-law basis that treats the right as a constant, not as something to be balanced against considerations of pain and necessity (Tribe 1988, 1363–65).

explicitly regulating adults' consent to medical treatment. Georgia is one state that does have such a law, even though Georgia is also one of the states that has authorized forcing unwanted procedures on a pregnant woman. The "Georgia Medical Consent Law of 1971" states that "nothing contained in this chapter shall be construed to abridge any right of a person 18 years of age or over to refuse to consent to medical and surgical treatment as to his own person" (Ga. Code Ann. § 31-9-7). This law played no part in the *Jefferson* case, which relied primarily on a misreading of *Roe v. Wade*. That court might have found persuasive an argument that the treatment was not "as to [Jefferson's] own person" but to that of her autonomous fetus.

No state has enacted any law that explicitly deprives competent, pregnant women of the right to choose and refuse medical treatment, but there has been a striking trend to deprive incompetent pregnant women of their rights in the area of living wills. California passed the nation's first living will law in 1976. By 1992, forty-six other states and the District of Columbia followed suit. Almost all of the thirty-seven states that specifically address pregnant women in their laws restrict women's decisions. Fully thirty-four of thirty-seven give pregnant women less authority to decide their fate than any other person signing a living will.

The purpose of a living will is to allow people to specify in advance what kinds of life-sustaining treatments they would want in the event that they are injured or develop a terminal illness and can no longer make and communicate decisions for themselves. A living will differs from a health care proxy or durable power of attorney in that the patient's own instructions govern; proxies are people designated by the patient to make decisions for them once they can no longer do so for themselves. I have focused on living will legislation because it reveals most sharply the conflict between pregnant women and the state over who gets to make life and death decisions.

Utah's law, ironically called the "Personal Choice and Living Will Act," spells out what is at stake in living will laws:

Developments in medical technology make possible many alternatives for treating medical conditions and make possible the unnatural prolongation of death. *Terminally ill persons should have the clear legal choice to be spared unwanted life-sustaining procedures, and be permitted to die with a maximum of dignity and a minimum of pain. In recognition of the dignity and privacy which all persons are entitled to expect, [the Legislature intends to] protect the right of individuals to refuse to be touched or treated in any manner without their willing consent.* (Utah Code Ann. § 75-2-1102; my emphasis)

Table 5.1. Pregnancy provisions in living will laws as of December 31, 1992

Provision	States
Women decide	Arizona, Georgia (only until viability), New Jersey
Silent on pregnancy	District of Columbia, Florida, Louisiana, Maine, New Mexico, North Carolina, Oregon, Tennessee, Vermont, West Virginia
Directive invalidated:	
If live birth is probable	Alaska, Colorado, Montana, Nebraska, Nevada, Ohio, Rhode Island
If live birth is possible; but treatment can be discontinued if it will harm or inflict pain on the woman	Kentucky, North Dakota, Pennsylvania, South Dakota
If live birth is possible	Arkansas, Illinois, Iowa, Minnesota
Automatically invalidated	Alabama, California, Connecticut, Delaware, Hawaii, Idaho, Indiana, Kansas, Maryland, Mississippi, Missouri, New Hampshire, Oklahoma, South Carolina, Texas, Utah, Virginia, Washington, Wisconsin, Wyoming
No living will law	Massachusetts, Michigan, New York

Of the forty-eight states that have living will laws, only three (6 percent) explicitly allow a woman to specify whether to carry out her instructions if she is pregnant at the time she becomes incapacitated, and in Georgia her instructions apply only before viability. Eleven states are silent on pregnancy (23 percent), leaving the question of what to do open to interpretation. The remaining thirty-four states (71 percent) all compromise or eliminate pregnant women's right to die. Of these, fifteen (31 percent of the total) require that life-sustaining procedures be continued if it is either "possible" or "probable" that the fetus could develop to the point of live birth (the statutes almost never define these terms), and nineteen (40 percent of the total) invalidate pregnant women's directives altogether, prohibiting them from having any force or effect "during the course of the pregnancy." Utah, despite its eloquence, is one of these states. Only Pennsylvania specifies that the state will pay the costs for keeping a pregnant woman alive against her wishes (20 Pa. C.S.A. § 5414) (Table 5.1).

Perhaps the most insidious thing about these statutes is that they never acknowledge the way they define pregnant women out of their guarantees. All living will laws define which people count as "qualified patients" for purposes of the law. Alabama's definition is typical: "A patient, who has executed a declaration in accordance with this chapter and who has been diagnosed and certified in writing to be afflicted with a terminal condition by two physicians who have personally examined the patient, one of whom shall be the attending physician" (Ala. Code § 22-8A-3 [5]). Also typical is the following proviso buried in another section of the law: "The declaration of a qualified patient diagnosed as pregnant by the attending physician shall have no effect during the course of the qualified patient's pregnancy" (Ala. Code § 22-8A-4 [a]). Nowhere is this disjuncture noted, that the pregnant woman is twice referred to as a qualified patient and yet she has just been disqualified.

To give women fair notice, "qualified patients" must be defined as those who are not pregnant women. The term *incompetent* must include all pregnant women, or pregnant women with possibly viable fetuses, as determined by each state. Perhaps the most jarring example of this blind spot is in the California law's provision on patient self-determination, which was amended in 1991 to *exclude* pregnant women (Ca. Health & Safety Code § 7189.5 [c]). Because the mere presence of an embryo or fetus overrides a pregnant woman's explicit instructions, pregnant women are deprived of the rights of the terminally ill, cannot exercise personal choice, cannot have natural deaths, or die with dignity.[16]

James Hoefler and Brian Kamoie note that the high level of legislative activity in this area is somewhat deceptive. Most states, they argue, enact narrow measures that do not deal with the complexities of the right to die that state courts have been grappling with and encouraging legislatures to address. This narrowness of scope makes it all the more remarkable that so many states have seen fit to regulate pregnant women's exercise of the right to die (Hoefler and Kamoie 1992, 362). Many states have based their living will laws on the model law, which imposes stricter restrictions on pregnant women's decisions in each of its three versions (*Uniform Laws Annotated* 1994). Hoefler and Kamoie attribute the restrictions on pregnant women to two things—the development of anti-abortion attitudes in state legislatures and the active lobbying by anti-abortion forces. Living will laws have been passed with very little interest-group activity by potentially interested groups, such as the elderly, but Catholic and right-to-life forces have been persistent and effective in influencing most of this legislation throughout the country (Hoefler and Kamoie 1992, 364). Feminist advocates presumably were less effective, or else were engaged in other political struggles.

---

[16] See, for example, the Alaska Rights of the Terminally Ill Act, the Alabama Natural Death Act, the Delaware Death with Dignity Act, and the Utah Personal Choice and Living Will Act.

A Washington woman and her doctor filed the only known court challenge to the exclusion of pregnant women from a living will law. Joann Lynn DeNino altered the living will to reflect her wishes that it should apply if she were to become terminally ill or disabled while pregnant; Washington's law automatically invalidates pregnant women's directives. When she asked her doctor to place it in her file, he refused, saying he feared civil or criminal liability for carrying out instructions contrary to the state's Natural Death Act. The trial court found that the pregnancy exclusion unconstitutionally violated the right to privacy, but the state supreme court reversed that decision. The high court essentially dismissed the case on the grounds that there was no controversy to resolve, as DeNino was neither pregnant nor terminally ill at the time. Three justices dissented from the majority opinion, arguing that if these issues could not be addressed once a woman drafted a living will, then they never would be, because a terminally ill pregnant woman would almost certainly die before the courts could resolve her case. The dissent also argued that the majority underestimated the public importance of the issue, which put all physicians at risk if they follow a patient's altered living will, and which affects the rights of all women of childbearing age (*DeNino v. State Ex Rel. Gorton* 1984).

An analysis of right-to-die cases in the absence of living wills revealed significant gender disparities in the adjudication of cases. The researchers found that courts treated evidence of women's preferences as emotional and unreflective, and hence dismissed it, while treating evidence of men's preferences as actual decisions needing to be respected. Courts were far more likely to delegate the decision about a woman patient to family or medical personnel than to use substituted judgment to reach the woman's own decision. The judges' gender-biased reasoning in right-to-die cases did not stem from particular assumptions about pregnant women, as there is no evidence that any of the women was pregnant, but reflected widespread assumptions about women in general (Miles and August 1990).

In limiting pregnant women's health care decisions, legislatures seem to be following the lead of the medical profession. Rosalind Ladd argues that the profession shares a pervasive presumption that women in labor are not competent to give consent. She argues that the broadly worded consent forms that pregnant women are required to sign in order to be admitted to the hospital for childbirth assume that pregnant women lose their competence the minute they walk in the door. Rather than constituting informed consent, these blanket forms amount to a waiver of the right to decide anything at all after admission, and they deny the value of a woman's actual experience in reaching an informed decision about the need for pain medication or other measures that doctors typically regard women in labor as being too emotional to make. People undergoing elective surgery or participating in medical research are also required to give their consent prior to the event, yet they can opt out if they decide to, whereas pregnant women cannot decide to defer labor and birth. "Preconsent is in a sense," Ladd concludes, "more coercive for them than for others" (1989, 39).

The court decisions, legislation, and research all demonstrate that, compared with men, women are not treated equally as medical patients and do not have self-determination. The current medical and political trends to aggrandize the fetus, seeking to give fetuses rights of their own in opposition to pregnant women, worsen the inequality. Women are not equal to men in terms of patient rights, and they now risk inequality with their own fetuses.

Public Opinion

What do people think about these developments? It is difficult to gauge public opinion about how perceived conflicts between pregnant women and fetuses should be resolved. There has been less public discourse about this issue than about either "fetal protection policies" in the workplace or the prosecution of pregnant women for taking drugs, as measured by high court opinions, government hearings, or news coverage and editorials. I identified only one public opinion poll that addressed pregnant women as medical decision makers. Conducted by Gallup for a health magazine, the telephone survey questioned one thousand adults on medical ethics (*Hippocrates* 1988). All such polls help to shape public opinion as well as to measure it, by the way they frame the issues and limit permissible responses, and later when the media report them as fact. Still, the survey demonstrates that many Americans hold women responsible for fetal health.

When asked, "Should a woman be held legally liable for harm done to her fetus because she refused to have a cesarean birth as recommended by her doctor?," 42 percent of respondents said yes, 41 percent said no, and 17 percent didn't know. To the follow-up question, "Should a woman be held legally liable for harm done to her fetus because she refused to let doctors operate on the fetus while it was still in the womb?," 32 percent said yes, 46 percent said no, and 22 percent didn't know. Finally, when asked whether a woman should "be held legally liable for harm done to her fetus because she chose to have surgery that was necessary to save her own life," 26 percent said yes, 63 percent said no, and 11 percent didn't know.

These responses yield two important conclusions. First, large numbers of the American public think it is appropriate to second-guess pregnant women's health care decisions and to punish them when something goes wrong. The results indicate a substantial willingness to hold women accountable for refusing treatment that doctors recommend on behalf of the fetus. Note that the question wording —"cesarean birth"—obscures the fact that a cesarean is major surgery. The question on fetal surgery met with the most uncertainty, probably because these techniques are still highly experimental and unfamiliar. Even so, one-third of those polled believe that a woman should be held liable for refusing to have this kind of surgery. Finally, one-fourth of respondents feel that women should be held liable for "choosing" surgery needed to save their own lives. This finding suggests that people commonly define motherhood as synonymous with selflessness and raises the following question: If the pregnant woman successfully discharges her maternal duty and sacrifices her life for the fetus, then who will mother it after it is born?

The second conclusion is perhaps the more politically important one. A large number of respondents said they did not know how to answer the questions: between 17 and 26 percent on every question. This significant segment of the American public is still forming its opinions, and thus can be influenced by arguments on either side, and perhaps more important, by courts' actions. If courts continue to take away women's power to make decisions, and there is no concerted protest, then people who are undecided are more likely to lean toward accepting state intervention in women's medical care.

Implications for the Future

Pregnant women's autonomy in the medical realm continues to be threatened by forced interventions and by developments in HIV policy in the post-1992 period. Late in 1993 a forced cesarean case once again made headlines. Tabita Bricci, a twenty-two-year-old Pentecostal Christian, refused to let doctors induce delivery or perform a cesarean when they predicted that her thirty-seven-week-old fetus would suffer brain damage or die from inadequate oxygen. The hospital contacted the Illinois state attorney's office, and Cook County Public Guardian Patrick Murphy (the county's lawyer for children) sought permission from the juvenile court to order Bricci to have the cesarean. When the juvenile court denied the order, Murphy appealed, arguing that the court must decide whether the viable fetus was "just a mass of human cells or a real life form being kept prisoner in a mother's womb" because of "primitive beliefs" (quoted in

Terry 1993, A22). Murphy said that Bricci should not be physically forced
to have the cesarean but should be held in contempt of court if she refused. Both the Illinois Supreme Court and the U.S. Supreme Court refused to review the appellate court's decision to deny the order, and two
weeks later Bricci gave birth to a healthy infant (*RFN* 1994).

While not the first such case to follow the final decision in Angela
Carder's case, this is the first one to gain widespread media attention. Does
it signal a renewed interest in using state authority to compel women to
have treatment to which they object? Illinois courts had authorized forcing women to have cesareans at least four times in the early 1980s, but they
appear to have learned from those past incidents, perhaps with help from
Bricci's American Civil Liberties Union (ACLU) attorneys: The courts
unanimously refused to order Bricci to submit to a cesarean. It is interesting, however, that the fetus in this instance was represented by the state's
attorney, not by the hospital's attorney. This situation suggests a fissure
within the state on issues of fetal personhood and women's rights.

Those fault lines emerged somewhat differently in a later conflict in Illinois. In 1996 a Jehovah's Witness named Darlene Brown had urethral
surgery when she was thirty-four weeks pregnant. She lost more blood
than was anticipated, doctors predicted that both she and the fetus would
die without a transfusion, and the hospital set the judicial machinery in
motion. This time the Public Guardian's office objected to being appointed to represent the fetus. The court nonetheless accepted a state's attorney's argument that Brown's situation could be distinguished from
Bricci's because a blood transfusion is so much less risky and invasive than
a cesarean; in other words, the court weighed the question according to its
own terms, not according to what mattered to Brown. The court awarded
the hospital temporary custody of the fetus and gave it the right to "consent" to blood transfusions on Brown's behalf. When Brown resisted, doctors "yelled at and forcibly restrained, overpowered and sedated her" (*In
re Fetus Brown*, 400). Even after an appellate court vindicated Brown's right
to make her own medical decisions, the state's attorney sought leave to appeal to Illinois's highest court. These shifting fissures within the state reveal that forced treatment remains contested terrain.[17]

Prominent on the public policy agenda since the mid-1990s is HIV test-

[17] See also Shirk 1991 and Marcus and Lundy 1997 on forced cesarean disputes in Missouri and Florida, and *In re Dubreuil* (1993) and *Stamford Hospital v. Vega* (1996) on forced
transfusions of women after giving birth in Florida and Connecticut. The Connecticut
Supreme Court strongly condemned the violation of Vega's bodily integrity but also made
clear that it did not answer the question of whether a pregnant woman may be given a blood
transfusion against her will for the sake of her fetus.

ing of pregnant women and newborns. Public discourse often reduces HIV-positive pregnant women to "vectors" of transmission to their innocent fetus.[18] Many HIV-positive women have intravenous or other drug addictions as well, and thus confront social scorn and a whole other set of problems with child custody and criminal justice (see Chapter 6).

As a condition of federal funding, the 1996 Ryan White Comprehensive AIDS Resources Emergency (CARE) Act requires states to implement mandatory newborn testing programs by the year 2000 if 95 percent of women do not choose to be tested, or if there is not a 50 percent reduction in the number of infants who are HIV-positive (Stein 1998, 115). Currently only New York tests and discloses results for all newborns, but many other states are considering doing so, or requiring pregnant women to be tested.

Pregnant women's test results only lead to more questions—about whether they can be forced to take the drug AZT or deliver by planned cesarean. The HIV-positive women who will feel the greatest impact of any change in protocol are by and large the same ones who have already borne a great burden of forced treatment: poor Blacks and Latinas (*JAMA* 1995).

Most policy debate ignores the limits of the research on perinatal transmission, which has found that under certain clinical conditions pregnant women who take AZT can reduce transmission from 25 percent to 8 percent (Farber 1995; Stein 1998, 109). The consequences for women of taking AZT before they need it are unknown (Stein 1998, 110, 112). So are the long-term effects on the fetus's developing nervous system (Stein 1998, 110, 112). Public debate minimizes the fact that AZT is a highly toxic drug that may not be appropriate for all pregnant women, and even the fact that the approximately 75 percent of children who would have been born without HIV infection in any case are subjected to a potentially dangerous drug for no reason. (Pregnant women in France and Switzerland who do not take AZT have lower transmission rates, probably owing to superior access to health care [*Science News* 1998].)

Testing newborns is a political compromise between advocates of mandatory testing for pregnant women and their opponents, including the American College of Obstetricians and Gynecologists, the American Academy of Pediatrics, and civil liberties groups. The American Medical Association changed its position in June 1996 to endorse mandatory testing (Stein 1998, 111). But all that such a test indicates for certain is the

---

[18] For an illuminating discussion of the cultural construction of AIDS through language, see Grover 1987.

woman's status, because all babies of HIV-positive women are born with their mothers' antibodies to the virus. A follow-up test several months later will be needed to determine which infants have the virus and which infants have seroconverted to negative status. Testing newborns, therefore, represents a significant violation of the woman's privacy rights, exposing her to potential discrimination if she has HIV, without giving a lot of information about the babies, and is opposed by many health professionals who work with women at risk for HIV infection *and* with infants who have HIV(Quindlen 1994). Good counseling and follow-up care are essential to make the testing worthwhile (Richardson 1998). These matters are not likely to be settled soon.

Several analysts have suggested the possibility that women could be prosecuted for giving birth to HIV-positive babies (Closen and Isaacman 1990; Bayer 1990). Certainly it is plausible that pregnant women who decline AZT or other medication will be challenged in court for depriving their fetuses of treatment. Michael Closen and Scott Isaacman identify several broadly worded state statutes making it a crime to knowingly infect another person with HIV.[19] At first glance the language of these provisions makes the possibility of prosecuting new mothers seem remote. But a decade ago few people would have thought that drug-trafficking laws could be used to prosecute a woman for taking drugs during pregnancy, as they have been in numerous states (discussed in Chapter 6). The political climate, more than the specific wording, is what makes such prosecutions possible, and this may be especially true if a woman has refused to take AZT.

Closen and Isaacman believe that "it is inconceivable that states could have intended to criminalize motherhood under these HIV-transmission statutes" (78). And yet Chicago's Patrick Murphy has proposed doing just that. He argues that all states should consider compelling all women who give birth to an HIV-positive infant to appear before a juvenile court judge who could order her to seek medical treatment and psychological counseling. "She would be told about birth control methods," Murphy continues, "and given advice about medications like AZT. If she became pregnant again, she would immediately be compelled to seek more medical aid and other counseling. But if she refused counseling and gave birth to a

[19] For instance, in Illinois someone violates the law when she knows she is HIV-positive and engages in contact involving "the exposure of one person to a bodily fluid of another person in a manner that could result in the transmission of HIV" (quoted in Closen and Isaacman 1990, 77). Presumably, application of these laws to pregnant women—and challenges to such application—would turn in part on the question of whether a fetus is "another person."

second child with H.I.V. . . . she should be prosecuted, perhaps on charges of criminal child abuse or assault. If found guilty, she should be put on probation or sent to jail (The children would be put into foster care.)" (Murphy 1996).

Murphy's scheme is rife with practical, legal, and social problems. Implementing it would require an enormously intrusive surveillance system to monitor the lives of all women of childbearing age. The legal basis to compel women to appear in court simply because they gave birth to a child with a life-threatening virus is unclear: HIV infection is a disease, not a crime. Murphy's proposal places the burden on women to "seek" assistance that often does not exist, instead of on the state to offer services. Already strained, the criminal justice and foster care systems are ill equipped to accommodate an influx of people with serious medical needs. But most of all, the proposal would rob women of their children, and children of their mothers, for absolutely no reason.[20]

The evidence presented in this chapter suggests that all pregnant women must live under the threat of intervention in order to prevent the very rare instances of irreparable harm to a woman or a fetus. This finding returns us to the question of who has the right to be wrong. The cases discussed in this chapter show that conflicts over medical treatment of pregnancy are always marked by uncertainty and the possibility of error. There is no question that these cases can be emotionally and ethically difficult for all the people involved—for the pregnant woman as well as the medical staff, lawyers, and judges. Yet coercion inflicts unacceptably high costs on pregnant women and has costs for women as a class and for society as a whole. The appearance of legitimacy that a court order confers cannot mask the fact that forced medical intervention amounts to state-sanctioned violence against pregnant women. Courts' participation in these conflicts for any reason other than to uphold pregnant women's rights to direct their treatment compromises judicial integrity and can lead to a loss of faith in government institutions. Certainly pregnant women's experiences compromise their faith in the integrity of the medical profession and can give many other women and men cause for concern as well. Fetal rights advocates may counter that honoring the pregnant woman's decision inflicts costs on the fetus and on the community that will absorb the extra financial costs for the services that a disabled child may require. Ultimately, the

[20] Murphy would extend his scheme to women who give birth to drug-exposed babies as well.

occasional fetal death or disability is the price society must pay for treating women as equals.

For all these reasons, if a woman refuses to follow professional advice, and either she or her fetus dies as a result, that is a politically acceptable outcome. Deaths that are considered "medically unnecessary" or "technologically avoidable" are still politically acceptable. While many people would regard such outcomes with outrage, disappointment, or sadness, those moral and emotional judgments are not cause for special legal restrictions on pregnant women.

As mentioned earlier, all women subjected to forced treatment should be entitled to some form of legal recourse, although most do not appear to pursue any. Susan Irwin and Brigitte Jordan indicate that Ayesha Madyun filed suit against the D.C. General Hospital but provide no details (Irwin and Jordan 1987). Angela Carder's survivors filed suit against the hospital for medical malpractice and wrongful death. Their settlement included a monetary award, something that is important to show hospitals that forcing patients to have medical procedures against their will has material consequences. The settlement also included new guidelines by the hospital to prevent future incidents of coercion against pregnant women. Some have hailed the rules as trend setting, but others see them as insufficiently woman-centered and doubt they will be effective (compare Thornton and Paltrow 1991 with Ikemoto 1992b, 1239).

Recall that when courts have upheld the rights of people engaged in alleged criminal activity or such morally suspect conduct as refusing to help a dying relative, they nonetheless honor the sanctity of the individual and paint vivid pictures of the consequences of doing otherwise. But courts do not honor pregnant women's individuality with the same consistency.

When doctors and courts force pregnant women to submit to unwanted medical procedures, they hold those women to standards of behavior that would not be enforceable against any other member of society. Even self-identified feminist scholars are willing to tolerate some level of medical coercion against pregnant women. Janna Merrick states that "claims on behalf of complete maternal autonomy ignore a number of important principles. For example, all people surrender some autonomy by living in an organized social system" (1993, 67). This statement glosses over the fact that pregnant women, like everybody else, have already given up some autonomy simply by virtue of living in a social world; additional justification is required to make them surrender additional freedom. Similarly, Merrick needs to make a case for why either moral obligations or medical diagnoses should be legally enforceable. She sees the essential question as one of maternal obligation to care for the born child, which she then reads backward onto the pregnant woman's obligation to her fetus. She finds that courts are ill suited to resolve these conflicts but does not call for legislation or offer any clear guidelines about who should resolve them. The last sentence of her article states that retrospective analyses of completed interventions "would shed enormous light on this very complex and clouded issue" (79). Her conclusion strongly suggests that she would not uphold the right of women to make decisions if such an analysis favored doctors (79). Merrick does not say how much more information is needed to find a definitive answer. The currently available data clearly support women's authority over doctors' predictions; even Merrick's own analysis rests on cases in which doctors calling for cesareans were wrong in at least six of seven instances.[21]

Merrick and I agree that the term *maternal-fetal conflict is incorrect*, but she sees the fundamental issue as how "the conflict affects the pregnant woman and the *born* child" (78; emphasis in original). The temporal impossibility of this formulation does not make clear precisely where Merrick thinks "the conflict" lies, and perhaps that is why it is difficult to find a solution to the dilemma she poses in her article.

Merrick considers Angela Carder's case "a tragic example of obstetrical intervention gone wrong," in which Carder became a "maternal martyr" (78). Isn't Carder better understood as a victim of powerful medical and state interests than as a martyr who gave herself to a cause, knowing the risks? There is a world of difference between a woman willingly risking her own life and the state risking a woman's life by forcing her to have an unwanted operation.

Compare the experiences of Carder and the other women described in this chapter with this story. In 1993 a fifteen-year-old Florida boy who was facing his third liver transplant and taking debilitating medication decided he would rather die than continue the painful treatments. State social service officials came to his house and took him by force to the hospital (five police cars came with the ambulance), claiming they were intervening in a case of child endangerment. "I should have the right to make my own decisions," Benny Agrelo told the *New York Times*, and a circuit judge agreed, even though he was a minor and Florida does not per-

---

[21] Merrick's review contains only one case in which the operation may have been necessary. In two instances, women were subjected to operations with no clear medical justification, with dire consequences for both woman and infant in one case. In the remaining four, women avoided the unwanted operation by their own wits (leaving the hospital) or by good fortune if they stayed within the hospital and legal systems. Surely, forcing women to flee hospitals and deliver at home without medical assistance is not in the best interest of the fetus that doctors, administrators, judges, and Merrick claim they want to protect.

mit minors to make their own medical decisions (see *New York Times* 1994a and 1994b).

In the very era when people have been gaining power over their medical care, then, pregnant women wind up with greater responsibility and less authority than anyone else. With pregnant women ordered to do for fetuses what no one is ordered to do for children or adults, the fetus has been endowed with super-rights that exceed those of any living human being.

6

Behaving Badly

Punishing Women for Conduct during Pregnancy

Forget about my rights,
I've got no money in the bank.

—Five Year Plan, from the song
"White Millionaires" (1988–90)

In 1992 the state of California tried unsuccessfully to prosecute a woman for murder because she had taken drugs while pregnant and delivered a stillborn infant. During oral argument, the deputy district attorney claimed that, "[under *Roe v. Wade*,] that baby that isn't born that happens to be over the age of twenty-four to twenty-eight weeks gestation has Constitutional rights, and somebody has to listen to that voice. Even though no one else can hear it, we hear it, and we intend to protect that child's Constitutional rights" (*People v. Jaurigue*, 27). Echoing the court orders forcing medical treatment, the district attorney's argument misconstrues the meaning of *Roe*. He transforms the state's compelling interest in protecting potential life in the third trimester into actual constitutional rights for fetuses. He also misconstrues the meaning of the state's homicide law, which was amended in 1970 to include the unlawful killing of a fetus but was meant to protect pregnant women from violent third-party assaults.[1] Moreover, the D.A. claims a privileged vantage point for the state

---

[1] California defines murder as "the unlawful killing of a human being, or a fetus, with malice aforethought" and specifies that the murder statute shall not apply to persons whose acts

in hearing the voice of the fetus, but comes to its aid only after it is too late, rather than assisting pregnant women in need of drug treatment.

This chapter examines the practice of prosecuting, incarcerating, and otherwise regulating women who use drugs or alcohol during pregnancy. The most frequently cited research estimates that 11 percent of babies born today, around 375,000 annually, have been exposed to street drugs prenatally (Chasnoff 1989). This number has been repeated so often that it has attained the status of fact. As early as 1985 medical researchers predicted that "crack babies" would fail in school and grow up to be less than human, wreaking havoc on society. These predictions lent legitimacy to harsh policies to control women's drug use. Throughout the 1990s, however, many have questioned the dire predictions for drug-exposed babies' future prospects, as well as the possibility of singling out any one definitive cause to account for the fate of drug-exposed children. In this chapter I assume that pregnant women's consumption of alcohol and drugs indeed causes some harm to some of the children they bear. What I seek to do in the following pages is critique the political response to the problem of drug-exposed babies, arguing that the response has been punitive, ineffective, and unfair to women and their children.

The *Jaurigue* case just described illustrates much of what is wrong with punitive practices toward pregnant drug users. First, it shows that the state is on shaky legal ground when it creates fetal rights to penalize women's conduct. Second, it shows that when the state does create rights for fetuses, it passes the costs on to women, even when they can't absorb them. In other words, the state burdens women with the responsibility for bringing healthy babies to term, even when they lack the resources to do so. As the cases in this chapter make clear, the state's enforcement of responsibility in this area has been quite selective: Poor women, especially poor Black women, have almost exclusively been held accountable. Recent legislation casts the net wider. Many of the state's actions in this area treat pregnant women as nothing more than carriers of fetuses, making their own needs invisible. These actions and attitudes do not succeed in promoting healthy babies. Given the failure of these policies to meet their stated goal of improving birth outcomes, what other agendas might ac-

---

result in the death of a fetus if the "mother of the fetus" solicits, aids, abets, or consents to the act (Cal. Penal Code § 187 [a] and [b][3]). The legislature amended the murder statute in 1970 to include the killing of a fetus, after the California Supreme Court ruled that a man who beat his estranged wife in order to kill her fetus could not be charged with murder. The fetus was stillborn, with fractures to the skull, when delivered by emergency cesarean. The court held that it would violate the defendant's due process rights and infringe on the legislature's authority to let the murder charge stand (*Keeler v. Superior Court* 1970).

count for the policy patterns evident in courts and legislatures throughout the nation? What is at stake for women, as directly affected individuals and as a group, in resisting this misguided "protection" of fetuses?

As I argue, the stakes are very high. Women may lose their freedom through imprisonment and lose permanent custody of their children. These absolute losses are at the extreme end of a spectrum of harm. Women may lose lesser degrees of freedom by coming under state surveillance during pregnancy and after giving birth. Fear of punishment may discourage pregnant women from telling health care providers about their drug use, thus compromising their care, or it may discourage them from seeking medical attention at all.[2] Insufficient medical care is correlated with poor birth outcomes, such as prematurity and low birth weight, that compromise newborns' health and development, as well as compromising women's own health. When they come under the jurisdiction of criminal and civil courts, women who have taken drugs during pregnancy are frequently deprived of due process. Due process means treating people fairly and according to the same rules as everyone else; in this way it is inextricably linked to equality. All of these experiences can make women lose faith in the social institutions of law and medicine that hold power over them. Punitive and paternalistic measures establish new standards of socially and politically acceptable behavior toward pregnant women.

These policies also sanction the use of pregnant women as scapegoats, as pawns in the power struggles of elected officials. Judges, prosecuting attorneys, and legislators use pregnant women to make political statements. Laura Gomez found legislative activity in California "fertile ground" for "symbolic politics" (1997, 40). Perhaps her most striking finding is that more than one-quarter of representatives introduced a bill on this subject between 1983 and 1996 (31). One in four legislators chose to sponsor a bill because it was an easy way to take positions on hot issues without having to spend much energy or face the consequences of the measure actually passing, as most of the sponsors did not have the committee placements or seniority to shepherd the bill to victory. Pregnant women's drug use came to be associated with crime, AIDS, abortion, and the "decline" of the family. The high number of bills introduced suggests that many law-

---

[2] Expression of this concern is widespread in the literature (see, for instance, AMA 1990; Barry 1991; Becker and Hora 1993, 554; Chavkin 1990; LaCroix 1989; Moore 1990, writing for ACOG; and *Pediatrics* 1990). Marilyn Poland and her colleagues report as their key finding "that our sample of low-income mothers in Detroit [85 percent Black] strongly believed that punitive legislation would further alienate pregnant substance-using women from needed health care" (Poland et al. 1993, 202). More recently, drug abuse counselors and patients in South Carolina raised this objection to reporting pregnant women (Dube 1997).

makers were able to use pregnant women as a convenient vehicle to achieve political gain. Unfortunately, such interest in political gain most often turns into grandstanding and comes at the expense of tackling such real problems as the shortage of substance abuse treatment for pregnant women.

Many commentators across the ideological spectrum have claimed that pregnant women owe a moral or a legal duty of care to their fetuses, one that may justify coercive government action against them (Balisy 1987; Burtt 1994; Dershowitz 1992; Robertson 1983; Shaw 1984). It is not my aim to engage in this debate to specify what the nature of pregnant women's duty is or might be. Rather, I want to ground my discussion in an examination of the consequences of enforcing unique standards of duty on pregnant women. However we view pregnant women's duties, these consequences represent largely counterproductive results that jeopardize the health of women and their fetuses.

In order to make this argument, I analyze several developments between 1973 and 1992. First, I set the context by describing the obstacles pregnant women encounter when seeking treatment and the way the media, medical researchers, and others constructed a sense of crisis about drug-exposed babies in the 1980s and 1990s. I then examine criminal cases against women for their conduct during pregnancy. Next I assess other mechanisms at the state's disposal to regulate and punish pregnant women's conduct. Finally, I analyze patterns of policy adopted by legislatures around the country. One of my goals in examining these policies is to undermine the false dichotomy between "punitive" and "public health" strategies to curtail pregnant women's use of drugs. The criminal justice system does not have a monopoly on punishment. Public health programs designed to increase surveillance of pregnant women can also be punitive, and such civil actions as terminating a parent's custody rights can be an extreme form of punishment. The important distinction is between policies of retribution and policies of assistance. Documenting the effect that the actual practices of government and medical institutions have on women and their fetuses shows that the creation of fetal rights in the substance abuse arena has been used to distribute the burdens of reproduction onto women in an unwise and unjust manner.

Women's Barriers to Treatment

Prosecutions and regulatory actions all take place in a context of acute treatment shortages for pregnant women to become sober and self-sufficient. Congress's major 1988 drug abuse law allocated less than 1 percent of its funding for pregnant women and women with infants (Segal 1991, 290). In 1990 the National Association of State Alcohol and Drug Abuse Directors estimated that less than 11 percent of pregnant women in the United States who need drug treatment receive it (reported in Becker and Hora 1993, 568n118).

Dependence on alcohol or drugs afflicts women of all class and race backgrounds, in rural, urban, and suburban communities. Addiction can be understood as "a biological, social, and psychological response to a drug, most usefully compared to a chronic illness in which relapse can be anticipated" (Wendy Chavkin, quoted in Cohen 1994, 94n17). When someone is addicted, she does not merely suffer from lack of willpower; rather, she has "impaired control" of the substance in use and continues drug-seeking behavior "despite adverse consequences" (Meyer 1995, 537). The U.S. Supreme Court has recognized addiction as an illness rather than a crime for almost forty years (*Robinson v. California* 1962).

U.S. drug policy emphasizes law enforcement over preventing drug use or treating drug users (Gomez 1997, 1–2). Begun under President Richard Nixon and solidified by Ronald Reagan's "war on drugs," this policy orientation creates special hardships for women. According to the AMA, "Even the most persistent pregnant woman is likely to fail to find a treatment program for her substance dependency," because, even if money was no obstacle, such programs are in short supply, and most will not accept pregnant women, partly because of fear of liability (AMA 1990, 2669). Withdrawal from opiates can harm or kill a fetus, as can sudden withdrawal from alcohol.[3] Women in at least two states have had to file class-action lawsuits to try to gain access to treatment programs in their communities.[4]

The following case illustrates the challenge. A twenty-seven-year-old pregnant woman living in Butte County, California, was addicted to heroin. She sought medical treatment but could not find a methadone maintenance program in her poor, rural county. Instead, she drove 140

---

[3] Medical practitioners generally recommend treating babies for withdrawal after they are born, citing the first and third trimesters as the most dangerous times for a pregnant woman to withdraw from opiates and preferring methadone maintenance even in the second trimester (Hoegerman and Schnoll 1991). Similarly, alcoholic women who suddenly stop drinking may experience seizures and other withdrawal symptoms that can threaten a fetus. The drug antabuse, prescribed for recovering alcoholics, is contraindicated during pregnancy (U.S. DHHS 1993, 13).

[4] The cases are *Elaine W. v. Joint Diseases North General Hospital* (1993) in New York, in which the plaintiffs prevailed, and an investigation by the Philadelphia Human Relations Commission, described in Cohen 1994, 94.

miles each day to Sacramento for methadone treatments, which cost $200 of her monthly welfare check, until her car broke down and she could no longer get to the clinic.

After failing again to secure treatment closer to home, and eight and one-half months pregnant, she did what one commentator has called the responsible thing: She started taking heroin again, to prevent stillbirth (*Youth Law News* 1990, 19). She told the medical staff about her drug habit when she gave birth in order to ensure proper treatment for her baby, and the child protection agency assumed custody of her child. She was also threatened with prosecution by the district attorney for illegal drug use. Negative publicity ultimately deterred the district attorney from pressing charges, but his office expressed interest in keeping its prosecution options open (Aronson 1989; LaCroix 1989).

This woman's dilemma is not unique. Her story dramatizes the barriers to treatment for pregnant women throughout the country. In New York City, 54 percent of programs categorically exclude pregnant women, 67 percent reject pregnant Medicaid patients, and 87 percent reject pregnant Medicaid patients addicted to crack cocaine—the group most likely to be prosecuted (Chavkin 1990). In Florida there are only 135 residential treatment beds for the 4,500 pregnant women who need them; in April 1990 the waiting lists reached a new high, with more than 2,000 women signed up (Blumner 1991). In Connecticut four new state-funded model programs for pregnant women will serve only 90 of the estimated 5,000 women in need (Stoddard 1990). Whatever the specific numbers, most state directors of alcohol and drug abuse programs identified women as an underserved group in fiscal year 1990 (U.S. DHHS n.d., 109).

Even when treatment is available, many people argue that programs are designed with men in mind. They argue that the typical confrontational style of therapy is not effective with women, whose paths to addiction require different kinds of treatment (Chavkin 1990; Cohen 1994; Kumpfer 1991). Another manifestation of male-centered treatment design is programs' failure to provide child care, even though the National Institute on Drug Abuse identified lack of child care as a major obstacle to women's treatment twenty years ago (Chavkin 1990). Child care is a pressing need because many pregnant drug users are already mothers, and others will become mothers before they kick their habits. Very few residential programs allow women's children to live with them at the treatment facility. In San Diego, for instance, such programs accommodate only twenty-six women (Roberts 1991, 1448n147). For many women who do not have someone to care for their children full time, entering drug treatment means giving up their children to foster care and risking permanent loss of custody. They may rightly view the trade-off as unacceptable. A study of services in California's Alameda County (Oakland and Berkeley) found places for only twenty infants and older children with their mothers in residential treatment programs (U.S. Public Health Service 1991). The report notes that this forced many women to choose between entering treatment and keeping their children (32).

Good treatment can make a difference in women's lives and the lives of their children. A substance abuse clinic for pregnant women created by the chief of obstetrics at Harbor/UCLA Medical Center in 1986 brings 80 percent of its patients to a drug-free delivery. The program continues to help women after their children are born; they remain in group therapy for six months and participate in parenting classes (ABA 1990, 56). Treatment is also cost-effective: An Alaska study estimated that residential alcohol treatment for a pregnant woman costs $6,000 per month, as compared with $2,400 per day for intensive care for an infant with fetal alcohol syndrome (Dineen 1994, 65).

In 1992 Congress amended the law governing the Alcohol, Drug Abuse, and Mental Health Administration (ADAMHA) block grant, adding several new provisions to facilitate pregnant women's access to treatment services. The most significant provision prohibits programs that receive federal funds from discriminating against pregnant women. Because almost all programs receive some federal money, this law potentially gives pregnant women access to virtually all treatment sites in the country. The law is only as good as its enforcement, however, and advocates worry that programs will take advantage of loopholes to justify their continued exclusion of pregnant women. The law's ultimate impact on pregnant women's lives will be determined by actual compliance rates and by women's ability to bring lawsuits to secure admission to recalcitrant facilities (Cohen 1994).[5]

The Social Construction of the "Drug Baby Crisis"

This information about pregnant women's difficulty finding treatment gets far less play than information about the possible effects of women's substance use on fetal development. The topic of "fetal abuse" became so

---

[5] Because the ADAMHA program is a block grant, the federal government does not collect, aggregate, or publish a great deal of information about how the various states administer it. Consequently, it is difficult to know how much the legal changes have actually improved pregnant women's access to services. Anecdotal reports continue to indicate problems. A Virginia news story, for example, reports that a pregnant cocaine addict was turned away from a facility whose fourteen "female-designated beds" were taken and was not provided interim services (Simpson 1999).

popular that every article focusing on drug abuse and state law published in the 1991–92 academic year concerned pregnant women (Nyberg 1991–92). No one argues that drinking or taking drugs during pregnancy is good for fetuses, but there is no consensus on how widespread fetuses' exposure is or on how harmful it is, especially in the long term.

Janet Fink observes that "as recently as 1982, medical texts on high-risk obstetrics maintained that cocaine had no harmful effect on fetuses" (1990, 37). Three years later, when crack cocaine appeared, that changed. Television, magazines, and newspapers unleashed a steady stream of stories about "the crack baby," with its characteristic high-pitched wail, irritability, and developmental deficits. For the past decade, news stories have heralded the advent of a "biologic underclass" and warned that "crack kids" have neurobehavioral deficits that "interfer[e] with the central core of what it is to be human" (quoted in Zuckerman and Frank 1992, 337). In 1990 *National Review* editor Jeffrey Hart claimed that it is impossible to treat crack babies, and that money is wasted on them because they often become violent and manic-depressive (quoted in *The Responsive Community* 1991, 72). Even though it is quite unlikely that anyone could have known how these children would turn out when the oldest ones were about five years old, the speculations have been influential: Laura Gomez interviewed California district attorneys who repeated these claims that "crack kids" without consciences would soon be flooding the criminal justice system (Gomez 1997, 72).

These accounts generated harsh policy proposals. Hart has proposed that all women addicted to cocaine be sterilized (quoted in *The Responsive Community* 1991, 72). Michael Dorris sympathetically quotes a social worker who suggests sterilizing alcoholic women of reproductive age in his best-selling 1989 book *The Broken Cord*, which describes his adopted son's struggles with fetal alcohol syndrome. Dorris and his son (both now deceased) were Native American, and this proposal is especially ominous given the history of forced sterilization of Native American women. The possibility of using the contraceptive Norplant to sterilize temporarily women who give birth to drug-exposed babies has been debated in the media and in state legislatures and courtrooms around the country.

The widely publicized 1985 study credited with starting the "crack baby" myth is based on a total of twenty-three infants born to women who used cocaine and thirty born to women who did not (Chasnoff et al.; see also Fackelmann 1991). Only six of 119 developmental studies follow drug-exposed children past the age of three years (Begley 1997). Most reviews of the literature now emphasize the limitations of the data, especially the small samples from which conclusions have been drawn. Another common problem in research design is failing to control for confounding variables, such as women's use of alcohol, tobacco, or other drugs; lack of prenatal care; poor nutrition; and the home environment after birth. All of the methods used to detect drug exposure—drug testing, self-reporting, and clinical observation—have shortcomings and may contradict each other. Linda Mayes and her colleagues report that only one study has ever evaluated infant outcomes according to their mothers' specific patterns of drug use (1992, 407).

An early nonalarmist review of the medical literature in *Youth Law News* emphasized that "at least as much is unknown about prenatal drug exposure as can be stated with any certainty," but concluded that women who use drugs during pregnancy are more likely to give birth prematurely and to have low-birth-weight babies, conditions that increase the risk of infant mortality and childhood disability (Lockwood 1990, 15, 16). In a 1992 commentary in *JAMA: The Journal of the American Medical Association,* a team of pediatric specialists criticized the country's "rush to judgment" that exposure to cocaine during gestation irrevocably damaged children. They oppose labeling drug-exposed children as hopelessly damaged because "labels have a way of becoming self-fulfilling" (Mayes et al. 1992, 407). Five years later, a conference convened by the New York Academy of Sciences reached similar conclusions, and found primarily subtle developmental differences between children who were exposed to cocaine and those who were not (Begley 1997).

Although there is no single reliable estimate of the number of newborns exposed to drugs, the estimate that 11 percent of babies are born exposed to drugs has great currency politically. Judges and legislators as well as reporters invoke this figure; Bill Grimm explains how a California appellate court reported this estimate without giving the original source, treating it as the factual context for its determination that a positive drug test at birth is sufficient to declare a newborn a dependent child of the court (*In re Troy D.*; see Grimm 1995, 8).[6]

Women giving birth in public inner-city hospitals have been subjected to the most systematic testing, creating the impression that drug use is primarily a problem of poor minority women. In addition, the findings that investigators choose to highlight contribute to a biased picture of preg-

[6] The 11 percent figure was derived by reviewing medical charts for the diagnosis of mothers and newborns discharged after birth from thirty-six hospitals around the United States. Together, these hospitals "represent a total annual delivery rate of 154,856," but the author does not give the actual number of charts reviewed. The data were reviewed for diagnoses of exposure to heroin, methadone, cocaine, amphetamines, PCP, and marijuana, and the incidence ranged from 0.4 percent to 27 percent (Chasnoff 1989).

nant women's drug use. W. H. Hollinshead and colleagues, for instance, report in the text of their article on Rhode Island that "cocaine was detected more commonly in women who were other than white," but not that white women tested positive more often for every other drug in the study. To learn that, readers must study the table where the findings are displayed (Hollinshead et al. 1990, 226).

Gideon Koren and colleagues uncovered another form of bias: against studies that do not show harmful effects from cocaine exposure during pregnancy (1989). Between 1985 and 1989 the Society of Pediatric Research accepted twenty-eight (57 percent) of the studies finding adverse outcomes for presentation but accepted only one (11 percent) study finding no such harm, even though the negative studies were on the whole more methodologically rigorous. This skewed selection distorts the public's understanding of the problem and contributes to a climate of panic in which coercive intervention into pregnant women's lives seems acceptable.

What do the doomsday accounts leave out? The roles of men and of government. Epidemiological evidence suggesting a link between men's drinking and cocaine use and prematurity and low birth weights made front-page news in 1991 but has not kept the nation's attention (Blakeslee 1991). A government survey of parents of 2,200 children found that "the more a mother smokes *after giving birth*, the more behavioral problems her children are likely to have." The survey did not even ask about fathers' smoking (*New York Times* 1992, C9; my emphasis).

A comparative perspective also suggests that the U.S. findings reflect in part the high level of poverty and problems with health care access in this country. According to Susan Boyd's review of the literature, most births to women suspected of using drugs are not remarkable, and most of these infants are neither premature nor small (Boyd 1994, 187). Studies in Glasgow and Liverpool found that when women who use drugs are provided with medical care and economic and social support, their birth outcomes are comparable to those of women who do not use drugs (187–88). Even in this country, prenatal care has a positive impact on fetal growth, regardless of drug use, and intensive early intervention programs have been successful at helping drug-exposed infants develop normally (Coles et al. 1992; Toufexis 1991).

What is especially striking is not just how similar cocaine-exposed children are to their nonexposed peers, but how much worse these poor children, enrolled in studies in cities such as Chicago, Detroit, and Philadelphia, fare than their counterparts in better-off communities. Koren's study of forty-seven drug-exposed children in Toronto who were adopted as infants found that they scored almost thirty points higher on IQ tests than children in Philadelphia (cited in Begley 1997).

Whatever the precise nature and extent of harm may be, there are better ways to try to avert it than to punish women. Prevention and treatment services are more effective at rehabilitation and improving health and come closer to paying for themselves than incarceration ever will.[7] Unfortunately, spending priorities favor the criminal justice system over education and other human services.[8] The politics of fiscal retrenchment and fetal rights ideology compound each other to distribute the costs of fetal health unfairly and unproductively to women.

Criminal Court Cases

The first known criminal case against a woman for using drugs during pregnancy occurred in 1977, when the state of California charged Margaret Velasquez Reyes with two counts of felony child endangerment for giving birth to twins addicted to heroin. An appeals court found that the child endangerment statute does not apply to fetuses and prohibited any further proceedings, except to dismiss the case (*Reyes v. California*).

It was not until ten years later that the issue of criminalizing pregnancy drew widespread media attention. The catalyst was the case of another California woman, Pamela Rae Stewart. After her infant son died of massive brain damage sustained when Stewart was pregnant, Stewart was charged under a 1926 statute that makes it a crime for a parent to "willfully omit" furnishing necessary medical attention to a *child*. She was also charged with failing to follow her doctor's orders. Stewart's son had been born with traces of amphetamines in his blood, and this was sufficient to trigger prosecution even though the delivering physician determined that the drugs had not caused the brain damage or death (McNulty 1990). A judge dismissed the charges, agreeing with Stewart's attorney, Richard Boesin, that the statute was intended to assure that fathers pay child support, not

[7] There is ample evidence of the fiscal wisdom of prevention and treatment programs (see generally Edelman 1987). According to the House Select Committee on Children, Youth, and Families, every dollar invested in programs on behalf of young children saves between three and ten dollars down the line, including prenatal care, immunizations, Head Start, and WIC, the supplemental food program for women, infants, and children (reported in *Youth Law News* 1991a).

[8] California's priorities have probably attracted the most publicity. Spending on prisons increased by 800 percent to $4.1 billion between 1981 and 1996, while the higher education budget has shrunk (Skelton 1996). The Rand Corporation predicts that prisons could take up as much as 21 percent of the budget by early next century if the "three strikes" mandatory sentencing law is fully implemented (Schrag 1995).

to prosecute pregnant women. Boesin hoped then that the ruling would send a message that such prosecution is "counterproductive and will do nothing but terrorize the hearts and minds of pregnant women" (quoted in Warren 1987).

But the prosecutions continued. By mid-1992 there were more than 150 documented cases of women who faced unprecedented criminal charges for using drugs or alcohol during pregnancy. No state has passed a law creating "special or additional penalties for becoming pregnant while addicted to drugs," and yet prosecuting attorneys have pressed charges in at least twenty-eight states by creatively invoking a number of existing statutes (Paltrow 1992, i).[9] Prosecutors have wide latitude in deciding whether, when, and against whom to bring charges. They also have ample discretion to "overcharge" a defendant in order to increase the state's leverage (Greene 1991). The charges against women have included possession of a controlled substance; delivering drugs to a minor; child abuse or neglect, cruelty to children, and contributing to the delinquency of a minor; assault with a deadly weapon; and, in cases of stillbirth, manslaughter or murder. District attorneys brought the charges against women during pregnancy and at any time up to a year after they had given birth. Anecdotal evidence suggests that there are additional cases that have not been fully documented.[10] It is not common practice for trial judges in criminal courts to write opinions explaining their sentences, so the record of a woman convicted of drug possession might not reflect the fact that she was pregnant, that her pregnancy is what brought her to the attention of criminal justice authorities in the first place, or that her pregnancy is the reason for the judge's sentence.

Race and Class Disparities in Prosecution

Of those cases in which the woman's race is known, 71 percent were Black, Latina, or Native American; only 29 percent were white. More than one-

---

[9] The states are Alaska, California, Colorado, Connecticut, Florida, Georgia, Idaho, Illinois, Indiana, Kentucky, Massachusetts, Michigan, Mississippi, Missouri, Nebraska, Nevada, New York, North Carolina, North Dakota, Ohio, Oklahoma, Pennsylvania, South Carolina, South Dakota, Texas, Virginia, Washington, and Wyoming.

[10] The best single source of information on prosecutions is a report published by the American Civil Liberties Union (Paltrow 1992). A later report by the Center for Reproductive Law and Policy cites cases in Oklahoma and Pennsylvania from this time period (CRLP 1996). Three cases reported elsewhere were brought in Nebraska, Ohio, and California (see *Los Angeles Daily Journal* 1992; United Press International 1991; and *San Diego Tribune-Union* 1989, respectively). Sources of anecdotal information on additional prosecutions include Gomez 1997 on several successful prosecutions in Riverside County, California (90–91); Moss 1990 on Colorado; and Parness 1993 on Winnebago County, Illinois. It is likely that more cases were brought prior to 1993 but were not widely publicized.

half of all the cases come from South Carolina, and while information about them is scarce, we do know that almost all the women are Black. There is a parallel in the higher incidence of court-ordered medical treatment of women of color, who are ordered to undergo procedures four times as often as white women (see Chapter 5).

Dorothy Roberts argues that the decision to single out Black women for prosecution is not an accident but the latest link in a chain of historical control over their reproduction, starting with slavery and including forced sterilization and government removal of children from Black homes (Roberts 1991). The women prosecuted used a range of drugs, but the majority used crack cocaine. Crack is a drug most often associated with inner-city Blacks. This is by and large the same group blamed for violent crime and intergenerational welfare dependence. Crack cocaine is not necessarily more likely to harm a fetus than powdered cocaine, heroin, alcohol, or other drugs. Roberts and others have pointed out that the decision to focus on prosecuting pregnant women who use crack is a decision to target poor Black women, one that cannot be justified medically but can be justified politically and ideologically (Roberts 1991; Greene 1991, 745). Crimes involving crack are punished one hundred times more harshly than crimes involving powdered cocaine (J. Miller 1996). Although the U.S. Sentencing Commission opposes this difference in punishment, President Bill Clinton, Attorney General Janet Reno, and Congress have held fast to it, further suggesting that the war on crack is a politically expedient war on Black Americans.[11]

Law enforcement officials get their information about women who use drugs from departments of social services or directly from medical facilities. Health care providers are far more likely to report pregnant women of color than pregnant white women for substance use. A study of women enrolled for prenatal care at public health clinics and private doctors' offices in Pinellas County, Florida, found that "the use of [alcohol and] illicit drugs is common among pregnant women regardless of race and socioeconomic status," yet it also found that Black women are nearly ten times more likely than white women to be reported to local authorities, and women of both races who were reported were more likely to be of low socioeconomic status (Chasnoff, Landress, and Barrett 1990). The white women were more likely to use marijuana and the Black women to use cocaine, a drug that, as we have just seen, carries more symbolic weight (the study does not distinguish between forms of cocaine). Florida requires

---

[11] Two psychiatry professors recently argued in *JAMA* that the discrepancy in sentencing cannot be justified on medical grounds and conclude that providing treatment is more cost-effective than imprisonment (Hatsukami and Fischman 1996, 1586–87).

that *all* infants born "physically dependent" on a controlled substance be reported to child welfare authorities. This study's findings suggest either that hospital workers test Black newborns for drugs at significantly higher rates than white infants or that they violate the mandatory reporting law with regularity. Racist stereotypes of drug use as a minority problem appear to exert a strong influence on reporting practices.

Illinois also requires that drug-exposed infants and their mothers be reported to government authorities. A study of pregnant women in four Illinois communities found that 12 percent of Black women and 9 percent of white women used illicit drugs, and yet fully 87 percent of the women reported were Black (Olen 1991). These two studies, along with trends in prosecution, confirm that punishment for drug use falls more heavily on women of color.

Tribal councils on Native American reservations are reported to detain against their will pregnant women who drink, in order to decrease the incidence of fetal alcohol syndrome (Magar 1991, 33). There is no way to know how prevalent the practice is because these reports are anecdotal. At least two tribes, the Cheyenne River Sioux of South Dakota and the Standing Rock Sioux of North Dakota, authorize the involuntary civil commitment of pregnant women for this reason. The Cheyenne River Sioux policy is included in its ordinance regulating alcohol on the reservation. The ordinance prohibits anyone from providing alcohol to a pregnant woman and subjects violators to a fine of up to five hundred dollars. The same fine applies to pregnant women who obtain alcohol, but the policy controls them further: Pregnant women whose drinking poses "serious danger of prenatal alcohol damage" can be committed to an alcohol abuse treatment center for the duration of their pregnancy (Dineen 1994, 37). The closest treatment center for pregnant women is in Nebraska and has a two- to three-month waiting list (*Alcoholism and Drug Abuse Week* 1992). The Standing Rock Sioux Tribal Court has put all pregnant women on notice that if they do not stop drinking and if commitment to treatment centers "doesn't work," then "mothers [*sic*] can be held in Contempt of Court and face imprisonment until the baby is born" (July 1993 letter from Chief Judge Michael Swallow, quoted in Dineen 1994, 50).

These practices raise thorny dilemmas about the relationship between women's civil rights and Native American tribes' sovereignty to set their own rules. Generally speaking, federally recognized Native American tribes have the authority to govern the conduct of their resident members. In 1968 Congress passed the Indian Civil Rights Act (ICRA), which applied many of the provisions of the Bill of Rights to Native American tribes. Ten years later, however, the U.S. Supreme Court ruled in *Santa Clara*

Pueblo v. Martinez that the ICRA did not authorize bringing civil actions to federal courts when tribal decisions violate civil rights. Therefore it is not clear what kind of legal recourse Native American women have to challenge their involuntary confinement.

These Native American practices arise in a different context from criminal actions against women for conduct during pregnancy. Most tribal governments have fewer resources at their disposal than either the federal or state government to spend on solving long-standing problems of poverty, unemployment, and substance abuse that afflict their communities. But there is an overriding similarity: It is largely pregnant women who are singled out to bear the burden of improving infant health. Detaining pregnant women is an easy course of action when confronted with problems whose solutions do not lie entirely within the communities' control.

How Court Decisions Punish Women

Of the 172 known prosecutions brought through 1992, I found 64 cases with relatively complete records of how the case was resolved. Those cases show that, collectively and individually, women suffer significant punishment for ad hoc crimes and for minor crimes for which they would never have been prosecuted if they were not pregnant.[12]

Almost one-fourth of the women (fifteen) were sentenced to prison, on average for three years each (sentences range from three months to twelve years; two women got suspended sentences of one and three years). Many others spent time in jail during the course of their case, including forty to fifty women in South Carolina alone. Another three women were sentenced to house arrest, on average for more than one year (the range is six months to two years). More than one-third (at least twenty-four) were put on probation, for an average length of three years (the range is eighteen months to fourteen years). The rest had their charges dismissed. Cases took up to three years to resolve, from arrest through final appeal.

Some women had prior criminal records, making it harder to strike a plea bargain. Records are incomplete, but it appears that other women may not have had prior histories and still received harsh sentences. Similarly, information is not available on whether most of these women's children were placed in foster care. Records do show that in several instances newborns removed by the state were returned after the department of social services conducted a home study. And finally, these women's lives have

---

[12] The information for this analysis comes from Paltrow 1992, newspaper articles, court documents, arrest records, and briefs.

been exposed to a degree of public scrutiny most people cannot imagine. With their names and details about their lives routinely published in local and national papers, they incur a loss of privacy they can never recover.

The following two cases give life to these statistics. When Dianne Pfannenstiel was four months pregnant, she came to an emergency room in Laramie, Wyoming, after her husband beat her. A twenty-nine-year-old white woman, Pfannenstiel had previously given birth to a baby with a fractured skull because of her husband's violence. She was arrested at the hospital and charged with felony child abuse because she was intoxicated (she was also charged with committing offenses against "the peace and dignity of the state of Wyoming"). Pfannenstiel spent the night in jail before charges were formally brought against her. Her husband, charged with aggravated assault, did not go to jail. A judge dismissed the charges, finding no probable cause to continue without proof that her drinking had harmed the fetus.[13]

Across the country in Charleston, South Carolina, an eighteen-year-old Black woman named Monica Young came to the hospital after being kicked in the abdomen. Unbeknownst to her, the staff tested her urine for cocaine, found positive results, and called the police, who arrested her at the hospital on charges of possession of cocaine and distributing cocaine to a minor. She spent the third trimester of her pregnancy under house arrest, with bond set at $80,000. Final disposition is unknown.[14]

With savvy legal representation, women can successfully challenge their charges. But public defenders are often overworked and inexperienced in these cases, and so the majority of women settle for plea bargains and incur penalties they don't deserve. For instance, prosecutors commonly charge a woman with both possession of a controlled substance and with child abuse or neglect. Typically, the woman agrees to plead guilty or no contest to the abuse charge in exchange for having the drug charge dropped.

This plea is not much of a bargain. The child abuse charge is not likely to be upheld, because the statutes were not intended to apply to fetuses or to women's conduct during pregnancy. The possession charge is similarly

[13] See Levendosky 1990a and 1990b and the *State of Wyoming v. Dianne Pfannenstiel* docket.
[14] See *State of South Carolina v. Young* (1989) in Paltrow 1992. South Carolina has the most egregious policies toward pregnant women who use drugs. The city of Charleston and the hospital for indigent patients jointly implemented a policy to threaten women who test positive for cocaine at their prenatal visits with prosecution if they do not stop taking drugs. There are numerous reports of women being arrested and removed from the hospital shortly after giving birth, even when they were bleeding and running fevers (Moss 1991, 15; CRLP 1996). The Charleston policy has been the subject of two federal investigations for racial discrimination and for ethics violations in human subjects research (CRLP 1996).

flawed. Courts' understanding of the crime of possession reflects common sense: Someone must know she has a tangible amount of an illegal substance and be able to dispose of it. The presence of a controlled substance or its metabolite in someone's body does not meet that test or constitute "possession" within the meaning of the law (see, for example, *Jackson v. State* 1992 and cases cited therein). Many women are charged with possession "between March and June," instead of on a specific date, making the charge even less credible.

When women have challenged the application of these various statutes to them or their fetus, courts have been extremely reluctant to let the charges stand. In fact, no state high court ruling on this question by 1992 validated the charges. To do so would undermine the separation of powers by violating legislative intent as well as deprive the accused of a number of due process guarantees regarding the proper interpretation of statutes (Smith and Dabiri 1991). In addition to due process concerns, judges have occasionally cited violations to the woman's constitutional rights to privacy.[15]

The Gap between Rhetoric and Reality

Many district attorneys maintain that their motivation for prosecuting women is to "encourage" women to get treatment and to deter other pregnant women from using drugs (or to deter drug users from getting pregnant).[16] Assistant Attorney General Belle Turner of Florida argues that "criminal penalties are one of the tools we have for getting somebody to seek treatment" (Hansen 1992, 18). Butte County, California, District Attorney Michael Ramsey told a reporter that "people with substance abuse problems do not voluntarily get into these treatment programs," but that he is confident that women will "choose" treatment over jail (quoted in LaCroix 1989, 586). Of his aggressive program to identify and threaten pregnant drug users, South Carolina prosecutor Charles Condon insists, "We are not really interested in convicting women and sending them to jail. We're just interested in getting them to stop using drugs before they do something horrible to their babies" (quoted in Lewin 1990; see also Logli 1990, 27).

Despite these statements, there is virtually no evidence of deterrence, except to deter women from seeking help at all, as in the forced cesarean

[15] For example, *People v. Bremer* (1991) in Michigan and *Commonwealth v. Pellegrini* (1990) in Massachusetts, summarized in Paltrow 1992, 17, 19.

[16] At least one state statute also explicitly promotes this policy. One of Oregon's goals is to develop pilot projects to "reduce the incidence of pregnancy among drug users through intensive family planning counseling" (Or. Rev. Stat. § 430.925, passed in 1989).

cases. San Francisco Deputy City Attorney Lori Giorgi reported an increase in the number of babies being born at home without medical supervision—in toilet bowls, in bathtubs, and on kitchen floors—because women are afraid of losing their children if they go to a hospital (LaCroix 1989, 586). In addition, many of these jurisdictions do not provide drug treatment for pregnant women, or these cases might never have arisen in the first place. Why, then, do prosecutors insist on this position? What is really driving these cases?

The following case offers an unusually explicit articulation of the fears and motives underlying criminal proceedings against pregnant drug users. This 1988 case was actually one of "preventive detention," in which women brought up on unrelated charges are given inappropriate sentences because they happen to be pregnant and using drugs. Brenda Vaughn, a twenty-nine-year-old Black woman from Maryland, was charged and convicted of forging $722 in checks. Vaughn had a drug history, and so the judge ordered her to submit to a drug test when she said that she was pregnant. After her results came back positive, the judge ordered her to spend 180 days in jail instead of giving her the probation typical for first-time offenders, to ensure that she would remain confined for the duration of her pregnancy (Moss 1988). The judge reasoned that

> it is true that the defendant has not been treated the same as if she were a man in this case. But then a man who is a convicted rapist is treated differently from a woman. She has also not been treated the same as a non-pregnant woman. But Ms. Vaughn became pregnant and chose to bear the baby who, like most criminal defendants the court sees so frequently, will start life with one other severe strike against it—no father is around. Arguably, Ms. Vaughn should have demonstrated even greater responsibility toward her child. (*U.S. v. Vaughn* 1989, 447)

Clearly the judge is punishing Vaughn for more than forging checks or taking cocaine while pregnant (which, in any case, is not the crime she is charged with). He punishes her for expressing her sexuality, for not getting married, and for not having an abortion. He blames her for the fact that she will be a single parent, and more than that, for contributing to crime by rearing a child without paternal influence.

In these remarks, the judge doesn't simply comment on the crimes and misfortunes of Brenda Vaughn as an individual. He taps into popular discourse and imagery about single motherhood, race, drugs, and crime to construct Vaughn as the carrier of a future degenerate who will grow to be a burden on the state. His remarks resemble popular media stories that, according to Patricia Williams, construct Black single mothers as "the universal signifiers for poverty, irresponsibility, drug addiction, and rabbit-like fertility" (Williams 1990, 86). In effect, he turns Vaughn into a symbol of the entire underclass debate.

The judge further dismisses Vaughn's very real concern about the treatment she will receive in jail. He belittles her complaints about bad prison diets as "ironic," "when her real craving is for a devastating drug" (*U.S. v. Vaughn* 1989, 447). Yet if the District of Columbia's facility is typical, Vaughn is not likely to kick her drug habit while in jail. In fact, she is more likely to have access to drugs and alcohol than she is to drug treatment or prenatal care, undermining the judge's express reason for jailing her (AMA 1990; Barry 1991). A survey of twenty-six correctional institutions found that most facilities deal with pregnant inmates on an ad hoc basis, without any official policy for their care, and in all but five cases seeing no need for any official policy (McHugh 1980). This policy vacuum persists, despite the fact that approximately 10 percent of women inmates are pregnant at any given time (Barry 1989). Between 1980 and 1995 the number of women entering federal and state prisons and local jails more than quadrupled to almost 116,000 (Holmes 1996b). In California the number grew from 1,316 in 1980 to 7,232 in 1993, the largest population of incarcerated women in the world (Bloom et al. 1994, 1; Becker and Hora 1993, 568). These numbers reflect the impact of mandatory sentencing policies. In 1979 one in ten women in U.S. prisons was doing time for drug offenses; by 1991 the figure was one in three. More than one-third of these women were incarcerated solely for possession (Bloom et al. 1994). More women in general means more pregnant inmates, placing extra pressure on already strained systems.

The abysmal health and sanitation conditions in women's jails and prisons are well documented—conditions that put pregnant women at risk of miscarrying (McCall et al. 1985). The influx of new inmates has led to overcrowding, with women's correctional facilities operating at up to 600 percent above capacity (Barry n.d.; Stein and Mistiaen 1988). Pregnant women are routinely deprived of nutritious diets, exercise, fresh air, accessible toilets and showers, and beds to sleep in, not to mention privacy (Barry 1989; McHugh 1980; Stein and Mistiaen 1988). They are the objects of hostility and harassment from staff people who perceive them as unworthy of motherhood, and are subjected to physically inappropriate work assignments as a result (McHugh 1980; Stein and Mistiaen 1988). Increasingly, they are the victims of sexual assault and coercion by male guards (Holmes 1996b). Prisons and jails expose pregnant women to such contagious diseases as measles, hepatitis, and tuberculosis, as well as lice and vermin (Barry 1989; Stein and Mistiaen 1988). In addition to going without drug detoxification services, pregnant women are denied access to basic medical services: Few institutions have obstetricians, gynecologists, or any full-time medical staff, and most lack basic medical facilities, including those for childbirth or emergencies (Barry 1989; McHugh 1980). Pregnant women are handcuffed, shackled, and chained around the belly when going to court or to the hospital, even when in active labor (Barry n.d., 1989; Stein and Mistiaen 1988). Many institutions do not initiate the process to transfer a woman to a hospital until she has already gone into labor, and bureaucratic delays often result in women giving birth while still in prison, even in their cells (Barry 1989; McHugh 1980).

Consequently, women inmates experience extremely poor birth outcomes. A 1983 study of health conditions in three California women's correctional facilities documents that among prison inmates, only 45 percent of pregnancies resulted in a live birth. Fully 34 percent miscarried, as compared with a miscarriage rate of less than 1 percent in the outside community. Among California's county jail inmates, only 21 percent of pregnancies resulted in live birth; their miscarriage rate was 55 percent, a rate fifty times higher than the statewide average (results reported in Barry 1985, 1989, and in *Youth Law News* 1985). This study was sponsored by the California Department of Health, and unfortunately there are no federally collected data with which to compare it (Harris 1993; Raeder 1993, 914n34, 945–46). Ten years later a Sacramento County, California, defense attorney reported seeing more clients miscarry in jail than out (Becker and Hora 1993, 554). Certainly the available information is sufficient to invalidate the wisdom of incarcerating pregnant women for the sake of their fetus. In the words of one prison lawyer, incarceration "is a potential death sentence" for inmates' unborn children (Ellen Barry, quoted in Stein and Mistiaen 1988, 6).[17]

Women inmates are caught in a complicated web of policy problems. Prenatal care and drug treatment are rare, while inappropriate treatment is all too common: Women are given prescription drugs contraindicated by pregnancy, including tranquilizers or mood-altering and anti-psychotic drugs administered indiscriminately at some facilities to control the inmate population (Barry 1985 and McHugh 1980). Another problem is the high rate of medically unnecessary hysterectomies performed on women in Ohio and California prisons (McHugh 1980 and Barry 1989).

---

[17] Incarcerated pregnant and postpartum women do have some legal recourse. In 1976 the U.S. Supreme Court ruled in *Estelle v. Gamble* that prisoners have a constitutional right to "adequate" medical care. To win a lawsuit, plaintiffs must demonstrate a pattern of "deliberate indifference" to their medical needs that violates the Eighth Amendment's prohibition of cruel and unusual punishment. Inmates in Massachusetts, Connecticut, and California have launched class-action suits to improve their care (Barry 1989, n.d.; Siegal 1997; Stein and Mistiaen 1988).

In many jurisdictions, women have trouble getting abortions. Beyond the problem of funding for poor women, there is the problem of arranging transportation to a clinic or hospital, something that anti-choice sheriffs have obstructed (see, for instance, *Houston Chronicle* 1996). In this sense health policy for incarcerated women resembles policy for poor women in general, favoring permanent sterilization over abortion. There are almost no prison nurseries in the United States that would allow women to stay with the babies they have chosen or been forced to bear, and they may lose permanent custody if their sentence is long and they cannot maintain a relationship with the child. In these circumstances, being forced to carry a pregnancy to term is nothing but punishment.

In light of the problems blocking women's access to treatment, some initiatives sound like a bad joke. The Eighteenth Judicial Circuit in Seminole County, Florida, has implemented a diversion program in which pregnant women can have charges against them deferred and ultimately dismissed if they successfully complete a drug program that includes a period of mandatory "no frills," "hard line" treatment while incarcerated for up to six months and meet other conditions of probation for two years. However, "the cost of participating in this program and any treatment or counseling shall be [their] responsibility." The reason for the program is clearly stated: to "lessen the burden on Law Enforcement and the Court System" (see the Cooperative Rehabilitation Abuse Contract, n.d.).

Some people have proposed mandatory treatment for pregnant drug users as an alternative to criminal sanctions. But Wendy Chavkin's comprehensive review of the research on mandatory treatment suggests that patients are more likely to succeed in overcoming their addictions when they themselves decide they need help. Forcing people into treatment is therefore a poor use of limited resources. Chavkin concludes that debates over mandatory treatment are "symbolic at best" and "meaningless in practical terms," given the shortage of treatment opportunities for people willingly seeking help (Chavkin 1991, 1560; see also Moss 1991).

For all these reasons, the organized medical and public health community has publicly rejected the criminal prosecution of pregnant women. The American Medical Association, the American College of Obstetricians and Gynecologists, the American Public Health Association, the American Academy of Pediatrics, and at least twenty other groups have gone on record with their opposition, in policy statements and in amicus curiae briefs on behalf of women in criminal cases (see, for instance, the list of amici in *Johnson v. Florida* 1992).

Trial judges are not all of one mind on these questions. Although many have dismissed charges brought against women for conduct during pregnancy out of concern for due process, others feel it is an appropriate use of their discretion to keep pregnant women who use drugs in custody. Peter Wolf, the District of Columbia judge who gave Vaughn jail time instead of probation, mentioned in his opinion that some of his colleagues have similarly sentenced pregnant drug users (*U.S. v. Vaughn* 1989, 447). Judge Howard Broadman of Tulare County, California, told a woman who had pleaded guilty to possessing and being under the influence of heroin that if she got pregnant he would send her to prison "because I want to protect the un-born child."[18] Stanley Golde is the judge responsible for determining the majority of sentences in California's Alameda County superior courts. He began sending all pregnant women brought in on narcotics charges to jail instead of giving them probation, in order to "protect their unborn babies." As a result, the number of pregnant women in the new county jail doubled in its first year of operation (Brewer 1990). Golde held to this policy despite a 1986 incident in which a heroin addict whom he sent to jail for the last three months of her pregnancy on a petty theft charge suffered violent "cold turkey" withdrawal that caused her to miscarry in the eighth month (Jacobus 1992).

To get a better picture of how legal actors respond to cases involving pregnant women who use drugs, Barrie Becker and Peggy Hora surveyed trial judges, prosecutors, and defense attorneys in ten California counties. The authors describe their survey as "the first empirical study of how trial judges are responding to this problem in the courtroom" (Becker and Hora 1993, 528n6). They say their survey asked about judges' "sentencing patterns," but the questions were phrased hypothetically—that is, "As a judge, would you sentence women to jail or prison to protect a fetus from maternal drug use?" (540, 548). Given this wording, all we can be sure they have measured is judges' attitudes, not their actual behavior. The attorneys' questionnaire, in contrast, seems designed to elicit actual experience. Despite the study's methodological flaws, its results are useful, especially because California sends more women to prison than any other state in the nation.

Becker and Hora argue that according to state, federal, and constitutional law, drug use should not be considered an aggravating factor in sentencing, release, or probation decisions, and that pregnancy *cannot* be considered in this manner (533–37). And yet their survey suggests that judges do treat pregnancy and drug use precisely this way.

---

[18] *People v. Zaring* (1992), 369. Judge Broadman placed Linda Gail Zaring on probation for five years and included as a term of probation the condition that she not get pregnant during that time. An appellate court overturned the ban on pregnancy, because it is impermissibly overbroad and impinges on the exercise of the constitutionally protected right to procreate.

Almost half of judges (46 percent) said they would sentence a woman to prison or jail to protect a fetus from drug use. Slightly more than half (56 percent) said they would decline to release a pregnant drug user or would set high bail before sentencing (547). When it comes to making these decisions, no more than half of the judges were concerned about the conditions in jails and prisons for prenatal care and delivery (47 percent), women's civil liberties (50 percent), or even whether they have the authority to take fetal health into account (45 percent) (549). The majority (64 percent) said they were equally likely to consider women's addiction to legal drugs as to illegal ones in their decisions (549).

Almost half of defense attorneys (45 percent) reported that judges had sentenced pregnant women to jail or prison based primarily on their concern for the fetus (551). This number accords almost exactly with judges' own responses: Forty-six percent said they would sentence a woman to prison or jail to protect a fetus from drug use (547). A substantial majority (78 percent) reported that they had seen judges decline to release pregnant defendants on bail or on their own recognizance, ensuring that they would remain in custody for as long as possible. Far fewer prosecutors, only 26 percent, reported that they had seen judges send women to jail or prison to protect a fetus, and slightly more than half (53 percent) reported that judges kept pregnant women in custody prior to sentencing for this reason (553). Prosecutors from two counties did not answer this question, including those from Alameda, where Judge Golde has gone on record with his policy to send addicted pregnant women to jail. Those gaps in data probably account for a good part of the discrepancies.

All of the respondents expressed a need for more treatment services and indicated that the availability of alternatives to incarceration—specifically, structured, residential drug treatment—affected judges' decisions about whether to send a pregnant woman to jail. It is not surprising that prosecutors and judges were more supportive of detaining pregnant women than were defense attorneys; it is disappointing, though, that they had so much less knowledge of resources in the community to help women (555).

Public Opinion

It has become commonplace for reporters and academic scholars to cite widespread public support for punitive measures against pregnant women who take drugs (see, for example, Condit 1995; Curriden 1990; Daniels 1993; Kantrowitz 1991; Young 1995). This claim rests on an incomplete analysis of one or two surveys. Between 1988 and 1991 at least six public opinion surveys addressed the issue. Overwhelmingly, respondents favored some form of criminal penalty for women who take drugs during pregnancy—usually at least 70 percent. Similarly, 60 percent of respondents in a 1991 survey approved of making the contraceptive Norplant mandatory for "drug abusing women of childbearing age" (Skelton and Weintraub 1991).

When given a choice between incarcerating a woman or treating her addiction, however, respondents also overwhelmingly chose treatment and favored keeping mothers and babies together (CBS 1989; Fogarty 1990; Sherman 1991; Drug Strategies Survey 1994). This suggests that people do want to express disapproval of women's behavior. But they may not actually want to punish women as much as observers ordinarily presume; they have simply been constrained by the structure of the survey from giving any other response.

Analysts of public opinion tell us that question order and wording matters. Typically, surveys include only one question, and it is posed in the context of a poll devoted to drugs, crime, or "controversial" issues. The question is usually included in response to a recent incident in the local community or to one that received national press attention, such as Jennifer Johnson's conviction in Florida (discussed in the next section), and is not repeated over time. Compare the questions *and* the strikingly different responses elicited to national ABC and CBS polls conducted the very same day (see ABC 1989 and CBS 1989). CBS asked, "(When a person is convicted for using drugs there can be a choice between sending them to jail or having them go to a drug treatment program instead.) What do you think is the best way to deal with a pregnant woman convicted for using drugs that might affect her baby—jail or treatment?" Only 15 percent opted for jail; 71 percent chose treatment. In contrast, ABC stated, "A pregnant woman who uses crack-cocaine and addicts her unborn child should be put in jail for child abuse." Eighty-two percent of people agreed; only 16 percent disagreed: virtually the opposite results.

As far as other sorts of potentially harmful but legal behavior are concerned, people's opinions tend to split down the middle on whether to hold women accountable. Responses to an *Atlanta Constitution* poll of the twelve southern states suggest that people are willing to create new categories of criminal behavior specifically for pregnant women (Hansen 1989). Forty-five percent of respondents think that criminal charges should be brought against a woman who drinks or smokes during pregnancy "if her baby is born seriously damaged." Eleven percent favor criminal charges against a woman who "eats the wrong foods or gets the wrong kinds of exercise." Twice as many opponents of legal abortion supported criminalizing diet and exercise as did supporters of abortion rights (correlation with abortion views was not reported for the other questions). Party affiliation did not significantly affect respondents' views. A nationwide Gallup poll reported comparable results (*Hippocrates* 1988). Forty-eight percent of respondents believed that a pregnant woman should "be held legally liable for harm done to her fetus because she smoked cigarettes or drank alcohol during her pregnancy." These responses suggest that people tend to blame women's behavior for infant morbidity and mortality instead of blaming more systemic problems such as poverty and the structure of the health care system. The tremendous variation in responses, depending on the choices given, may give advocates some ammunition to lobby government for improved services for pregnant women.

Prosecuting Jennifer Johnson: The State and the Drama of Public Morality

Perhaps the most famous prosecution of all is that of Jennifer Johnson in Seminole County, Florida, a case that exemplifies many of the problems identified in this chapter. With more than thirty known cases, Florida has prosecuted more women for drug-related behavior during pregnancy than any other state except South Carolina. Johnson's conviction under drug-trafficking laws was both the state's first major success and the downfall of its policy.

At the time the state began its case against her in 1989, Jennifer Johnson was twenty-three years old and a mother of four. Johnson, who is Black, had begun using crack at age twenty and became addicted. Having given birth to one child while using crack, Johnson sought out drug treatment when she became pregnant again. But the program she contacted turned her away. During her eighth month of pregnancy, Johnson called paramedics because she was concerned about her fetus. She also told hospital staff about her crack habit during labor. Because neither of Johnson's two young children appears to suffer drug-related impairment, the state dropped its child abuse charges against her. But it still pressed forward with drug charges. The prosecution twisted Johnson's attempts to get help into a story of her criminal intent to harm her fetus: Johnson's actions, they argued, demonstrated her awareness of the damage she might be inflicting.

Prosecutor Jeff Deen had been looking for a test case to try his theory that pregnant women "deliver" drugs through their umbilical cords in the moments after the baby is born and attains the legal status of person but before the cord is cut (Davidson 1989). The state legislature had already decided not to define exposing a fetus to drugs as criminal child abuse, so

Deen had to find another way to prosecute pregnant drug users. The trial judge accepted Deen's theory and convicted Johnson of two counts of distributing drugs to a minor—one for the baby she had just had and one for her son born two years earlier. Johnson was the first woman in the country to be convicted of this "crime." The judge sentenced her to fifteen years probation, including one year of strict supervision in a rehabilitation program, random drug tests for at least one year, educational and vocational training, two hundred hours of community service, and court-approved prenatal care should she become pregnant again (*Los Angeles Times* 1989).

An appeals court upheld the convictions in a two-page opinion, saying that they are only "logical." The court maintained that there was evidence that Johnson knew that "cocaine use by the mother within 48 hours before delivery would result in transmittal of that cocaine to a child after its expulsion from the birth canal" and prior to the clamping of the cord (*Johnson v. State* 1991, 420). The court's language dehumanizes Johnson. In its eyes she does not give birth to a baby; she expels it. A more thorough opinion by the one dissenting judge assailed the prosecution's case on the following grounds: that the statute was not meant to apply to pregnancy; that there was no proof that a "delivery" actually occurred, even if the statute did apply; and that there was no evidence of Johnson's intent to deliver drugs. Judge Winifred Sharp based her opinion on legislative history and on due process considerations that require interpreting criminal statutes narrowly.

The Florida Supreme Court adopted the dissenting argument, quoting it at length and adding only one substantive point of law. The court found that the rule of lenity as well as the rule of strict construction applies; that is, when a criminal statute is open to competing interpretations, the court must use the interpretation that is most favorable to the accused. The court stated that it "declines the State's invitation to walk down a path that the law, public policy, reason and common sense forbid it to tread," and accordingly reversed Johnson's two convictions (*Johnson v. State* 1992, 1297). By this time Johnson was already three years into her sentence.

Extending the State's Punitive Reach

Criminal prosecutions like the one brought against Jennifer Johnson are the most visible of the state's attempts to control pregnant women's behavior. Criminal proceedings are public and therefore accessible to the media and researchers; one of the courts' public functions is to serve as a forum for the state to issue authoritative moral discourse. But these proceedings represent only a fraction of the state's intervention into the lives of pregnant women who use drugs. The state has an array of other mechanisms—family and juvenile courts and legislation—to regulate pregnant women and new mothers. All of these mechanisms have the potential to be punitive.

There have been isolated reports of private actors going to civil court to prevent pregnant women from using drugs. In Tennessee, for instance, a pregnant woman's estranged husband got a family court judge to order her not to drink alcohol or use drugs during pregnancy (Mitchell 1990). A Maryland doctor asked a juvenile court to order his patient to stop taking drugs during her pregnancy (*New York Times* 1983).

In another instance, a coroner's inquest was held after a woman gave birth prematurely at twenty to twenty-four weeks to an infant who lived only one hour. The woman had used cocaine during pregnancy, and the coroner's jury ruled the newborn's death a homicide. The inquest was held as a substitute for filing criminal charges to draw attention to the incident (Enstad 1993).

Far more common is Child Protective Services involvement. Typically, these proceedings are private, only becoming available for analysis if they reach a court of appeals. In some of these cases, the state takes away a woman's child at birth, arguing that evidence of drug use during pregnancy constitutes prima facie evidence of neglect or abuse.[19] In others, especially during the height of crack's popularity, babies remained hospitalized at great public expense, languishing in a sort of legal limbo until authorities decide what to do. These infants are commonly referred to as "boarder babies," whose medical condition allows them to be discharged but who are officially on hold (Bussiere and Shauffer 1990).

Bonnie Robin-Vergeer's research on California in the 1980s uncovered significant confusion over whether drug use during pregnancy could be considered neglect and significant variation in practice from county to county. In 1987, presumably in the wake of Pamela Rae Stewart's case, the attorney general's office directed agencies not to report acts by pregnant women to the Justice Department, including positive infant drug tests, because a fetus is not legally a "child" (Robin-Vergeer 1990, 752–53). At least one of four Bay Area counties studied nonetheless continued to place

[19] The two state supreme courts to rule on this question held that a finding of abuse or neglect could not be based solely on a woman's conduct during pregnancy; see *In re Valerie D.* (Conn. 1992) and *Nassau County Department of Social Services v. Denise J.* (New York 1995), reported in CRLP 1996, 17n5. Many other state appellate courts, however, have reached the opposite conclusion; see Grimm 1995.

drug-exposed infants in protective custody without first investigating for other factors that might place them at risk of neglect or abuse. These findings suggest that practices may be arbitrary and uneven in other states without specific legislative guidance.

Becker and Hora's survey of trial judges and attorneys in California also asked under what conditions judges declare children dependents of the juvenile court. Contrary to both federal and state mandates, 36 percent of judges said that they would not order the county to make reasonable efforts to help keep families together before removing a drug-exposed infant from a mother's custody (Becker and Hora 1993, 559). Roughly half of defense and prosecuting attorneys reported having seen judges remove an infant from a woman's custody solely because of an infant's positive drug test (50 percent and 54 percent, respectively) (563–64). Both federal and California law require state agencies to make "reasonable efforts" to prevent placing a child in foster care and to reunify foster children with their families. "Reasonable efforts" might include drug or alcohol treatment; family counseling; homemaking and parenting classes; emergency cash assistance; help in accessing available resources such as food stamps, housing assistance, and medical care; or other services parents need to become capable of caring adequately for their children (Grimm 1995).

It is more difficult to determine the role pregnant women's drug use plays in judicial decisions to sever a parent's custody, a necessary step before children can be adopted by someone else. The problem is that the survey doesn't ask respondents to report observations before and after a change in California law went into effect in 1991. Even given this ambiguity, the judges' answers raise concern (Becker and Hora 1993, 560–65). Because parental rights are considered fundamental and the termination of parental rights is permanent, due process should be held to the highest standards.

The state has a legitimate interest in ensuring that children have adequate care. Probably almost everyone would agree that drug-addicted or alcoholic parents are not ideal parents, but they may be able to provide sufficient care, especially with help.[20] Up until the 1970s the child welfare

---

[20] The California Medical Association and District IX of the American College of Obstetricians and Gynecologists support this view (CRLP 1996, 16n47). Very little work has been done to document women's experiences with drugs and parenting. In 1993, Avril Taylor published the first book-length ethnographic study of drug-using women (Taylor 1993). She studies a community of women in Glasgow, Scotland, who inject heroin. Many of the women are mothers, and she examines their child-rearing practices and the support systems available to them. Taylor concludes that women addicted to heroin *can* be adequate parents, although many are not up to the task.

system focused on "rescuing" children from "bad homes." State laws defined neglect in loose terms that allowed children to be removed because of how social workers and judges felt about their parents' lifestyles. The result was often that children were placed in foster care without specific plans for their future (Matthews and McKee 1993, 2). By 1980 a different standard for coercive intervention on behalf of allegedly neglected children had emerged: "a well-founded belief that the child faces imminent and serious harm" (Robin-Vergeer 1990, 758). According to this standard, it is not in the state's interest to remove children from their homes on the grounds that their parents fail to provide optimum care. "Many troubled families go unserved and unsupported," writes Los Angeles County juvenile court judge Paul Boland, because the social service delivery system is underfunded, fragmented, and difficult to access. "A tragic consequence," he concludes, is that "in too many cases, children are removed unnecessarily from their parents' homes" (Boland 1990, 103–104).

State Legislation

In the criminal cases described in this chapter, district attorneys used laws written for other purposes to prosecute women for their conduct during pregnancy. Increasingly, states are passing laws specifically addressing pregnant women's behavior. My research found that between 1973 and 1992 two-thirds of the states in the country (thirty-three and the District of Columbia) passed legislation on women's drug and alcohol use during pregnancy (Table 6.1).

As we saw in Chapter 5, state legislatures' response to perceived conflict between pregnant women and their fetuses in the medical arena was fairly consistent: Where legislatures chose to regulate women's ability to make medical decisions, they largely chose to constrain them. The response to pregnant women's use of drugs and alcohol has been both more prolific and less uniform. Legislatures have adopted a range of policies concerning child abuse and neglect, the provision of drug treatment, and the education of health care providers, among others. Looking just at the numbers, education- and treatment-oriented laws outnumber punishment and surveillance measures. But a closer examination reveals serious implications for women in some of the seemingly benign acts.

When states regulate pregnant women's behavior, they say their goal is to increase healthy birth outcomes, and to do so as cheaply as possible. By this states certainly mean to reduce the number of babies born exposed to

Table 6.1. States with and without legislation on women's drug and alcohol use during pregnancy

States with legislation	States without legislation
Alaska	Alabama
Arizona	Arkansas
California	Hawaii
Colorado	Idaho
Connecticut	Maryland
Delaware	Michigan
District of Columbia	Mississippi
Florida	Montana
Georgia	New Jersey[a]
Illinois	North Carolina
Indiana	North Dakota
Iowa	Pennsylvania
Kansas	South Carolina
Kentucky	Texas
Louisiana	Vermont
Maine	West Virginia
Massachusetts	Wyoming
Minnesota	
Missouri	
Nebraska	
Nevada	
New Hampshire	
New Mexico	
New York	
Ohio	
Oklahoma	
Oregon	
Rhode Island	
South Dakota	
Tennessee	
Utah	
Virginia	
Washington	
Wisconsin	

[a] New Jersey has a law predating this period, allowing the Division of Youth and Family Services to apply for custody of endangered children, including "unborn child[ren]" (N.J. Sat. Ann. § 30:4C-11, enacted 1951 and amended 1962). A review found "no reported cases prosecuting pregnant women for fetal neglect under this statute" (Smith and Dabiri 1991, 96n181).

drugs or alcohol. Most efforts to improve women's health appear to be inadvertent side effects. Consider Missouri's law, known as "An Act Relating to the Protection of Certain Children," enacted in 1991. This law puts in place a system for identifying drug- or alcohol-exposed newborns and for determining when to involve child protective services. It also prohibits publicly funded treatment programs from discriminating against pregnant women and gives them priority for treatment. Yet those elements are not reflected in the name. "An Act Relating to the Improvement of Pregnant Women's Health" apparently would not have had the same political capital as one protecting "children." Calling fetuses "children" designates fetuses as the party in need and as the recipient of services.

An Alaska statute vividly illustrates the problem with making the fetus instead of the woman the recipient of services. In 1990 Alaska passed a law requiring the Department of Health and Social Services to make available to patients in public hospitals and clinics information regarding "fetal alcohol effects and the fetal health effects of chemical abuse and battering during pregnancy" (Alaska Stat. § 18.05.037). The state is trying to do something important by bringing attention to the problems of substance abuse and domestic violence. Yet the language on fetal effects is ludicrous because it makes women disappear. The only way to have a "battering effect" on a fetus's health is to hit or kick a pregnant woman. Rather than train prenatal care providers to look for signs of abuse among their patients and to talk with them about their lives, the state instead authorizes the creation of literature to educate pregnant women *themselves* about the dangers to their fetus of drinking alcohol, taking drugs, or being battered. The policy assumes that, once armed with this knowledge, the women will automatically be able to change their situations and make the battering stop. It also effectively places the burden of ending the violence on women. To accomplish that goal, the state must focus on the needs of the woman and not just on her fetus and offer women real, material assistance.

As the earlier section showed, this rhetorical erasure of pregnant women plays out in flesh-and-blood situations as well. Pregnant women have come to emergency rooms after being beaten only to find themselves turned over to the police because the hospital considers them "child abusers" for being drunk or high.

While Congress has held several hearings on drug-exposed babies, it has generated little in the way of legislation. In 1989 then-Senator Pete Wilson introduced the "Child Abuse during Pregnancy Prevention Act." If successfully passed into law, Wilson's bill would have provided grants to states for substance abuse services for pregnant women, on the condition that states certify that giving birth to an infant exposed to drugs or alcohol

Table 6.2. Summary of state legislation on women's substance use during pregnancy as of
December 31, 1992

Treatment

Arizona, California, Colorado, Connecticut, District of Columbia, Georgia, Illinois, Iowa,
Kansas, Kentucky, Louisiana, Maine, Minnesota, Missouri, New York, Ohio, Oregon, Rhode
Island, Tennessee, Virginia, Washington, Wisconsin

Education

Alaska, Arizona, California, Connecticut, Delaware, District of Columbia, Georgia, Illinois,
Kansas, Kentucky, Minnesota, Nebraska, New Hampshire, New Mexico, New York, Oregon,
Rhode Island, South Dakota, Wisconsin

Abuse/neglect[a,b]

California, Florida, Illinois, Indiana, Iowa, Kentucky, Massachusetts, Minnesota, Missouri,
Nevada, Oklahoma, Rhode Island, Utah, Wisconsin

Administration

California, Colorado, Connecticut, Illinois, Iowa, Kansas, Kentucky, Louisiana, Minnesota,
Missouri, New Hampshire, Ohio, Oklahoma, Oregon, Rhode Island, Virginia, Wisconsin

[a] Indiana, Kentucky, Missouri, Nevada, and Utah apply to alcohol as well as controlled
substances
[b] California, Florida, Iowa, Kentucky, and Missouri, as well as Kansas and Virginia, prohibit
criminal prosecution or removal of children solely on the basis of a positive drug test.

is a crime. Women convicted of this crime would have been sentenced to
three years of mandatory rehabilitation in a custodial setting (Ikemoto
1992b, 1271–72). Wilson's bill died after debate on the Senate floor.

The legislation I identified falls essentially into four broad categories:
treatment, education, abuse/neglect, and administration (Table 6.2).
Statutory provisions are classified according to the language in 1992.
Where an earlier version exists, I mention it for the reader's information.

Treatment

Twenty-two of the thirty-four states had some type of treatment-oriented
legislation. As explained earlier, there is a serious shortage of substance
abuse treatment for pregnant women. This is both because many programs do not provide the full range of medical and counseling services
that pregnant women need and because many programs refuse to accept
them, mostly out of fear of liability should anything go wrong with the
pregnancy.

States have taken several approaches to increase women's access to treatment. One is to prohibit discrimination in admission on the basis of pregnancy. Four states have adopted such laws (Iowa, Kansas, Louisiana, and Missouri). A second approach is to give pregnant women priority for treatment. Six states either have policies or have directed government agencies to develop policies that give pregnant women priority for available treatment slots (the District of Columbia, Georgia, Illinois, Kansas, Louisiana, and Missouri). Two of these states limit somewhat pregnant women's priority: In the District of Columbia pregnant women share priority with minors and with parents or guardians of minors needing treatment, and in Illinois the priority is for residential treatment only.

Three states provide weaker guarantees of access. Virginia, for instance, requires the state Boards of Mental Health and Substance Abuse to issue regulations ensuring that licensed treatment programs develop their own policies and procedures to provide for timely and appropriate treatment for pregnant women. For one year (1991), New York's mission statement on delivering substance abuse services explicitly mentioned pregnant women. But when the legislature overhauled its provisions in 1992, it codified language to state merely that New York's legislature "recognizes that the distinct treatment needs of special populations, including women and women with children . . . merit particular attention" (N.Y. Mental Hygiene Law § 19.01). California's Health and Safety Code states that "every county drug and alcohol abuse treatment or recovery program *which serves women* gives priority to pregnant women" (§ 11998.1 [f] [9]). This language was adopted in 1989, backtracking from the stronger commitment in the original 1988 law that applied to all programs. The small number of treatment programs serving pregnant women is a problem in the first place. Moreover, the goals set forth in this law are "advisory."

Fourteen states have passed laws concerning the direct provision of drug treatment for pregnant women. Authorizing new treatment is a very important step toward universal access. Many of the laws create pilot programs, which are the most likely to be comprehensive and tailored to pregnant women's needs. Yet by their very nature pilot programs and demonstration projects are also likely to serve a small number of patients and are not stable sources of care—in order to be renewed, they must show that they are effective, but such evaluations are usually made after only a few years of the program's operation.

Of these fourteen states, five say simply that the state shall make treatment available, and two identify funding mechanisms that include drug treatment as an optional service for which some women may be eligible (for example, those enrolled in a special program for uninsured women whose incomes are above the Medicaid threshold). But ten states are explicit that providing the treatment is contingent on the availability of funds—federal, private, or their own.[21]

For instance, Kentucky passed a law in 1992 allowing the Cabinet for Human Resources to establish four or more pilot projects, specifying that "the Cabinet may use any state appropriation and any gifts, grants, or federal funds that become available for the purposes of implementing the provisions of this section" (Ky. Rev. Stat. Ann. § 222.037). Also in 1992, Minnesota passed a law providing for programs for pregnant women and women with children "within the limits of funds available" (Minn. Stat. Ann. § 254A.17 Subd. 1[a]). None of the other programs specified in the statute has this qualification. Rather, the commissioner of human services "shall" fund, develop, or provide grants for those programs. Minnesota's lack of commitment to providing treatment is all the more inexcusable given its adoption—three years earlier—of punitive and coercive policies toward pregnant drug users (discussed later).

At least one state (Wisconsin) specifies dates at which its legislation will automatically be repealed. The legislature would have had to pass a new bill in 1993 to keep its programs alive, just a few years after they were authorized.

Although I have listed together all states enacting any type of treatment-oriented legislation, the programs vary considerably. Some are comprehensive in scope, addressing a range of women's psychological, medical, and economic needs, while others are restricted to one type or component of treatment, such as "behavioral counseling against smoking, alcohol, or other drug use" (R.I. Gen. Laws § 23-13-18 [b] [7]). Seven of the nine states that explicitly list a comprehensive set of services or that authorize pilot projects make provision of services contingent on securing the necessary funds.

Two states, Maine and Wisconsin, passed laws to provide child care to parents in treatment; neither is specific to pregnant women. Wisconsin's law specifies that provision is limited to available funds, again raising questions about implementation.

Oregon has two apparently unique provisions relating to the actual medical treatment of pregnant women. Physicians are permitted to ad-

[21] California, Colorado, Illinois, Ohio, and Wisconsin say the state shall make treatment available; Colorado and Rhode Island identify special funding mechanisms. The ten contingent states are Arizona, California, Connecticut, Illinois, Iowa, Kentucky, Minnesota, Oregon, Tennessee, and Washington. Because California, Colorado, and Illinois show up in more than one group, the number is still fourteen.

minister or prescribe controlled substances to pregnant women to ease withdrawal. Pregnant women may also be treated with synthetic opiates without first having to go through detoxification, which is a standard practice in state-run programs. Detoxification, or withdrawal from heroin, can cause miscarriages. I came across no other state laws concerning this issue, and so I cannot speculate about whether state policies interfere with the appropriate treatment of pregnant women.

What this range of laws suggests is that providing adequate drug-treatment services to pregnant women is a problem that will not be solved without strong federal leadership. The same federal law that made it illegal to turn away a woman solely because she is pregnant also mandated that states set aside at least 10 percent of their federal funds for pregnant women and women with dependent children, and that all programs receiving funds give preference in admission to pregnant women. If a facility cannot admit a pregnant woman, then it must refer her to the state, which is responsible for finding another facility or arranging interim services within forty-eight hours.[22] Yet these mandates were not attached to a new infusion of funds. Congress merely replaced an existing requirement for states to set aside 10 percent of their funds for programs for *women* with a requirement to set aside those funds for pregnant women and mothers. This requirement pits one set of women against another, instead of recognizing that all women remain underserved. This policy also values fetal health above the health of women and men in need of services. Ultimately, to ensure access to effective treatment, the government needs to allocate more money for drug treatment across the board, with explicit provisions for meeting pregnant women's specific treatment needs, and to ensure that programs receiving public funds comply with laws to admit pregnant women.

Education

Twenty states have some type of measure intended to educate the population at large, or most often pregnant women, of the health risks associated with drug and alcohol consumption during pregnancy. Only two states, Kansas and Kentucky, specifically recognize men's role in unhealthy birth outcomes from alcohol or drugs, even though epidemiological evidence suggests that men's drinking and cocaine use can contribute to prematurity and low birth weight (Blakeslee 1991). In 1992 Kansas mandated a public awareness campaign directed to both men and women on the pre-

[22] Programs that serve intravenous drug users must also give preference to pregnant injecting drug users (45 *CFR*: 96.131).

Figure 6.1. Oregon sign warning pregnant women of alcohol-related birth defects. Reproduced by permission of the Oregon Liquor Control Commission.

conceptual and perinatal effects of the use of tobacco, alcohol, and controlled substances. Kentucky passed two laws the same year, requiring private physicians and retail establishments with liquor licenses to post government signs "with gender neutral language, which shall warn that drinking alcoholic beverages prior to conception or during pregnancy can cause birth defects" (Ky. Rev. Stat. Ann. § 311.378 and § 243.895).

Six kinds of measures fall under the education rubric. The most common (adopted in fourteen states) is consumer education in the form of warning signs where people purchase alcohol.[23] Oregon's sign includes a picture to assist people who can't read (Figure 6.1). (The warning labels on alcoholic beverage containers were mandated by Congress in 1988 [see Wagner 1991, 167].) The next most common is education for health care settings. Six states require or encourage training for health care professionals (or medical/nursing students) on how to identify, counsel, and

---

[23] Alaska, Arizona, California, the District of Columbia, Georgia, Illinois, Kentucky (gender-neutral), Minnesota (encourages, but does not require, signs), Nebraska, New Hampshire, New Mexico, New York, Oregon, and South Dakota.

refer pregnant women in need of drug or alcohol treatment, and five have some requirement for giving information to women receiving prenatal care or to patients in general (via waiting room signs or literature).[24] Five states mandate giving information on fetal alcohol syndrome to marriage license applicants or recipients (Illinois, New Hampshire, Oregon, Rhode Island, and Wisconsin). Wisconsin also requires giving information about the effects of cocaine and other drugs. Kansas and Minnesota passed laws to conduct general public awareness campaigns. And finally, California and Missouri passed laws requiring the development of primary and secondary school curricula, but Missouri's will only be implemented if federal funds can be secured. These measures, especially the warning signs, are probably as common as they are because they are some of the least costly and easiest steps that governments can take to try to reduce the number of babies born exposed to alcohol or drugs.

Abuse/Neglect

A third category of legislation makes policy based on a paradigm equating pregnant women's use of alcohol or drugs with abuse and neglect. This approach triggers civil or criminal procedures for investigating reports of child abuse. Thirteen states have adopted some version of this paradigm. Eight of the states' laws apply only to controlled substances; five include alcohol, too.

Seven states have amended their definitions of child abuse or neglect (Florida, Illinois, Indiana, Massachusetts, Minnesota, Nevada, and Oklahoma). The definitions take two forms: (1) the presence of any alcohol or drugs in the newborn's or woman's blood after birth or (2) the "dependence" or "addiction" of the newborn to alcohol or drugs. This means that infants meeting the above criteria *must* be reported to the local child protective services agency, which in turn must investigate the family situation, regardless of whether there are any indications besides the positive toxicology test that the woman will abuse or neglect her child. Remember that these women are being investigated for child abuse or neglect based on something they did when they were pregnant, not based on any interaction with a baby.

Six additional states have not redefined child abuse to include prenatal

---

[24] Medical education: California, Connecticut, Kansas, Missouri, Oregon, and Wisconsin. Patient information: Alaska, Delaware, Illinois, Kentucky, and Missouri. Connecticut had a policy for one year requiring hospitals to give information to any patient showing symptoms of substance abuse "who is pregnant or who has recently given birth." In 1991 the legislature changed the language to refer to all patients, not just pregnant women (Conn. Gen. Stat. Ann. § 17a-661).

exposure to controlled substances but still have laws triggering a report. In Utah reports are mandatory, whereas in California and Missouri they are permitted. In Wisconsin all positive tests must be reported, but the test cannot be performed without the parent or guardian's consent. In Kentucky health care providers are authorized to test either the woman after giving birth or the infant for drugs or alcohol. The woman must be informed of the test, but the statute does not require her consent. After the test results come in, the health care worker can decide whether an abuse investigation is needed, taking other factors into account. Iowa's statute is the broadest, allowing health practitioners to test a child up to one year of age for controlled substances. Unless the "natural mother" has shown "good faith" in seeking appropriate treatment, the practitioner shall report any positive results to the Department of Human Services for an abuse investigation (Iowa Code Ann. § 232.77[2]). As demonstrated earlier, laws like these have had an unfair and discriminatory impact on African American women.

Most of these provisions take effect after a child is born and has tested positive for drugs or alcohol. Although a number of states have laws to identify pregnant drug users (discussed later in the chapter), only one state explicitly specifies the *testing* of women while they are pregnant.[25]

In Minnesota physicians are authorized to test pregnant women they suspect are using drugs, and then to report them to the local welfare agency, which assesses the woman's needs and offers her services. The agencies are further empowered to seek an emergency involuntary commitment if the woman either refuses services or "fails" recommended treatment. "Failing" treatment is so common that many state statutes forbid treatment centers from refusing to admit someone because he or she has previously relapsed or left a program without completing it. An involuntary commitment is admitting a person to a treatment facility against her will. The facility should be a hospital or other therapeutic institution. Some states, however, have put women into correctional facilities instead because they didn't have enough room in treatment programs. It is unlikely that pregnant addicts will receive proper care in these settings. In order to be legitimate uses of coercive state power, involuntary commitments need to be therapeutically beneficial and distinguishable from incarceration (Chavkin 1991; Moss 1991). Taking pregnant women who use drugs into government custody is the most extreme and coercive pol-

---

[25] As the data presented in this chapter show, hospitals in many states test pregnant women, women who have just given birth, or newborns without specific legislative guidance or authority. In western Massachusetts, many private physicians test pregnant women, often without telling them (Turner 1999).

icy yet sanctioned by a state legislature to deal with this problem. Pregnant women in several states are exposed to more subtle forms of government surveillance, as I discuss later.

In contrast, Missouri's overall approach, adopted in 1991, is not punitive. Doctors are required to use a risk-assessment tool developed by the Department of Health to identify women using drugs or alcohol. If the woman consents, then she will be reported to the Department of Health, which is to offer to coordinate services for her. Doctors may report exposed infants to the Department of Health without a woman's consent, but the information cannot be used in any criminal prosecution.

Five of the thirteen states adopting an abuse paradigm have made it clear that women are not to be subject to criminal investigation or prosecution solely on the basis of a positive drug test, nor to have children removed from their custody on that basis (California, Florida, Iowa, Kentucky, and Missouri). Two other states that do not fall under the abuse paradigm do the same: Kansas and Virginia (the latter put this protection into place while waiting for a task force to develop a policy on how hospitals should handle cases of drug exposure).

After giving birth, women may still be subject to civil proceedings. Civil proceedings can be more severe, because they can lead to termination of parental rights, whereas a criminal conviction might result in jail time but not necessarily permanent loss of custody. As discussed earlier, federal law requires governments to make "reasonable efforts" to keep families together. This includes providing the services and counseling that parents need in order to take care of their children. But biases against women who use drugs mean that women who could be or become competent parents sometimes lose their children anyway. Only one-third of the states embracing an abuse paradigm require the state to coordinate health and social services for women found to be using drugs: Illinois, Minnesota, Missouri, and Wisconsin (Wisconsin's provision applies after the baby is born). If more states did this, it might decrease the likelihood that women and their infants would come into the child protection system in the first place.

One other state that has a potentially onerous policy is Ohio. The language is ominous and unclear: The Department of Alcohol and Drug Addiction Services is to "provid[e] an effective means of intervention to eliminate the addiction of pregnant women to drugs of abuse prior to the birth of their children" and "monitor" women after birth, in addition to making treatment available. The department is also responsible for defining what "intervention" means.[26]

[26] See Ohio Rev. Code Ann. §§ 3793.15, 3793.02 (D), passed in 1990 and 1991. Oregon's policy, too, is ambiguous, declaring in 1989 that health care providers should "encourage

Finally, three states require the development of hospital discharge protocols for drug-exposed babies (California, Rhode Island, and Virginia). The protocols are to establish when infants or their parents should be referred to child protective services or other government agencies for preventive assistance before leaving the hospital.

Administration

The final category is the most diffuse: administration. It includes a variety of measures pertaining to understanding and managing the problems associated with drug use during pregnancy. Seventeen states have enacted these measures.

The set of administrative statutes with the most significant impact on pregnant women's lives is that authorizing the identification of pregnant drug users. Ten states have adopted laws either encouraging or requiring health care workers to identify pregnant women using drugs or alcohol, and often to refer them to government social service agencies (or, in Minnesota, to law enforcement). In Illinois, for example, all service professionals who are required to report child abuse may report addicted "pregnant persons" to the Health Department for assistance and monitoring (325 ILCS 5/7.3b).

Of the ten states authorizing the identification of pregnant drug users, seven follow through with drug treatment. Five of these make an express commitment to providing some form of treatment. Two give pregnant women priority for existing treatment slots and prohibit discrimination against them, two promise treatment only if the money can be found, and one makes no statutory provision for treatment at all.[27]

Assessing a woman's drug use is an important part of taking an accurate medical history and designing a course of care, and most states allowing pregnant drug users to be identified have also taken positive steps to meet their health care needs. Yet the development of protocols to identify pregnant drug users also serves to bring women into the regulatory apparatus of the state. This increases the likelihood that officials will assume custody of babies who test positive for drugs without necessarily doing anything to

---

and facilitate counseling, drug therapy, and other assistance to the patient in order to avoid having the child, when born, become subject to protective services," while the state was waiting for federal funds to implement pilot projects for pregnant women (Or. Rev. Stat. §§ 430.915, 430.925).

[27] California, Colorado, Illinois, Ohio, and Wisconsin "shall provide" treatment; Kansas and Missouri give pregnant women priority for existing treatment slots and forbid discrimination against them; Minnesota and Oregon make treatment contingent on securing funds; and Virginia appears to make no provision whatsoever.

decrease the possibility that women will give birth to drug-exposed babies. This may be the case for some women in all ten states, given the overall shortages of drug treatment.

Interestingly, Colorado's law encourages health care workers to identify only pregnant women who qualify for government assistance to an agency that assesses needs. Although this may be because the government will only assist low-income women in need of treatment, it incorrectly suggests that higher-income women do not abuse drugs and would not derive equal benefit from a needs assessment.

Three states (Illinois, Kansas, and Missouri) provide either a toll-free hot line or a published directory of substance abuse services to assist prenatal care providers in locating treatment for their patients, and two (California and Iowa) have established a state office or council entirely devoted to "perinatal substance abuse," instead of assigning responsibility to an existing agency.

Five states (California, Colorado, Illinois, Missouri, and Oregon) have enacted an array of laws dealing with the management of programs — establishing standards for counties applying for grant money, designating agencies responsible for overseeing a program, and so on. California and Colorado specify that pilot programs be evaluated by a state agency.

Finally, eleven states have enacted measures charging a task force or other body with investigating the problem of drug use during pregnancy in their state; these task forces assess the prevalence of pregnant women's drug use, the ability of current programs to serve women and their infants, and the status of current laws related to child abuse.[28]

Implications for Women

Embedded in this array of legislation is an implied right of fetuses to be born without exposure to alcohol or controlled substances. Sometimes this right is enhanced to include government intervention to control pregnant women's actions. Other times, the right is tempered to limit government action against women.

Studies of government responses to pregnant women's drug use have often focused on the question of whether the state constructed it as a criminal problem or a medical one (AMA 1990; Chavkin 1990). Along these lines, they have sought to categorize legislation as either punitive or public health–oriented. Kathryn Moore's summary of state laws for the American College of Obstetricians and Gynecologists provides an exemplary

[28] California, Connecticut, Illinois, Kentucky, Louisiana, Missouri, New Hampshire, Oklahoma, Oregon, Rhode Island, and Virginia.

construction of this dichotomy: "Broadly speaking, state laws can be characterized as taking two different and opposing approaches to the problem of illicit drug use by pregnant women and drug-exposed and drug-addicted newborns. The difference is rooted in the contrary view of drug addiction as either a criminal or a medical matter. The first legislative approach is punitive [and the second] is public health oriented" (Moore 1990, 1).

My aim is different. I want to present not only the stated purpose of government policy but also to illuminate its effect on women. I am especially interested in whether policies have punitive effects on women, beneficial ones, or are simply neutral. In some cases only information about a statute's implementation can provide a definitive answer, but the language of a statute can still tell us where the state's priorities lie. It can also show that *punitive* and *public health* are neither mutually exclusive terms nor accurate synonyms for *criminal* and *civil*.

What are the results of revisiting the legislation with questions of purpose and effect in mind?

The treatment provisions can have universally beneficial effects. Regardless of whether their express purpose is to help *women*, they all have the potential to do so. They can serve to lift some of the burden of fetal health off of pregnant women's shoulders and transfer it to the state. Their effectiveness depends on the strength of the state's commitments, as measured by allocation and duration of funds; its enforcement of policies guaranteeing access; the breadth and depth of treatment offerings; and so on.

Administrative measures fall all across the spectrum. Mandates to coordinate services for pregnant women benefit them insofar as there are services to coordinate. Establishing a task force, one of the most common state actions, can only be regarded as neutral in effect. There is no way to know if the task forces will ever meet, what course of action they will recommend, whether their suggestions will be adopted by the legislature or accepted by the governor. At the other end are protocols to identify pregnant drug users, which are potentially very punitive, by bringing women under state surveillance without facilitating their access to needed resources.

Laws equating women's conduct during pregnancy with child abuse purport to protect fetuses, but they actually punish women. Exceeding the child abuse provisions already on the books, they treat women like criminals who are guilty until proven innocent. They imply that women have failed at motherhood before the child is even born. Because motherhood is normatively synonymous with selflessness, maternal duty is supposed to come before, and be able to overcome, any other need or problem. These norms have material consequences, punishing women for bringing their pregnancies to term by depriving them of their children.

The abuse paradigm assumes that requiring reports of all positive drug tests will give children greater protection under the law than they currently have. Child welfare experts disagree. Abigail English of the National Center for Youth Law contends that laws relying on positive drug tests are both too narrow and too broad—because the tests are not completely reliable, they will inevitably result in some false positives and some false negatives. Because virtually all medical and social service personnel are already legally obligated to report suspected instances of abuse, English argues, it makes more sense for them to use their experience and training to take into account each infant's situation when determining whether to make a report of suspected child endangerment, as current child abuse laws provide (English 1990).

Health education is generally beneficial and an appropriate government responsibility. Medical wisdom about drinking during pregnancy has changed dramatically in the past thirty years. Women were often told that a little alcohol, especially beer, was good for pregnancy and breast-feeding. Many pregnant women may still get this advice from their mothers or older acquaintances. The specific policies, however, are problematic in a number of ways.

Half the provisions to train health care workers to detect substance use by pregnant women and to educate them about its effects were either optional (California) or repealed within a few years (Connecticut and Wisconsin), demonstrating only a modest effort to help the medical community improve its delivery of prenatal care. All of the patient education measures address birth defects, but few mention the risks of harm to a pregnant woman herself.

Almost all of the proposals single out pregnant women in their message, ignoring the fact that men's alcohol and drug consumption can lead to birth defects. Although it can be argued that women's consumption stands to have the greatest impact on the fetus, this oversight exposes a general problem underlying most regulatory schemes: They reinforce the notion that only pregnant women's actions matter in determining fetal health, rather than also the actions of others or the conditions under which pregnant women live (such as poverty, pollution, violence). This is because pregnant women have been socially constructed as the single biggest threat to their fetuses, even though many things influence pregnancy outcome. Violence against women is endemic in the United States and often begins or intensifies when a woman is pregnant (Berenson et al. 1994,

1760). Women who are beaten during pregnancy have been found to have twice as many miscarriages as women who are not (Moran 1993, 110) and run four times the risk of having a low-birth-weight infant (McFarlane 1989, 73). Although the surgeon general recommended in 1986 that routine prenatal care include screening for battering, health care providers still largely fail to ask the right questions and to identify abuse (Beveridge 1991; Coeling and Harman 1997). Alaska's is the only statute to address domestic violence, and it does so in an ineffective way, because it reduces the injured pregnant woman to an invisible medium between the fetus and the batterer.

Of the more than 150 provisions included in this study, only five were enacted before 1987, so the real window of legislative activity is only six years. Were there noticeable policy shifts during that period?

All the states that flatly defined prenatal exposure to drugs or alcohol as child abuse or neglect did so before 1990. Massachusetts is the clear forerunner here, having changed its abuse definition in 1973. In contrast, only one of six states giving women some legal protection did so before 1990. Measures about reporting drug-exposed newborns, including hospital-discharge protocols, were more likely to rely on physicians' discretion than on blanket requirements during 1990–92. And provisions increasing pregnant women's access to drug treatment increased substantially from 1990 to 1992, with the number more than doubling during the latter period.

Certain other potentially punitive measures continued to be enacted during the 1990s, however. Half of the measures granting authority to test women or newborns for drugs were passed in 1990 or after. And measures authorizing the identification of pregnant drug users, which first appeared in 1989, continued regularly throughout the 1990s.

The positive shifts in policy—away from a punitive model and toward a beneficial one—are testament to the mobilization of the feminist, civil liberties, and health professional communities against legislation that would infringe on women's autonomy and endanger their health.[29] It is worth noting that the medical community's interests here dovetail with pregnant women's. While both have an interest in maximizing the delivery of effective health care, medical professionals, especially the American Medical Association, have long opposed government efforts to usurp their power (AMA 1990, 2665).

---

[29] See Gomez 1997, chap. 3, on the role played by California Advocates for Pregnant Women in influencing the direction of legislation in California. Judith Rosen, who defended Pamela Rae Stewart along with Richard Boesin, helped found the organization.

These shifts do not signal a total victory over the threat of punishment and government surveillance. Punitive measures continue to be introduced in high numbers across the country; defeating them requires ongoing vigilance.[30]

Resource constraints also indicate the need for continued advocacy and mobilization. Budget concerns were widespread in the legislation. Oregon's policy statement emphasizes minimizing costs to taxpayers, and other states directed agencies to obtain materials for free if possible. There is at least some evidence that states are not following through on the commitments made in their legislation. For instance, in 1990 California mandated the creation and dissemination of a model needs assessment protocol to assist people working with pregnant women who use drugs. This protocol is part of a "buffer law" between law enforcement and social services, specifying that a positive drug test is not in and of itself sufficient evidence to report a woman or infant to the child protection agency, but that any indication of drug use should trigger an assessment of the woman's and child's needs for services. Becker and Hora report, however, that "no funding was allocated for implementation of the law, and most hospitals, doctors, and judges are unaware of it" (Becker and Hora 1993, 571).

The gap between legislation and implementation is an important area for further study. As Jerome Miller says, "The only way to judge commitment to a policy is to follow the budget" (1996, 169). Knowing whether states follow through on their commitments to provide services to pregnant women, or whether they in essence give themselves unfunded mandates, will help answer whether states are making policy for symbolic or instrumental purposes.

Comprehensive, woman-centered drug treatment is expensive, but the price is less than incarceration, neonatal intensive care, or foster care after birth. In addition to the direct savings reaped from treating pregnant women's addictions, there are longer-term benefits. A 1991 *New York Times* editorial called "The Cost of Not Treating Crack" reported that two city programs for drug-dependent pregnant women and mothers averted foster care placement in 75 percent of cases, saving $22.7 million in foster care alone. Cumulative four-year savings were projected at more than $250 million. Unfortunately, the *Times* reported in 1995 that budget cuts had reduced these vital services (McLarin 1995).

More important, the number of children in foster care is growing faster

---

[30] See *Reproductive Freedom News*, 1993 to the present, passim; Gomez 1997, 60, on California; and Chapter 7.

than states can find families for them, and foster care too often fails to provide children with safe, stable home environments and access to medical care (Barden 1990). Between 1976 and 1994 foster children and their advocates brought class-action lawsuits against child welfare systems in at least ten states and the District of Columbia to try to improve case management and service provision. Because many children could be kept safely in their parents' homes given supportive services and because of the problems plaguing foster care systems, relocating these children often simply relocates their problems without solving them.[31]

Treatment also has the advantage of being a preventive service that can eliminate or at least minimize the need for other services. Successful rehabilitation benefits the individual, family, and community in terms of enhanced stability and productivity. Especially as responsibility for the poor devolves to the states, researchers and advocates should emphasize that providing humane services to those in need is cost-effective.

Together, courts and legislatures create a powerful system to regulate the lives of women who use drugs or alcohol during pregnancy. The regulation of pregnant women through state policy, criminal prosecutions, and civil proceedings creates fetal rights at women's expense. State actions are constructed to value fetal health above women's health, jeopardizing both. They deny women fair, equal treatment under the law and diminish women as individuals.

This diminution takes place at rhetorical and material levels. By failing to acknowledge women's needs explicitly in their legislation, policy makers deny pregnant women as individuals with their own problems and life plans, erasing them from public view except as the bearers of potential citizens.

In Oklahoma, for example, the legislature criminalized the act of giving birth to a drug-exposed infant in 1987. It appointed a task force to study the issue four years later, acknowledging that it was still wrestling with whether to punish or treat pregnant women (U.S. DHHS n.d., App. D). Another state, Minnesota, adopted a stick-without-a-carrot approach. It authorized the state to take custody of a pregnant drug addict three years before it even conditionally provided for treatment for pregnant women. This might be more acceptable if the state already provided adequate treatment resources, but Minnesota reported in fiscal year 1990 that re-

---

[31] The states are Alabama, Arkansas, Connecticut, the District of Columbia, Illinois, Louisiana, Maryland, Massachusetts, New Mexico, New York, and Utah. For information see Matthews 1992; Grimm 1992, 1994.

sources "are especially inadequate for treatment programs for pregnant women and women with children. The three existing programs all have waiting lists, an exception in Minnesota, which does *not* generally have a waiting list problem" (U.S. DHHS n.d, App. E; emphasis in original).

Women across the country have been prosecuted and jailed for crimes that no state legislature has recognized. The charges are an illegitimate abuse of prosecutors' discretion. When judges accept the charges, they enforce upon pregnant women a different and more exacting standard of duty than any other member of society must live up to. Enforcing that standard creates real, material costs that pregnant women must bear.

The prosecutions have continued since 1992: from the one brought in Washington in January 1993 to the one that ended in Massachusetts in May 1998 when a woman pleaded guilty to involuntary manslaughter after her premature stillborn infant tested positive for cocaine (*RFN* 1996b; A.P. 1998). And for the first time, a state supreme court ruled that pregnant women's drug use *can* be considered child abuse. The South Carolina Supreme Court ruled three to two in 1996 that the word *person* includes viable fetuses for purposes of the child abuse law. Women thus convicted of child abuse face up to ten years in prison (*New York Times* 1996b). The decision reinstates an eight-year sentence given to Cornelia Whitner, who had been freed by a lower court after serving more than one year.

One thing that makes it easier for civil and criminal courts to render decisions that punish women, for states to pass laws that penalize women, and for lay people to support both is that the arguments purporting to balance women's and fetuses' rights often misidentify the rights at stake. Those who advocate restricting pregnant women's actions typically cast the choice as one between women's right to use legal and illegal drugs and a fetus's right to be born free of exposure to them. John Robertson argues that laws forbidding pregnant women from using alcohol, drugs, or tobacco would be constitutional, "because there is no fundamental right to use psychoactive substances" (Robertson 1983, 443). Similarly, Sam Balisy's argument sets up a conflict between a fetus's right to be born free from damaging substances and women's right to pursue a particular "lifestyle" that includes smoking, drinking, or using illegal drugs for "physical and psychic pleasure" (Balisy 1987, 1219). And Alan Dershowitz maintains that women do not have the right to harm their future children "simply in order to satisfy a momentary whim for a quick fix" (Dershowitz 1992, 217). These arguments falsely characterize all women's experiences with drugs as recreational choices, denying the reality of addiction for many women, and they ignore the constitutionally protected rights that women do have—rights to privacy, bodily integrity, due process, and equal

444

protection that shield them from being singled out for unique restrictions and penalties. Fetal rights proponents would have a harder time making their case if they took these rights into account.

When evaluating these state practices toward pregnant women and new mothers, it is important to remember that no one else in this society would or could ever be held accountable for these "crimes." These approaches make women and their needs disappear. Their architects rush ahead to penalize women without giving them resources to manage their problems themselves. Women pay the cost by retreating from needed medical attention and by criminal or civil court intervention into their lives.

Meanwhile, politicians turn the plight of pregnant drug users to their advantage in their quests for personal fame and higher elected office. Tony Tague of Muskegon County, Michigan, appeared on PBS's *MacNeil/ Lehrer News Hour* after prosecuting two women for using cocaine (Greene 1991, 742). Paul Logli of Illinois became a public figure after charging Melanie Green with involuntary manslaughter when her newborn died of causes attributed to her cocaine use. He is quoted in newspapers and contributes to such academic journals as *Criminal Justice Ethics* (see, for example, Logli 1990).

Stephen Goldsmith used his position as Marion County prosecutor as a launching pad to the mayor's office in Indianapolis in 1992. He built a reputation for fighting drug crime and publicly advocated prosecuting women who smoke crack during pregnancy (Stattmann 1989). Charles Condon blazed his trail to the state attorney general's office and national prominence by prosecuting pregnant women in Charleston, South Carolina. One of his latest causes is to keep the confederate flag flying at the state capitol (Bragg 1996). This cause lends credence to the argument that prosecutions against Black women are often racially motivated.

This is not the first time politicians have exploited women's lives for their own gain: The very public campaign against illegal abortionists following World War II provides a telling parallel. Mayors, police, prosecutors, and the press all worked together to expose abortion providers and their clients in coordinated raids. These busts ended long-standing agreements under which, as long as no one died, law enforcement would look the other way. Seeking to generate publicity for his re-election campaign in 1951, the district attorney in Portland, Oregon, raided the downtown offices of Ruth Barnett and other illegal abortionists. Barnett had been practicing for thirty years and had never lost a patient. She was arrested again periodically, until a new district attorney was elected in 1965 and "determined to make his mark" by resurrecting the "tried-and-true strategy" of cracking down on abortionists and arrested her five times in two years (Solinger 1994, 230). The illegal abortion trials made women's "immorality" visible and vilified both female abortionists and the women they served in order to reconsolidate traditional gender roles. According to Rickie Solinger, the "core issue" in the trials was "much more the charge of murdering motherhood than it was the charge of murdering the 'unborn child'" (Solinger 1994, 209).

While not everyone may feel sympathetic toward pregnant drug users, a policy of retribution rather than compassion makes little sense in practical terms. Retribution scores political points but fails to accomplish any significant policy objective: improved health, increased family stability, deterrence, or fiscal savings. Those who favor retribution seek an individual solution to a set of societal problems, making women wholly and solely responsible for the work of reproduction while ignoring the material reality of their lives that makes them unable to fulfill their assigned duties without assistance.

7

The Costs of Inequality

> Women must have the ability to make responsible decisions
> concerning a pregnancy without losing other opportunities for
> a fulfilled life.
>
> —North Dakota Legislature, 1991 Policy Statement
> on "Aid to Pregnant Women"

In times of fiscal retrenchment and declining commitments to the public good, how we conceive of a problem and the terms we use to describe it assume even greater importance. In this book I have been fundamentally concerned with developing an adequate framework to understand the operation of fetal rights claims.

Women's poor access to resources to maximize healthy pregnancies is a critical problem. Ensuring healthy pregnancies without erasing women's selfhood, however, is also always at stake. In all three policy domains explored in this book, particular women's actions conflict with cultural expectations about how women, especially potential mothers, ought to behave. These two problems converge in the medical arena, where the power to make decisions and women's bodies themselves become contested resources.

As a society, we have a variety of choices to make about collective responsibility for children and for all generations, including whether to allocate resources to prevention or to reserve them for crisis management.

American hospitals, for example, boast the finest high-technology diagnostic and life-saving equipment, and yet in 1995, 40 million Americans had no health insurance whatsoever (Rosenthal 1997). This number includes millions of full-time workers and their families (*CDF Reports* 1996). Indeed, the gap between rich and poor has not been greater since World War II (Holmes 1996a). Similarly, focusing on possible fetal harm diverts attention from more blatant risks in the workplace, like the job-related injuries that kill 10,000 people and permanently disable 70,000 others each year (Lacayo 1991).

This critique of budget and policy priorities relates to another theme implicit in this book: Equality is a more effective argument than privacy as a means to increase women's autonomy and improve their lives. Claims of equality demand remedial action in a way that claims of privacy do not. Although privacy has positive meanings, it is a harder realm in which to ground claims on the state or collective resources. This is especially relevant for medical self-determination and drug use, areas in which women's challenges to being singled out for different treatment are usually framed as violations of constitutional rights. Privacy does not shield women from bodily invasions; their experiences of subordination to doctors and judges expose the costs of unequal treatment. Women's claims of due process proved their best defense in fighting charges of drug-related fetal abuse. In the employment realm, equality is already a goal written specifically into law, thanks to Title VII of the Civil Rights Act. Were it appropriate to frame the fight against fetal protection policies as a violation of constitutional rights, then claims to equal protection in the workplace would go further than claims to privacy toward securing women's access to jobs *and* a safe workplace for both sexes. Companies would not be allowed to say, "You can make your private decision to work here, and suffer any consequences in private as well."

Real political and sexual equality for women means being able to make choices and take action in the world. In life as we know it, making choices necessarily entails uncertainty and risk. Opposing the creation of fetal rights does not insulate women from accountability for the consequences of their actions. Rather, it rejects unique standards of accountability solely for women.

The Powerful Fiction of Third-Party Pregnancy

The legal construction of fetuses as independent third parties is a significant political innovation and a striking new emphasis in the history of Anglo-American law. Yet even more amazing is how women themselves have been treated as third parties in relation to their own pregnancies. When pregnancy is constructed in these ways, fetuses gain rights, and women lose them.

Courts have given potential fetuses independent identities in a number of ways. In the employment domain, potential fetuses (and their partial predecessors—women's ova) have been designated as visitors to the workplace. As "business visitors," potential fetuses were entitled to a greater degree of protection from the risks of industrial production than the women and men employed there. Courts have also designated fetuses as "innocent third parties" in medical and substance use contexts. They depict fetuses as distinct patients trapped within women's bodies and trapped by women's selfish and irrational decisions. Prosecutors and courts treat fetuses as crime victims, whether of violent assault or forced drugging. This designation of the fetus as a rights-bearing subject splits the fetus from the pregnant woman of whom it is a part. It also splits the pregnant woman from herself. Politically, the construct of fetal rights has the power to turn women into third parties to themselves.

The following cases illustrate this phenomenon. In 1994, nineteen-year-old Kawana Ashley had one child, was pregnant, and could not afford an abortion. So she put a pillow over her stomach and shot herself. The very premature fetus—weighing only two pounds—was delivered by emergency cesarean and lived for two weeks. When the baby died, the state of Florida charged Ashley with murder, manslaughter, and criminal abortion. A judge let the manslaughter charge stand, and Ashley appealed all the way to the state supreme court. The high court found no basis in legislation or its own power to "trump the common law and pit woman against fetus in criminal court," and ruled that the charges could not stand (*Ashley v. Florida* 1997, 343).

Florida has a manslaughter law specifically for fetuses, but the district attorney did not charge Ashley under that statute. It reads, "The willful killing of an unborn quick child, by any injury to the mother of such child which would be murder if it resulted in the death of such mother, shall be deemed manslaughter" (Fla. Stat. Ann. § 782.09). Because this law clearly refers to someone besides a pregnant woman, to charge Ashley under this law would render her a third party to herself.

This is exactly what happened in New York. A family court held that a newborn's positive test for cocaine was sufficient to uphold a charge of neglect against the mother. The court denied the woman's motion to dismiss the charges. The court did not rule in the typical way, by finding that drug use during pregnancy is in itself neglect or is indicative of a likelihood of future harm, but turned instead to tort law. It considered the charge "as one alleging neglect of a child *in esse*"—that is, an actual existing child, rather than a fetus.[1] Having thus split the fetus from the "mother," the court explained that tort law recognizes that a child born alive has a right to recover for injuries inflicted prior to birth. All of the court's examples concerned suits against third parties, like doctors, who had injured fetuses. By treating the dependent fetus as an independent person and analogizing the pregnant woman to an outsider, the court treated the woman like a third party to herself. In effect, the court acted as if the woman existed outside her body. The decision had the effect of turning the pregnant woman into two entities, one of whom (the "mother") acted tortiously toward the fetus, while the other was reduced to an invisible incubating medium between self and fetus.

Women themselves have attempted on occasion to invoke fetal rights. Sometimes this attempt has been cynical, as in the case of a pregnant inmate who claimed that it was unconstitutional to imprison her fetus because it had not been charged, tried, or sentenced. Here the inmate tried to use the fetus's "innocence" as a way to escape punishment for a forgery conviction (*New York Times* 1989; Williams 1990, 91). Other instances have been more poignant, as in the case of a battered woman who sought an order of protection against her husband on behalf of herself, her children, and her fetus. A family court held that it had jurisdiction to protect the fetus and issued a protection order on its behalf.[2] Realizing that society often values fetal life more than it values babies, children, or adults, these women tried to turn that assessment to their advantage.

These cases raise important questions. How is it that a woman can be considered a third party in relation to herself? The stories in this book have exposed the ways that fetal rights politics depends on pervasive assumptions that fertile and pregnant women are not capable of making decisions for themselves. But fetal rights politics does not stop there. It also renders pregnant women as something other than normal human beings—they no longer fit any of the existing categories. The refusal to consider pregnant women as ordinary human beings has caused some courts to resort to strained legal analogies when deciding cases involving pregnant women. This dynamic is clearly expressed in the first opinion about Angela Carder, who was forced to have a cesarean against her will. The three-judge panel that ordered the operation claimed to analyze Carder's case "within the context of its closest legal analogues: the right of an adult to refuse medical treatment and the right of a parent to refuse medical

---

[1] *DSS v. Felicia B.* 1989, 637. This case is discussed in Moss 1990, 291–92.
[2] *Gloria C. v. William C.* (1984) is also discussed in Chavkin, Walker, and Paone 1992, 304.

treatment on behalf of offspring" (*In re A.C.* 1987, 615). But why did the court consider the first situation an "analogue"? It was in fact precisely Carder's situation: She was an adult exercising her right to refuse treatment. In this case the court understood pregnant women as suspended between adulthood and parenthood. The logic of this opinion exemplifies the notion of pregnant women as confounding and as categorically different from other human beings.[3] This construction of pregnant women makes it easier to impose costs on them.

The cases also raise a different question: In what kind of society is a woman's claim of bodily harm insufficient to trigger the state's protection? The kind of society in which women are so conscious of their limited worth that they ask for help on behalf of their fetuses, as if fetuses *were* independent and existed outside of them. The kind of society in which, in Patricia Williams's terms, women "attempt to assert their own interests through that part of themselves that overlaps with some architecture of the state's interest" (Williams 1990, 92). Under these constraints, women assume the identity of fetal guardian, instead of claiming entitlement to assistance as a pregnant woman, a citizen, a victim of violence, or simply a human being.

These examples illustrate two meanings of the expression "disembodying women." Fetuses are disembodied from pregnant women as a precondition to independent status. But pregnant women are also disembodied. They are treated as if disembodied from their own experience, as if they have loaned out their bodies for nine months and so have no claim over what happens to them during that time. This conception of pregnancy has no basis in reality. Women who become pregnant have not merely invited in a houseguest or given shelter to a recluse but have conceived a being that will develop within their bodies for almost a year. For some women, that experience of embodiment is more pleasure; for others, it is more pain. But it is always theirs.

Treating pregnancy as a disembodied state is just another way of pretending that pregnancy has no costs to women. This pretense thus has the same effect as fetal rights rhetoric. But no matter what language judges, doctors, or legal scholars dream up, pregnancy isn't something that happens somewhere outside of women's bodies. Defeating fetal rights is necessary literally to make women whole.

The point of this analysis isn't simply to illustrate the social construction of women as an exotic "other." It is to demonstrate how a distinct, and dis-

---

[3] The final decision in Carder's case retreated from this line of reasoning, although too late to benefit Carder.

tinctly worse, *legal status* is being carved out for pregnant women. That formal status has profoundly negative consequences for women's well-being and for their equality with men. Inferior legal status is the cost women bear when fetuses are given rights. Two equal rights-bearing subjects cannot exist in one body.[4]

A problem for women who want to advance fetal rights on their own behalf and for those well-meaning individuals who see fetal rights as a way to help pregnant women is that those claims can only go so far in a country that does not really care about children at the level of public policy. The United States can be described as pronatalist, but it cannot be described as pro-child.[5] The number of children without a doctor, a good school, a safe place to play, or any place at all to live reveals the gap between the rhetoric and reality of America's commitment to children as our most valuable resource. As Katha Pollitt says, "Concern for the fetus may look like a way of helping children," but is really "a substitute for it" (Pollitt 1990, 414). The only thing fetal rights does effectively is penalize women.

Fetal Abuse as Metaphor

Racine County, Wisconsin, is the scene of another prosecution against women for conduct during pregnancy.[6] On a March night in 1996, Deborah Zimmerman was brought to the emergency room, very close to her due date and very drunk. She told a surgical aide that she wanted to drink herself and "this thing" to death. The baby was born by emergency cesarean and showed signs of fetal alcohol syndrome. After the birth, an assistant district attorney charged Zimmerman with attempted murder, arguing that her statements expressed a clear intent to kill her unborn child. Zimmerman was miserable, alcoholic, and pregnant. None of these things is illegal. But put them together and suddenly a new crime is created. A judge refused to dismiss the charges against Zimmerman, and her appeal is pending before the Wisconsin Supreme Court. After the birth, Zim-

---

[4] Except perhaps in the extremely rare cases of conjoined twins who are not merely joined at the hip or the head but who share one set of legs and one torso and yet have two hearts and minds (K. Miller 1996). In contrast to pregnancy, these human phenomena *are* anomalies.

[5] This pronatalism is clearly selective. Many women, such as those who receive welfare payments, are discouraged from bearing children. Mink 1998 shows how welfare policy undermines the reproductive rights and disparages the reproductive labor of women receiving assistance.

[6] Since 1992 new cases of the kind analyzed in Chapter 6 have been brought in several states, including—for the first time—Arizona, New Jersey, and Wisconsin (CRLP 1996).

merman enrolled in a court-ordered residential treatment program, and the state assumed custody of her daughter. She sees her daughter on weekends and can regain custody if she completes the treatment program. To go forward with the prosecution after restoring custody would seem to put the state in a contradictory position; the only way to make sense of this prosecution is to see it as the desire to punish women.[7]

The stories of women like Zimmerman are the most unsettling for many people. Pregnant women's use of drugs or alcohol seems unforgivable. Prosecutors act on those sentiments and charge women with crimes of fetal abuse in courts of law. Yet these criminal cases simply make explicit something that underlies fetal rights claims in general: The idea of fetal abuse is a powerful metaphor for women's actions. We have seen how courts compared potential fetuses that would be exposed to hazardous substances at work to deprived children. Similarly, courts have based their decision to force medical treatments on women on the grounds that the fetus is being neglected.

As Anna Tsing explains, "Both feminist and nonfeminist ideologies that glorify nurturant mothering . . . encourage as their hidden complement the conceptual space of the 'anti-mother.' Its monsters are created, and women are condemned, in the very real space of courtrooms and prisons" (1990, 284). Tsing writes about criminal charges brought against women who give birth outside of hospitals and whose babies die, but her comments apply to the situations examined here as well. Judges and others often condemn women for violating the norms of selfless devotion that are the hallmark of good mothering when they refuse medical intervention, drink alcohol or take drugs, or even work for a living. Whether working in factories or choosing vaginal birth, women's actions are suspect. These acts are taken as proof that women are abusing their fetuses and are bad mothers. Rejecting the politics of fetal rights means rejecting this understanding of pregnant and fertile women's actions.

It is important to make clear that taking this stand is not the same as saying that there are in fact no bad mothers. Rather, it is to insist on distinguishing between two different things: parents' harmful treatment of children and superimposing the construct of "bad motherhood" onto

---

[7] See Terry 1996 and *Wisconsin State Journal* 1996 for details of Zimmerman's case. The November 21, 1996 episode of the hit television show *ER* included a scene based on this case, giving its weekly audience of thirty-five to forty million people a crash course in the politics of fetal rights. The physicians in charge of the emergency room criticized the medical student who called the police for doing something that might scare away those women who most need medical attention.

women's lives. American society has not done a very good job of protecting children from the wrath of adults. Children suffer all too often at the hands of their parents, in situations where authorities are found to have known of ongoing abuse. Consider the fate of Joshua DeShaney in Wisconsin. At the age of four, Joshua's father beat him into a coma, and he sustained such severe brain damage that he is expected to spend the rest of his life in an institution for the profoundly retarded. The Winnebago County Department of Social Services had been following Joshua's case for two years before the fateful beating, even assuming custody of him at one point. Joshua's mother (who did not have custody) sued the department for violating Joshua's civil rights by failing to protect him when the agency knew that he was in danger. The U.S. Supreme Court ruled in 1989 that states have no affirmative obligation to protect children under the Fourteenth Amendment (Bussiere 1989).

Stories about pregnant women who abuse drugs grip the public's imagination. Because these stories resonate with a larger tale of social crisis, they become confused with stories about women addicts who abuse their children. In 1995 the story of Elisa Izquierdo mesmerized the nation. According to the *Time* magazine cover story, six-year-old Elisa was repeatedly tortured and eventually killed by her mother, who is Puerto Rican and addicted to crack. Neighbors, teachers, and the child welfare agency knew Elisa was being abused (Van Biema 1995; Kozol 1995). Gender, race, and crack combined to make a story that fit neatly into popular debates about fetal abuse, child abuse, and urban pathology.

But the greater significance of this story is the evidence it provides of our poor commitment to child welfare and our short historical memory. It was only in 1987 that a little girl named Lisa Steinberg was murdered in New York City by a parent. For weeks afterward, the press reported endless debate about the father's culpability versus the system's. According to a *New York Times* columnist, after Steinberg's death "the city devoted more resources to child protection. Training improved, just as it has now [after Izquierdo's death]. But then came the inevitable budget cuts, and services and training deteriorated" (Purnick 1996, B1).

One lesson of these tragedies is that women's advocates cannot further the cause of women's equality by denying that child abuse occurs. But it is wrong not to distinguish between what mothers do to children and what pregnant women do to themselves (and *for* themselves, like working) that may affect fetuses or future children. Fundamentally, there is a difference between drug exposure in utero and being starved, beaten, or molested by an adult. The motivation is completely different. People who conflate pregnant women's drinking or use of drugs with child abuse fail to make this distinction. It is also crucial to challenge the popular media's construction of monster mothers and to insist on accurate coverage of child abuse. The fact that some women are bad parents is no reason to circumscribe all women. Nor should women be held to higher standards of good parenting than are men simply because our culture defines mothering as nurturing and fathering as a combination of impregnation and economic support.

The Role of the State

Because my goal has been to explore the legal and political implications and consequences of creating fetal rights, I have emphasized women's legal rights and responsibilities over moral ones. My findings are nonetheless morally relevant. They demonstrate that by creating a regime of fetal rights the state has not facilitated women's ability to fulfill any moral responsibilities they may have—to fetuses, themselves, or others. Nor has this regime helped the state to fulfill its own responsibilities.

Instead, fetal rights exacerbate women's economic inequality with men, diminish women's freedom, and erode women's standing as citizens. Coercive government intervention in women's lives is therefore acceptable only after birth. In principle, the state cannot justify restricting the freedom, choices, and opportunities of an entire class of people in order to benefit (possibly) another class, that of potential and actual fetuses. In practice there is nowhere to draw the line once any intervention before birth is allowed.

Accordingly, conduct or status during pregnancy should not be considered evidence of abuse or neglect. When social workers investigate allegations of abuse, they should not apply lesser standards of due process or hold women to different standards simply because their children entered the child protection system as a result of a positive drug test at birth. These newborns should not be automatically removed from their mothers' custody; the abuse report was not triggered because of how the women related to their babies. The question of exactly what kind of intervention is appropriate still remains. How best to protect children is a source of longstanding conflict among child welfare professionals themselves: Does the government intervene too freely, needlessly disrupting families, or is it to blame for failing to intervene, leaving children vulnerable to harm and even death? As Chapter 6 makes clear, foster care is not a viable option for all the drug- and alcohol-exposed babies born in the United States. Even if it were, removing babies automatically on the basis of a positive drug test at birth without assessing parental fitness not only violates women's rights to due process but may not serve the child's best interests. All a single test result conveys is that a woman used drugs recently; it tells nothing about the woman's patterns of drug use, history of dependence, or capacity to meet a child's basic needs, nor about support systems available to her at home or through government programs. If social workers ultimately determine that a new mother who tests positive for drugs is not capable of being a parent, and the state fulfills its obligations to provide legal representation and to make reasonable efforts to help her become a capable parent, then it is appropriate for the state to remove the child.[8]

The following case provides an example of casting the net too wide, and it cautions against relying solely on toxicology screens at birth to determine abuse. A Long Island woman smoked marijuana to ease her pain during labor. In accordance with county policy, the hospital social worker reported the positive drug tests to the county Department of Social Services, which took emergency protective custody of the child and filed a neglect petition on the basis of the drug tests. The woman endured a nine-month court battle for custody of her child, despite her doctors' testimony that she was a fit parent and not addicted to drugs in any case. Even the hospital social worker who had reported her drug test testified on her behalf. Despite her ultimate victory in court, the woman's name will remain in the child abuse registry for the state until 2016 (Singer 1990). This is precisely the kind of result that policies should be designed to avoid.

In the criminal realm, legislatures and attorneys general should discourage district attorneys from charging women with drug-related crimes of "fetal abuse," and judges should vigilantly enforce fair treatment of any women so accused. Regardless of whether someone is convicted, simply being processed through the criminal justice system can make it harder to find a job (J. Miller 1996, 118). The negative impact on job prospects is one of the many broad implications that perversely makes it harder for women to succeed at taking care of their children.

The state should be equally vigilant in enforcing women's employment opportunities and health care decisions. Government actors at all levels must simultaneously enforce civil rights laws and occupational safety and health laws, and ideally expand the scope of both. This requires undermining the false dichotomy between opportunity and safety on which fe-

---

[8] This conclusion about the appropriate role of the state accords with recommendations set forth by the Center for the Future of Children and the American Academy of Pediatrics (Behrman et al. 1991; *Pediatrics* 1990).

tal protection policies depend and challenging the social relations of reproduction that make it easy to assign costs to women. Government actors need also to enforce common-law and constitutional guarantees of bodily integrity so that doctors do not dominate their pregnant patients. And finally they must enforce constitutional guarantees of due process so that prosecutors do not advance their careers by exploiting women.

The Persistence of Fetal Rights

The kind of right being created for fetuses in theory and in practice is an enforceable entitlement. In other words, it is a right to be born with a sound mind and body, or a right to a "maternal environment" free of hazards. A right to a sound mind and body may sound incredible, because biology and genetics intervene in ways we cannot control. Around 5 percent of newborns, for example, have birth defects for no known reason. But the fact that such a right cannot actually be guaranteed has not stopped fetal rights advocates and courts from trying to enforce it on women. The logic of this right dictates that social institutions hold women accountable for its fulfillment. The first step is to seek to enforce this new fetal right against women, only picking up the tab when a woman lacks the resources to provide what the right requires, as she usually does in these situations. Hence society's ultimate resource allocation is more costly and punitive than it has to be.

As I observe in Chapter 2, there has always been a line of feminist argument advocating abortion as an equality right for women in an unequal world. There are direct links between fetal rights politics and anti-abortion politics: Both use reproduction as a site to control women. Both undermine women's autonomy and power of self-determination. Consider Wisconsin's legislative record for 1998. The state passed three relevant laws, permitting involuntary commitment of pregnant women who take drugs or drink alcohol, creating new crimes of fetal battery and feticide that recognize the fetus as an independent victim from the moment of conception, and banning late-term abortions in such broad terms that doctors stopped providing abortions altogether until the attorney general assured them that they would not be prosecuted (*New York Times* 1998a; Herbert 1998). This package of laws underlines what the effort to codify rights for fetuses is all about: women's subordination.

The new legislation in Wisconsin is just one of many indications that the politics of fetal rights has not abated, and may even have recently accelerated. Consider what else happened in 1998. On the abortion front, judges continued to award fetuses rights in direct conflict with women and the Constitution. An Alabama judge, for instance, took the unprecedented step of appointing a guardian for the fetus when a teenager sought judicial permission instead of parental consent for an abortion (Bailey 1998). In Ohio a judge abused her power by sentencing a woman to six months in jail instead of probation in order to keep her from obtaining a second-trimester abortion (*New York Times* 1998c). And the war on legal abortion claimed another casualty, when a sniper killed Dr. Barnett Slepian in his own home (Berger 1998). This latest murder represents the most extreme form of the intimidation that anyone involved with abortion routinely experiences (Rodriguez 1998).

South Dakota passed a law like Wisconsin's to allow the state to take custody of pregnant women who use drugs through involuntary civil commitment procedures. These two states go further than their predecessor in Minnesota: They permit commitment of women who use alcohol as well as controlled substances, and South Dakota permits judges to order women into two-day detoxification at the behest of family or friends, or to confine a woman for nine months. South Dakota now defines drinking during pregnancy as a form of child abuse (*New York Times* 1998b).

Minnesota is not far behind. The legislature passed a law that allows reporting of pregnant women who drink to child abuse authorities. Some, like the state's first lady, regret that reporting is not required (Carlson 1998). Rounding out the states with significant new fetal rights laws, Virginia now includes prenatal exposure to drugs or alcohol as a reason to report suspected abuse (Simpson 1999). Some in Alabama hope to join this group; the Juvenile Justice Coordinating Council in Mobile County voted unanimously to ask the legislature to pass a law to incarcerate pregnant women who use cocaine (Rabb 1998). Meanwhile, the residents of Minot, North Dakota, said "not in my backyard" to a residential treatment facility for pregnant women, and a group of private citizens in Southern California began offering women who use drugs $200 to get a tubal ligation or Norplant (Zent 1998; Smith 1998).

At the national level, the House Government Reform and Oversight Committee held a hearing on the possibility of creating a federal "fetal abuse" law, with South Carolina Attorney General Charles Condon as star witness (Zeller 1998). The U.S. Supreme Court let stand the South Carolina ruling that a viable fetus is a person for the purposes of child abuse law, and Condon is stepping up the prosecutions of pregnant drug users in response.

There is nothing in the South Carolina decision to prevent the arrest of women for engaging in lawful activity that poses a possible threat to fetal health (*Whitner v. South Carolina* 1997). With this ruling, there is no doubt that we are embarked down the slippery slope. Federal lawmakers' interest in imposing South Carolina's values on the rest of the nation suggests the work yet to be done to secure women's reproductive self-determination as equal citizens. The past twenty-five years of reproductive politics are culminating in violence and injustice as we approach the twenty-first century.

For a society that promises equality, these costs are too great. We can't afford fetal rights.

Appendix: Selected State Statutes

In 1990 Wendy Chavkin observed the need for a national survey of state legislation and practice relating to pregnant women and substance abuse (Chavkin 1990, 483). This book seeks to provide that information for substance use and other areas of perceived conflict between women and fetuses in the *Roe v. Wade* period (1973–92).

I focus on state statutes rather than administrative regulations because state representatives are elected and therefore accountable for their actions in a way that administrative personnel are not. The following excerpts were selected to give the texture of the statutes by highlighting specific wording, variations, and changes over time. Several publications report more fetal "child abuse" laws than I do because I interpret those laws more narrowly. It is possible, then, that I may have underestimated the extent of states' punitive response to pregnant women in my own survey of state statutes. Readers wishing more background and additional excerpts may consult Roth 1997.

State Statutory Provisions on Pregnancy and the Right to Die, as of December 31, 1992

The purpose of living will laws is to empower patients to declare, in Missouri's terms: "I have the primary right to make my own decisions concerning treatment that might unduly prolong the dying process" (Missouri Ann. Stat. § 459.015 [Vernon 1992]). These safeguards are necessary, as Kansas puts it, "in order that the rights of patients may be respected even after they are no longer able to participate actively in decisions about themselves" (Kansas Stat. Ann. § 65-28,101 [1992]).

This is a fast-changing field of law; readers primarily interested in restrictions in place today should check statutes for current language.

Alaska Stat. Ann. § 18.12.040 (c) (Oct. 1994 Supp.), "Rights of the Terminally Ill Act," was passed in 1986. An attorney general opinion issued the same year questions the constitutionality of the provision requiring treatment if live birth is probable.

Arizona Rev. Stat. Ann. § 36-3262, Statement 3 (1993), "Medical Treatment Decisions Act," was passed in 1992 to respect pregnant women's wishes. A prior law from 1985 had no pregnancy clause.

California Health & Safety Code § 7189.5 (c) (West 1994 Supp.), "Natural Death Act," was passed in 1991 and changed the original 1976 law, which was silent on pregnancy, to invalidate pregnant women's directives.

Florida Stat. Ann. § 765.101 et. seq. (West 1994 Supp.), "Health Care Advance Directives Act," was passed in 1992. A hybrid living will/health care proxy law, it addresses pregnancy only in regard to the latter function of the law. A prior law stated that pregnant women's living will declarations had no effect (former § 765.08 (West 1986), enacted 1984).

Georgia Code Ann. § 31-32-3, 5 (1994 Supp.), "Living Wills Act," was passed in 1992 and contains the following: "If I am female and I have been diagnosed as pregnant, this living will shall have no force and effect unless the fetus is not viable and I indicate by initialing after this sentence that I want this living will to be carried out." Giving pregnant women a choice before viability is a change from the blanket provision enacted in 1984 that invalidated all pregnant women's living wills. (Because it provides *any* degree of choice, this provision was included among the three that allow pregnant women to decide whether their living wills will be implemented.)

Note that Section 31-32-11 (b) (1994 Supp.) from the 1984 law remains on the books. It reads, "Furthermore, nothing in this chapter shall be construed to condone, authorize, or approve abortion."

Idaho Code § 39-4504 (4) (1993), "Natural Death Act," was passed in 1988 and cancels pregnant women's directives. This is a change from the 1977 version of the law, which was silent on pregnancy.

Illinois "Living Will Act," 755 Ill. Comp. Stat. Ann. 35/3 § 3 (c) (West 1992), was passed in 1987–88 and cancels pregnant women's directives if live birth is possible. Previously, the act had completely invalidated pregnant women's directives (1983–84).

Kentucky Rev. Stat. Ann. § 311.622 et. seq. (Michie 1994 Supp.), "Living Will Act," appears to require medical treatment to be provided to a pregnant patient with a terminal condition unless such medical treatment will not lead to the live birth of the unborn child, will be physically harmful or unreasonably painful to the patient, or will prolong pain that cannot be alleviated by medication.[1]

---

[1] The statute contains other provisions that contradict this one. Section 311.625 (7) (c) (Michie 1994 Supp.) defines a "qualified patient" to mean "an adult patient of sound mind

Nevada Rev. Stat. Ann. § 449.624 4 (Michie 1991), "Withholding or Withdrawal of Life-Sustaining Treatment Act," was passed in 1991 and requires treatment as long as it is probable that the fetus will develop to the point of live birth. The original 1977 law had cancelled women's directives altogether during pregnancy.

New Jersey Stat. Ann. § 26:2H-56 (West 1994 Supp.), "Advanced Directives for Health Care Act" was passed in 1991, and specifies that "a female declarant may include in an advanced directive executed by her, information as to what effect the advance directive shall have if she is pregnant." This language is the clearest expression of women's right to decide what shall happen if they are pregnant.

Oklahoma Stat. Ann. tit. 63, § 3101.8, C (West 1994 Supp.), "Rights of the Terminally Ill or Persistently Unconscious Act," was passed in 1992 and invalidates pregnant women's directives. Leaving nothing to chance, the law further specifies that "if it is not known if the patient is pregnant, the said physician shall, where appropriate considering age and other relevant factors, determine whether or not the patient is pregnant."

Pennsylvania "Advance Directive for Health Care Act," 20 Pa. Cons. Stat. Ann. § 5414 (1994 Supp.), was passed in 1992 and specifies that the state shall pay the cost of keeping pregnant women alive.

State Statutes on Alcohol, Drugs, and Pregnancy, as of December 31, 1992

Arizona Rev. Stat. Ann. § 36-141 (B) (1993) requires that allocations of any new or existing undedicated monies shall give priority to treatment services for pregnant abusers of alcohol and other drugs (passed in 1991). This language is an example of "contingent" funding plans.

California passed a "buffer" law in 1990 to direct hospitals on how to deal with pregnant women and drug-exposed infants. California Health

---

who . . . is not known to be pregnant," and instructs the physician to test for pregnancy all adult women of childbearing age who have made declarations and been diagnosed with a terminal condition. The suggested form of the living will also excludes pregnancy (1990).

I nonetheless coded this provision in Chapter 5 as one that invalidates a pregnant woman's living will if live birth is possible and if treatment will not harm or inflict pain on the woman. James Hoefler and Brian Kamoie describe the Kentucky statute as one that requires medical treatment of pregnant patients under these conditions (Hoefler and Kamoie 1992). They cite the 1990 version of the law, but no specific provisions therein. In 1994 the legislature repealed and replaced its law with the "Living Will Directive Act," which states at the outset that pregnant women's living wills have no effect but later in the statute modifies that statement (compare § 311.625[1] with § 311.629[4]). My suspicion is that the 1990 law also contained both provisions, and that I missed the later, modified one. Because I have not been able to verify the earlier version of the law, and because Hoefler and Kamoie's research is the best I have seen, I gave Kentucky the benefit of the doubt in my summary statistics.

and Safety Code §§ 10900 to 10902 (West 1991) instructs the Health and Welfare Agency to develop and disseminate a model needs-assessment protocol for pregnant and postpartum women by July 1, 1991. It further requires each county to establish protocols between health and welfare departments and hospitals regarding such assessments of substance-exposed infants and referrals pursuant to Penal Code § 11165.13 (discussed next). Before an infant is released from the hospital, a health practitioner or medical social worker must (1) identify any needed services and (2) determine the newborn's level of risk upon release and what level of intervention, if any, is needed to protect his or her health and safety, including a referral to the county department for child welfare services. Intended funds to be provided in the annual Budget Act.

The law's counterpart, Penal Code § 11165.13 (West 1992), explains that a positive toxicology screen at birth is not in and of itself a sufficient basis for an abuse or neglect report. Any indication of maternal substance abuse shall lead to an assessment pursuant to Health and Safety Code 10901. Reports based solely on a parent's inability to provide care because of substance abuse shall be made only to county welfare departments and not to law enforcement agencies. Penal Code § 11166 (g) (West 1992) reiterates that reports do not go to law enforcement.

Colorado Rev. Stat. Ann. § 25-1-213 (West 1994 Supp.) illustrates what a comprehensive set of services looks like; it lists necessary components of treatment for high-risk pregnant women: risk assessment; care coordination; nutrition assessment; psychosocial counseling; intensive health education, including parenting education and education on risk factors and appropriate health behaviors; home visits; transportation services; and other services deemed necessary by the Division of Alcohol and Drug Abuse in the Department of Human Services (passed in 1991; amended in 1994).

Colorado Rev. Stat. Ann. § 26-4-302 (1)(s) (West 1994 Supp.) illustrates funding dilemmas. Optional services for which federal funds are available include alcohol and drug counseling and treatment, including "outpatient and residential care but not including room and board while receiving residential care" for pregnant women enrolled for services pursuant to "baby and kid care" or Aid to Families with Dependent Children (passed in 1991). The bill designating these optional services (SB 91-56 [chap. 171, p. 934]) included an application to the federal government for a waiver *not* to apply Section 26-4-302 statewide if there were not enough funds.

Illinois puts safeguards into law (305 Ill. Comp. Stat. Ann. 5/5-5 [West 1993]). It requires medical professionals to recommend treatment referrals to any pregnant welfare recipient suspected of using drugs. The Department of Public Aid shall cover the costs in accordance with Medicaid and the state Department of Alcohol and Substance Abuse. Women's substance use shall not entail any kind of economic sanction (passed in 1989).

Kansas Stat. Ann. § 65-1,160 to § 65-1,167 (1992), "Preconception and Perinatal Programs," passed in 1992, illustrates a comprehensive statutory approach. The law requires the secretary of health and environment (1) to conduct a public awareness campaign directed to both men and women on the preconceptual and perinatal effects of the use of tobacco, alcohol, and controlled substances; (2) to provide materials and guidance to health care professionals serving pregnant women to ensure proper patient education about these substances, and about the services available to pregnant women; (3) to provide an educational program to health care professionals to help them educate their patients, take accurate drug histories, and counsel women to comply with drug treatment to which they are referred, in collaboration with the secretary of social and rehabilitation services; (4) to develop a risk-assessment profile; and (5) to maintain a toll-free information hot line. The act permits referral of pregnant women to local health departments for service coordination with their consent (service coordination must be offered within seventy-two hours), provides immunity from civil and criminal liability for rendering or failing to render any services under this section, and provides immunity from criminal prosecution for pregnant women. The act also gives pregnant women referred for treatment priority status for treatment available through the department of social and rehabilitation services, prohibits facilities receiving public funds from refusing to treat women solely because they are pregnant, and reasserts that records are confidential. The act "shall not be construed in any way to create any new programs."

Minnesota Stat. Ann. § 253B.02 Subd. 2 (West 1994) defines "chemically dependent person" for the purposes of involuntary commitment to include "a pregnant woman who has engaged during the pregnancy in habitual or excessive use, for a nonmedical purpose, of any of the following controlled substances or their derivatives: cocaine, heroin, phencyclidine, methamphetamine, or amphetamine" (passed in 1989).

Minnesota § 626.556 Subd. 2 (c) (West 1994 Supp.) defines "neglect" to include "prenatal exposure to a controlled substance" and mandates reporting to police, sheriff, or local welfare agency (who, in turn, notify one another) (passed in 1989).

Nevada Rev. Stat. Ann. § 432B.330 1 (b) (Michie 1991) defines a child in need of protection to include one "suffering from congenital drug addiction or the fetal alcohol syndrome, because of the faults or habits of a person responsible for his welfare" (passed in 1985). Children needing protection may be taken into custody.

Oklahoma Stat. Ann. tit. 21, § 846 A.2 (West 1994 Supp.) requires physicians and others "attending the birth of a child who appears to be a child born in a condition of dependence on a controlled dangerous substance" to promptly report to the county department of human services (which then investigates and reports to the district attorney and child welfare division) (passed in 1987). Title 21 is the criminal child abuse statute.

Oklahoma Stat. Ann. tit. 10, § 1101, 4 (West 1987) defines "deprived child" to include "a child in need of special care and treatment because of his physical or mental condition including a child born in a condition of dependence on a controlled dangerous substance," and whose parent or guardian "is unable or willfully fails" to provide treatment (passed in 1987). Actions taken under this title ("Children") can lead to court jurisdiction over a child.

Rhode Island Gen. Laws § 23-13-18 (b) (7) (1989) makes "available as appropriate" optional services to pregnant women through this program or through the Rhode Island medical assistance program. These services include "outpatient counseling for drug-alcohol use" as part of the reenacted "maternity care payor of last resort program" for pregnant women ineligible for Medicaid, lacking health insurance, and whose family income is below 185 percent of the federal poverty level (passed in 1989).

Rhode Island Gen. Laws § 42-72-5 (1993), Department of Children, Youth, and Families, Section (b)(24) on "Powers and Scope of Activities," includes developing "multidisciplinary service plans, in conjunction with the department of health, at hospitals prior to the discharge of any drug exposed babies. The plan shall require development of a plan using all health care professionals" (passed in 1991).

Utah Code Ann. § 62A-4a-404 (1993 and 1994 Supps.) requires any person attending the birth of a child or caring for a child, and determining that the child, at time of birth, has fetal alcohol syndrome or fetal drug dependency, to report that determination to the division of family services as soon as possible (passed in 1988). Although child abuse is not defined to include prenatal exposure, all reports filed pursuant to this section must be investigated (see also § 62A-4a-101 and § 62A-4a-411).

Washington Rev. Code Ann. § 74.09.790 (6) (West 1994 Supp.) specifies that under the "Maternity Care Access Act," "support services" may include "alcohol and substance abuse treatment for pregnant women who are addicted or at risk of being addicted to alcohol or drugs to the extent funds are made available for that purpose" (passed in 1989). Like that of Arizona's statute, this language illustrates the contingency of funding plans.

Bibliography

ABC News/*Washington Post*. 1989. Poll, 6 September.

Adler, Stuart. 1989. "Cytomegalovirus and Child Day Care: Evidence for an Increased Infection Rate among Day-Care Workers." *New England Journal of Medicine* 321 (9 November): 1290–96.

Alcoholism and Drug Abuse Weekly. 1992. "Advocates Urge Passage of FAS Prevention and Treatment Bill" 4, no. 11 (11 March): 4.

Alderman, Ellen, and Caroline Kennedy. 1995. *The Right to Privacy*. New York: Knopf.

American Bar Association (ABA), Center on Children and the Law. 1990. *Drug Exposed Infants and Their Families: Coordinating Responses of the Legal, Medical, and Child Protection System*. Washington, D.C.: ABA.

American College of Obstetricians and Gynecologists (ACOG). 1987. "Patient Choice: Maternal-Fetal Conflict." Committee Opinion No. 55. Washington, D.C.: ACOG.

American Medical Association (AMA). 1990. "Legal Interventions during Pregnancy: Court-Ordered Medical Treatments and Legal Penalties for Potentially Harmful Behavior by Pregnant Women." Board of Trustees Report. *JAMA: The Journal of the American Medical Association* 264, no. 10 (28 November): 2663–70.

Amott, Teresa. 1993. *Caught in the Crisis: Women and the U.S. Economy Today*. New York: Monthly Review Press.

Anderson, Sarah. 1995. "OSHA under Siege." *The Progressive*, December, 26–28.

Andrews, Lori. 1993. "Social Control of Women: Regulating Pregnancy." Panel chair, Annual Meeting of the Law and Society Association, Chicago, 29 May.

———. 1994. "Policing Pregnant Women Who Use Drugs in the United States: A Contested Policy Domain." Discussant, Annual Meeting of the Law and Society Association, Phoenix, 16 June.

Angier, Natalie. 1996. "Ultrasound and Fury: One Mother's Ordeal." *New York Times*, 26 November, C1.

Arney, William Ray. 1982. *Power and the Profession of Obstetrics*. Chicago: University of Chicago Press.

Aronson, Peter. 1989. "Crackdown on Use of Drugs While Pregnant: Mothers Face Charges for Addicted Babies." *Recorder*, 4 April.

Artlett, Carol; Bruce Smith; and Sergio Jimenez. 1998. "Identification of Fetal DNA and Cells in Skin Lesions from Women with Systemic Sclerosis." *New England Journal of Medicine* 338 (23 April): 1186–91.

Associated Press (AP). 1998. "Mother Pleads Guilty to Manslaughter in Cocaine Induced Birth," 7 May.

Baer, Judith. 1978. *The Chains of Protection: The Judicial Response to Women's Labor Legislation.* Westport, Conn.: Greenwood Press.

Bailey, Stan. 1998. "Guardian in Teen Abortion Case to Appeal Ruling." *Birmingham News*, 23 July.

Balisy, Sam. 1987. "Maternal Substance Abuse: The Need to Provide Legal Protection to the Fetus." *Southern California Law Review* 60: 1209–38.

Barden, J. C. 1990. "Foster Care System Reeling." *New York Times*, 21 September, A1.

Barry, Ellen. n.d. "Pregnant Women Prisoners Win Major Victories against Two County Jail Systems in California." San Francisco: Legal Services for Prisoners with Children.

———. 1985. "Quality of Prenatal Care for Incarcerated Women Challenged." *Youth Law News* 6, no. 6: 1–4.

———. 1989. "Pregnant Prisoners." *Harvard Women's Law Journal* 12: 189–205.

———. 1991. "Pregnant, Addicted, and Sentenced: Debunking the Myths of Medical Treatment in Prison." *Criminal Justice* 5, no. 4: 23–27.

Bayer, Ronald. 1990. "AIDS and the Future of Reproductive Freedom." *The Milbank Quarterly* 68 (Suppl. 2): 179–204.

Becker, Barrie, and Peggy Hora. 1993. "The Legal Community's Response to Drug Use during Pregnancy in the Criminal Sentencing and Dependency Contexts: A Survey of Judges, Prosecuting Attorneys, and Defense Attorneys in Ten California Counties." *Southern California Review of Law and Women's Studies* 2: 527–75.

Becker, Mary. 1994. "Reproductive Hazards after *Johnson Controls*." *Houston Law Review* 31: 43–97.

Begley, Sharon. 1997. "Hope for 'Snow Babies': A Mother's Cocaine Use May Not Doom Her Child after All." *Newsweek*, 29 November, 62.

Behrman, Richard, et al. 1991. "Recommendations." *The Future of Children* (Spring): 8–16.

Bennett, Belinda. 1991. "Pregnant Women and the Duty to Rescue: A Feminist Response to the Fetal Rights Debate." *Law in Context* 9, no. 1: 70–91.

Benton, Elizabeth Carlin. 1990. "The Constitutionality of Pregnancy Clauses in Living Will Statutes." *Vanderbilt Law Review* 43: 1821–37.

Berenson, Abbey, et al. 1994. "Perinatal Morbidity Associated with Violence Experienced by Pregnant Women." *American Journal of Obstetrics and Gynecology* 170, no. 6: 1760–69.

Berger, Joseph. 1998. "Beliefs Pushed Doctor to Keep Abortion Role." *New York Times*, 25 October, A1.

Bertin, Joan. 1983. "Workplace Bias Takes the Form of 'Fetal Protectionism.'" *Legal Times*, 1 August, 18.

———. 1989. "Reproductive Hazards in the Workplace." In *Reproductive Laws for the 1990s*, edited by Sherrill Cohen and Nadine Taub, 277–305. Clifton, N.J.: Humana Press.

Beveridge, Dawn. 1993. "Violence against Pregnant Women." In *Encyclopedia of*

Childbearing: Critical Perspectives, edited by Barbara Katz Rothman, 416–17. Phoenix: Oryx Press.

Blakeslee, Sandra. 1991. "Research on Birth Defects Turns to Flaws in Sperm." *New York Times*, 1 January, A1.

Blank, Robert. 1993. *Fetal Protection in the Workplace: Women's Rights, Business Interests, and the Unborn*. New York: Columbia University Press.

Bloom, Barbara; Meda Chesney Lind; and Barbara Owen. 1994. *Women in California Prisons: Hidden Victims of the War on Drugs*. San Francisco: Center on Juvenile and Criminal Justice.

Blumner, Robyn E. 1991. "Prosecuting the Persecuted: Addicted Mothers-to-Be." *Miami Herald*, 28 April, C1.

Boland, Paul. 1991. "Perspective of a Juvenile Court Judge." *The Future of Children* (Spring): 100–104.

Boling, Patricia, ed. 1995. *Expecting Trouble: Surrogacy, Fetal Abuse, and New Reproductive Technologies*. Boulder, Colo.: Westview Press.

Bowes, Watson A., and Brad Selgestad. 1981. "Fetal versus Maternal Rights: Medical and Legal Perspectives." *Obstetrics & Gynecology* 58, no. 2 (August): 209–14.

Boyd, Susan. 1994. "Women and Illicit Drug Use." *The International Journal of Drug Policy* 5, no. 3: 185–89.

Bragg, Rick. 1996. "Time to Lower Rebel Flag, a Southern Governor Says." *New York Times*, 27 November, A18.

Brewer, Boni. 1990. "Incarceration of Pregnant Women Doubles at Jail." *Valley Times*, 17 June, 1A.

Brill, Alida. 1990. "Womb versus Woman." In *Nobody's Business: Paradoxes of Privacy*, 69–95. Reading, Mass.: Addison-Wesley.

Brown, Harriet. 1994. "The Other Pain of Childbirth." *Health* 8, no. 2: 120.

Burtt, Shelley. 1994. "Reproductive Responsibilities: Rethinking the Fetal Rights Debate." *Policy Sciences* 27, nos. 2–3: 179–96.

Buss, Emily. 1986. "Getting beyond Discrimination: A Regulatory Solution to the Problem of Fetal Hazards in the Workplace." *Yale Law Journal* 95: 577–98.

Bussiere, Alice. 1989. "No Constitutional Right to Protection from Parental Harm, Says High Court." *Youth Law News* 10, no. 2: 1–2.

Bussiere, Alice, and Carole Shauffer. 1990. "The Little Prisoners." *Youth Law News* 11, no. 1: 22–26.

California Senate Judiciary Committee. 1997–98. Bill analysis AB 310.

Carlson, Susan. 1998. "Pregnant Drinkers Need Help, and Law Offers Way to Provide It." *Star Tribune*, 27 June, 21A.

CBS News/*New York Times*. 1989. Poll, 6–8 September.

CDF Reports. 1996. "Children of Working Parents Squeezed Out of Health Care" 17, no. 11: 1–2.

Center for Reproductive Law and Policy (CRLP). 1996. "Punishing Women for Their Behavior during Pregnancy: An Approach That Undermines Women's Health and Children's Interests." New York: CRLP.

———. 1998. "The International Criminal Court: Ending Impunity for Reproductive Rights Violations Involving Sexual Violations." 26 October. New York: CRLP.

Chasnoff, I.; H. Landress; and M. Barrett. 1990. "The Prevalence of Illicit-Drug or Alcohol Use during Pregnancy and Discrepancies in Mandatory Reporting in Pinellas County, Florida." *New England Journal of Medicine* 322: 1202–1206.

Chasnoff, Ira J., et al. 1985. "Cocaine Use in Pregnancy." *New England Journal of Medicine* 313 (12 September): 666–69.

Chasnoff, Ira J. 1989. "Drug Use and Women: Establishing A Standard of Care." *Annals of New York Academy of Science* 562: 208–10.

Chavkin, Wendy. 1984. "Walking a Tightrope: Pregnancy, Parenting, and Work." In *Double Exposure: Women's Health Hazards on the Job and at Home*, edited by Wendy Chavkin, chap. 10. New York: Monthly Review Press.

———. 1990. "Drug Addiction and Pregnancy: Policy Crossroads." *American Journal of Public Health* 80, no. 4: 483–87.

———. 1991. "Mandatory Treatment for Drug Use during Pregnancy." *JAMA: The Journal of the American Medical Association* 266, no. 11 (18 September): 1556–61.

Chavkin, Wendy; Nancy Walker; and Denise Paone. 1992. "Drug-Using Families and Child Protection: Results of a Study and Implications for Change." *University of Pittsburgh Law Review* 54: 295–324.

Chira, Susan. 1996. "Study Says Babies in Child Care Keep Secure Bonds to Mothers." *New York Times*, 21 April, A1.

Closen, Michael, and Scott Isaacman. 1990. "Are AIDS-Transmission Laws Encouraging Abortion?" *American Bar Association Journal* (December): 77–78.

Coelign, Harriet, and Gloria Harman. 1997. "Learning to Ask about Domestic Violence." *Women's Health Issues* 7, no. 4: 263–68.

Cohen, Alys I. 1994. "Challenging Pregnancy Discrimination in Drug Treatment: Does the ADAMHA Reorganization Act Provide an Answer?" *Yale Journal of Law and Feminism* 6: 91–142.

Coleman, Linda, and Cindy Dickinson. 1984. "The Risks of Healing: The Hazards of the Nursing Profession." In *Double Exposure: Women's Health Hazards on the Job and at Home*, edited by Wendy Chavkin, chap. 2. New York: Monthly Review Press.

Coles, Claire, et al. 1992. "Effects of Cocaine and Alcohol Use in Pregnancy on Neonatal Growth and Neurobehavioral Status." *Neurotoxicology and Teratology* 14: 23–33.

Committee for Abortion Rights and Against Sterilization Abuse (CARASA). 1988. *Women under Attack: Victories, Backlash, and the Fight for Reproductive Freedom*, edited by Susan Davis. Boston: South End Press.

Condit, Deirdre. 1995. "Fetal Personhood: Political Identity under Construction." In *Expecting Trouble: Surrogacy, Fetal Abuse, and New Reproductive Technologies*, edited by Patricia Boling, chap. 3. Boulder, Colo.: Westview Press.

Cook, Christopher. 1996. "Congress Proposes Brazen New World for Workers." *Z Magazine* (February): 20–23.

Copelon, Rhonda. 1990. "From Privacy to Autonomy: The Conditions for Sexual and Reproductive Freedom." In *From Abortion to Reproductive Freedom: Transforming a Movement*, edited by Marlene Gerber Fried, 27–43. Boston: South End Press.

Corea, Gena. 1985. *The Mother Machine*. New York: Harper & Row.

Curriden, Mark. 1990. "Holding Mom Accountable." *American Bar Association Journal* (March): 50–53.

Daniels, Cynthia. 1993. *At Women's Expense: State Power and the Politics of Fetal Rights.* Cambridge, Mass.: Harvard University Press.

Davidson, Jean. 1989. "Newborn Drug Exposure Conviction a 'Drastic' First." *Los Angles Times*, 31 July, 1.

Davis, Angela. 1983. "The Legacy of Slavery": Standards for a New Womanhood"; "Rape, Racism, and the Myth of the Black Rapist"; and "Racism in the Reproductive Rights Movement." In *Women, Race, and Class.* New York: Vintage Books.

Davis, Devra. 1991. "Fathers and Fetuses" (op-ed). *New York Times*, 1 March, A27.

Dawson, T. Brettel. 1990. "*Re Baby R:* A Comment on Fetal Apprehension." *Canadian Journal of Women and the Law* 4: 265–75.

Dershowitz, Alan. 1992. *Contrary to Public Opinion.* New York: Pharos Books.

Dineen, Claire. 1994. "Fetal Alcohol Syndrome: The Legal and Social Responses to Its Impact on Native Americans." *North Dakota Law Review* 70: 1–65.

Dougherty, Charles. 1985. "The Right to Begin Life with a Sound Body and Mind: Fetal Patients and Conflicts with Their Mothers." *University of Detroit Law Review* 63: 89–117

Dorris, Michael. 1989. *The Broken Cord.* New York: Harper & Row.

"Drug Strategies Survey." 1994. Washington, D.C.: Peter D. Hart Research, February.

Dube, Jonathan. 1997. "Case Raising Questions about Pregnant Drug Users." *Tampa Tribune*, 28 December, 18.

Duden, Barbara. 1993. *Disembodying Women: Perspectives on Pregnancy and the Unborn.* Translated by Lee Hoinacki. Cambridge, Mass.: Harvard University Press.

Dyke, Molly. 1990. "A Matter of Life and Death: Pregnancy Clauses in Living Will Statutes." *Boston University Law Review* 70: 867–87.

Eastman, Crystal. 1978. "Birth Control in the Feminist Program" (1918) and "Now We Can Begin" (1920). In *Crystal Eastman on Women and Revolution*, edited by Blanche Wiesen Cook. Oxford: Oxford University Press.

Edleman, Marian Wright. 1987. *Families in Peril: An Agenda for Social Change.* Cambridge, Mass.: Harvard University Press.

Elkins, Thomas E., et al. 1989. "Court-Ordered Cesarean Section: An Analysis of Ethical Concerns in Compelling Cases." *American Journal of Obstetrics and Gynecology* 161, no. 1: 150–54.

English, Abigail. 1990. "Prenatal Drug Exposure: Grounds for Mandatory Child Abuse Reports?" *Youth Law News* 11, no. 1: 3–8.

———. 1995. "Does Prenatal Drug Exposure Trigger an Obligation to Report Child Abuse?" *Youth Law News* 17, nos. 4–5: 3–7.

Enstad, Robert. 1993. "Cocaine Use Killed Baby, Jury Rules." *Chicago Tribune*, 23 January, L1.

Essence. 1991. "Lowdown on Lead Poisoning," January, 80.

Estrich, Susan. 1987. *Real Rape.* Cambridge, Mass.: Harvard University Press.

European Union Pregnancy Directive. 1992. Council Directive 92/85, in *Official Journal of the European Communities* No. L 348.

Fackelmann, Kathy. 1991. "The Crack-Baby Myth." *Washington City Paper*, 13 December, 25+.

Faludi, Susan. 1991. *Backlash: The Undeclared War against American Women*. New York: Crown.

Farber, Celia. 1995. "AIDS Words from the Front." *Spin*, April, 189–93, 214.

Federal Register. 1978. "Occupational Exposure to Lead" 43(220), 14 November, and 43(225), 21 November.

Field, Martha A. 1989. "Controlling the Woman to Protect the Fetus." *Law, Medicine, and Health Care* 17: 114–29.

Fink, Janet. 1990. "Reported Effects of Crack and Cocaine on Infants." *Youth Law News* 11, no. 1: 37–39.

Fisher, Sue. 1986. *In the Patient's Best Interest: Women and the Politics of Medical Decisions*. New Brunswick, N.J.: Rutgers University Press.

Five Year Plan. 1988–90. "White Millionaires," song on *Passage*. San Francisco. Used with permission.

Flannery, Michael. 1992. "Court-Ordered Prenatal Intervention: A Final Means to End Gestational Substance Abuse." *Journal of Family Law* 30: 519–604.

Florida. n.d. Eighteenth Judicial Circuit, Seminole County. "Cooperative Rehabilitation Abuse Contract."

Fogarty, Thomas. 1990. "Iowans Favor Child-Abuse Law for Drug Babies." *Des Moines Register*, 15 April.

Fried, Marlene Gerber. 1998. "Abortion in the United States: Legal but Inaccessible." In *Abortion Wars: A Half Century of Struggle, 1950–2000*, edited by Rickie Solinger, chap. 9. Berkeley: University of California Press.

Gallagher, Janet. 1984. "The Fetus and the Law: Whose Life Is It Anyway?" *Ms.* (September): 62.

———. 1987. "Prenatal Invasions and Interventions: What's Wrong with Fetal Rights." *Harvard Women's Law Journal* 10: 9–58.

Galston, William. 1995. "Needed: A Not-So-Fast Divorce Law" (op-ed). *New York Times*, 27 December, A15.

Ginsburg, Faye. 1989. *Contested Lives: The Abortion Debate in an American Community*. Berkeley: University of California Press.

Ginsburg, Ruth Bader. 1985. "Some Thoughts on Autonomy and Equality in Relation to *Roe v. Wade*." *North Carolina Law Review* 63: 375–86.

Glanton, A. Dahleen. 1988. "Job Bias Plea Clashes with Firm's Fetus Safety Rules." *Los Angeles Times*, 15 May, pt. 1, 35.

Goldstein, Leslie Friedman. 1988. *The Constitutional Rights of Women: Cases in Law and Social Change* (2d ed.). New York: Longman.

Gomez, Laura. 1997. *Misconceiving Mothers: Legislators, Prosecutors, and the Politics of Prenatal Drug Exposure*. Philadelphia: Temple University Press.

Gordon, Linda. 1976. *Woman's Body, Woman's Right: A Social History of Birth Control in America*. New York: Penguin Books.

———. 1982. "Why Nineteenth-Century Feminists Did Not Support 'Birth Control' and Twentieth-Century Feminists Do: Feminism, Reproduction, and the Family." In *Rethinking the Family: Some Feminist Questions*, edited by Barrie Thorne and Marilyn Yalom, 40–53. White Plains, N.Y.: Longman.

Gorney, Cynthia. 1988. "Whose Body Is It, Anyway? The Legal Maelstrom That Rages When the Rights of Mother and Fetus Collide." *Washington Post*, 13 December, D1.

Greene, Dwight. 1991. "Abusive Prosecutors: Gender, Race, and Class Discretion and the Prosecution of Drug-Addicted Mothers." *Buffalo Law Review* 39: 737–802.

Greenhouse, Linda. 1991. "Court Voids Limits to Women in Jobs on Basis of Fetus." *New York Times*, 21 March, A1.

Grimm, Bill. 1992. "*Angela R.* Is Latest Chapter in Systemic Child Welfare Litigation." *Youth Law News* 13, no. 2: 8–14.

———. 1994. "Triumph in Utah Child Welfare Litigation; Long Road Ahead in Implementing Reforms." *Youth Law News* 15, no. 5: 1–8.

———. 1995. "Juvenile Courts Seek Appropriate Response to Prenatal Drug Exposure." *Youth Law News* 17, nos. 4–5: 8–16.

Grover, Jan Zita. 1987. "AIDS: Keywords." *Scientific American*, January, 17–30.

Guillemin, Jeanne Harley. 1993. "Cesarean Birth: Social and Political Aspects." In *Encyclopedia of Childbearing: Critical Perspectives*, edited by Barbara Katz Rothman, 59–62. Phoenix: Oryx Press.

Hall, Trish. 1998. "You Are Getting Very Confused: Psychologists' Split Decisions." *New York Times*, 14 June, sec. 4, 7.

Hansen, Jane O. 1989. "Southerners Back Penalties for Moms Whose Drug Use Hurts the Unborn." *Atlanta Journal-Constitution*, 30 July, A1.

Hansen, Mark. 1992. "Courts Side with Moms in Drug Cases." *American Bar Association Journal* (November): 18.

Harris, Jean. 1993. "The Babies of Bedford: It's Wrong to Separate Infants from Their Imprisoned Mothers. An Insider's Account." *New York Times Magazine*, 28 March, 26.

Hartouni, Valerie. 1997. *Cultural Conceptions: On Reproductive Technologies and the Remaking of Life*. Minneapolis: University of Minnesota Press.

Hatsukami, Dorothy, and Marian Fischman. 1996. "Crack Cocaine and Cocaine Hydrochloride: Are the Differences Myth or Reality?" *JAMA: The Journal of the American Medical Association* 276, no. 19 (20 November): 1580–88.

Herbert, Bob. 1998. "Hidden Agendas." *New York Times*, 14 June, sec. 4, 15.

Hewson, Barbara. 1992. "Mother Knows Best." *New Law Journal* (6 November): 1538+.

Hippocrates. 1988. "*Hippocrates*/Gallup Poll," May–June, 40–41.

Hoefler, James, and Brian Kamoie. 1992. "The Right to Die: State Courts Lead Where Legislatures Fear to Tread." *Law & Policy* 14, no. 4: 337–80.

Hoegerman, Georgeanne, and Sidney Schnoll. 1991. "Narcotic Use in Pregnancy." *Clinics in Perinatology* 18: 51–76.

Hoffman, Jan. 1990. "Pregnant, Addicted—and Guilty?" *New York Times Magazine*, 19 August.

Hollinshead, W. H., et al. 1990. "Statewide Prevalence of Illicit Drug Use by Pregnant Women—Rhode Island." *MMWR: Morbidity and Mortality Weekly Report* 39, no. 14 (13 April): 225–27.

Holloway, Marguerite. 1990. "Heavy Metal Rap." *The Nation*, 19 February, 228.

Holmes, Steven. 1996a. "Income Disparity between Poorest and Richest Rises." *New York Times*, 20 June, A1.

———. 1996b. "With More Women in Prison, Sexual Abuse by Guards Becomes a Troubling Trend." *New York Times*, 27 December, A18.

Horovitz, Bruce. 1990. "Two Volvo Ads Rev Up Controversy." *Los Angeles Times*, 7 November, D2.

Houston Chronicle. 1996. "Pregnant Inmate Sues," 4 April, 28.

Ikemoto, Lisa. 1992a. "Furthering the Inquiry: Race, Class, and Culture in the Forced Medical Treatment of Pregnant Women." *Tennessee Law Review* 59: 487–517.

———. 1992b. "The Code of Perfect Pregnancy: At the Intersection of Motherhood, the Practice of Defaulting to Science, and the Interventionist Mindset of Law." *Ohio State Law Journal* 53: 1205–1306.

Irwin, Susan, and Brigitte Jordan. 1987. "Knowledge, Practice, and Power: Court-Ordered Cesarean Sections." *Medical Anthropology Quarterly* 1, no. 3: 319–34.

Jacobus, Patricia. 1992. "Prosecutors' New Drug War Target: The Womb." *Los Angeles Daily Journal*, 2 April, 1.

JAMA: The Journal of the American Medical Association. 1995. "Update: AIDS Among Women—United States, 1994" 273, no. 10 (8 March): 767–68.

Jasso, Sonia, and Maria Mazorra. 1984. "Following the Harvest: The Health Hazards of Migrant and Seasonal Farmworking Women." In *Double Exposure: Women's Health Hazards on the Job and at Home*, edited by Wendy Chavkin, chap. 4. New York: Monthly Review Press.

Johnsen, Dawn. 1986. "The Creation of Fetal Rights: Conflicts with Women's Constitutional Rights to Liberty, Privacy, and Equal Protection." *Yale Law Journal* 95: 599–625.

Jurow, Ronna, and Richard H. Paul. 1984. "Cesarean Delivery for Fetal Distress without Maternal Consent." *Obstetrics & Gynecology* 63, no. 4 (April): 596–98.

Kantrowitz, Barbara. 1991. "The Pregnancy Police." *Newsweek*, 29 April, 52–53.

Kaplan, Laura. 1995. *The Story of Jane: The Legendary Underground Feminist Abortion Service*. New York: Pantheon Books.

Kaus, Mickey. 1992. *The End of Equality*. New York: Basic Books.

Kenney, Sally. 1992. *For Whose Protection? Reproductive Hazards and Exclusionary Policies in the United States and Britain*. Ann Arbor: University of Michigan Press.

Kilborn, Peter. 1991. "Employers Left with Many Decisions." *New York Times*, 21 March, B12.

Knapp, Caroline. 1996. *Drinking: A Love Story*. New York: Delta.

Kolder, Veronika; Janet Gallagher; and Michael Parsons. 1987. "Court-Ordered Obstetrical Interventions." *New England Journal of Medicine* 316 (7 May): 1192–96.

Koren, Gideon, et al. 1989. "Bias against the Null Hypothesis: The Reproductive Hazards of Cocaine." *Lancet*, 16 December, 1440–42.

Kozol, Jonathan. 1995. "Spare Us the Cheap Grace." *Time*, 11 December, 96.

Kreiger, Linda, and Patricia Cooney. 1993. "The Miller-Wohl Controversy: Equal Treatment, Positive Action and the Meaning of Women's Equality." In *Feminist Legal Theory: Foundations*, edited by D. Kelly Weisberg, 156–79. Philadelphia: Temple University Press.

Kumpfer, Karol. 1991. "Treatment Programs for Drug-Abusing Women." *The Future of Children* (Spring): 50–60.

LaCroix, Susan. 1989. "Birth of a Bad Idea: Jailing Mothers for Drug Abuse." *The Nation*, 1 May, 585–86, and 588.

Lacayo, Richard. 1991. "Death on the Shop Floor." *Time*, 16 September, 28–29.

Ladd, Rosalind Ekman. 1989. "Women in Labor: Some Issues about Informed Consent." *Hypatia* 4, no. 3: 37–45.

The Lancet. 1997. "Canadian Fetal-Rights Case Decided," 11 January, 112.

Larson, Carol. 1991. "Overview of State Legislative and Judicial Responses." *The Future of Children* (Spring): 72–84.

Law, Sylvia. 1984. "Rethinking Sex and the Constitution." *University of Pennsylvania Law Review* 132: 955–1040.

Leary, Warren. 1996. "Childbearing Deaths Underreported." *New York Times*, 31 July, B7.

LeBlanc, Ann Marie Curran. 1991. "Louisiana's Fair Employment Statutes: A Cry for Clarity amid Expansive Federal Civil Rights Protection." *Loyola Law Review* 37: 313–51.

Leiberman, J. R., et al. 1979. "The Fetal Right to Live." *Obstetrics & Gynecology* 53, no. 4 (April): 515–17.

Levendosky, Charles. 1990a. "Turning Women into Two-Legged Petri Dishes." *Star-Tribune*, 21 January, A8.

———. 1990b. "Using the Law to Make Justice the Victim." *Star-Tribune*, 4 February, A8.

Lewin, Tamar. 1987. "Courts Acting to Force Care of the Unborn." *New York Times*, 23 November, A1.

———. 1990. "Drug Use in Pregnancy: New Issue for the Courts." *New York Times*, 5 February, A14.

Lockwood, Susan. 1990. "What's Known—and What's Not Known—about Drug-Exposed Infants." *Youth Law News* 11, no. 1: 15–18.

Logli, Paul. 1990. "Drugs in the Womb: The Newest Battlefield in the War on Drugs." *Criminal Justice Ethics* (Winter–Spring): 23–29.

Lopez, Iris. 1993. "Agency and Constraint: Sterilization and Reproductive Freedom among Puerto Rican Women in New York City." *Urban Anthropology* 22, nos. 3–4: 299–323.

Los Angeles Daily Journal. 1992. "Mother Charged with Prenatal Abuse," 14 July, 4.

———. 1996. "Drug Use Is Abuse by Mothers-to-Be," 17 July.

Los Angeles Times. 1989. "Cocaine Mother Gets 15 Years Probation," 26 August, pt. 1, 2.

Lowry, Susan Steinhorn. 1992. "The Growing Trend to Criminalize Gestational Substance Abuse." *Journal of Juvenile Law* 13: 133–43.

Luker, Kristin. 1984. *Abortion and the Politics of Motherhood*. Berkeley: University of California Press.

Mackay, R. D. 1993. "The Consequences of Killing Very Young Children." *Criminal Law Review* (January): 21–36.

MacKinnon, Catharine. 1987. "Difference and Dominance." In *Feminism Unmodified: Discourses on Life and Law*, chap. 2. Cambridge, Mass.: Harvard University Press.

————. 1989. *Toward a Feminist Theory of the State*. Cambridge, Mass.: Harvard University Press.

Magar, Michele. 1991. "The Sins of the Mothers." *Student Lawyer* 20, no. 1: 30–34.

Maher, Lisa. 1990. "Criminalizing Pregnancy: The Downside of a Kinder Gentler Nation?" *Social Justice* 17, no. 3: 111–35.

————. 1992. "Punishment and Welfare: Crack Cocaine and the Regulation of Mothering." In *The Criminalization of a Woman's Body*, edited by Clarice Fineman, 157–92. New York: Haworth Press.

Maher, Lisa, and Richard Curtis. 1992. "Women on the Edge of Crime: Crack Cocaine and the Changing Contexts of Street-Level Sex Work in New York City." *Crime, Law, and Social Change* 18: 221–58.

Malnory, Margaret. 1993. "Electronic Fetal Monitoring." In *Encyclopedia of Childbearing: Critical Perspectives*, edited by Barbara Katz Rothman, 120–21. Phoenix: Oryx Press.

Marcus, Noreen, and Sarah Lundy. 1997. "Woman Agrees to C-Section, Has Girl; Case Propels Debate on Fetus Representation." *Sun-Sentinel*, 5 March, 1A.

Maschke, Karen. 1989. *Litigation, Courts, and Women Workers*. New York: Praeger.

Matthews, Jessica. 1996. "Why Do We Feed Highways and Starve Rail?" (op-ed). *Portland Press Herald*, 3 July, 9A; reprinted from the *Washington Post*.

Matthews, Martha. 1992. "Major Victory for Arkansas Children." *Youth Law News* 13, no. 2: 1–7.

————. 1994. "HHS Issues Family Preservation and Support Program Instructions." *Youth Law News* 15, no. 2: 1–4.

Matthews, Martha, and Estelle McKee. 1993. "Family Preservation Programs May Benefit Legal Services Clients." *Youth Law News* 14, no. 3: 1–5.

May, Elaine Tyler. 1995. *Barren in the Promised Land: Childless Americans and the Pursuit of Happiness*. Cambridge, Mass.: Harvard University Press.

Mayes, Linda, et al. 1992. "The Problem of Prenatal Cocaine Exposure: A Rush to Judgment." *JAMA: The Journal of the American Medical Association* 267, no. 3 (15 January): 406–408.

McCall, Carolyn; Jan Casteel; and Nancy Shaw. 1985. *Pregnancy in Prison: A Needs Assessment of Perinatal Outcome in Three California Penal Institutions*. Report to the State of California Department of Health Services, Maternal and Child Health Branch.

McCann, Carole. 1994. *Birth Control Politics in the United States, 1916–1945*. Ithaca, N.Y.: Cornell University Press.

McElroy, Pat. 1993. "California Supreme Court Eases Standards for Parental Rights Termination." *Youth Law News* 14, no. 3: 14–17.

————. 1997. "Statute Doesn't Violate Prop. 13, Says State Supreme Court: California Can Impose Fees on Industry for Cost of Lead Poisoning." *Youth Law News* 18, no. 4: 7–10.

McFarlane, Judith. 1989. "Battering during Pregnancy: Tip of an Iceberg Revealed." *Women & Health* 15, no. 3: 69–84.

McHugh, Gerald Austin. 1980. "Protection of the Rights of Pregnant Women in Prisons and Detention Facilities." *New England Journal on Prison Law* 6: 231–63.

McLarin, Kimberly. 1995. "Panel Presses to Combat Drug Use in Pregnancy." *New York Times*, 16 October, B3.

McNulty, Molly. 1990. "Pregnancy Police: Implications of Criminalizing Fetal Abuse." *Youth Law News* 11, no. 1: 33–36.

Meredith, Robyn. 1996. "New Blood for the Big Three's Plants: This Hiring Spree Is Rewarding Brains, Not Brawn." *New York Times*, 21 April, F3.

Merrick, Janna. 1993. "Caring for the Fetus to Protect the Born Child? Ethical and Legal Dilemmas in Coerced Obstetrical Intervention." *Women & Politics* 13, nos. 3–4: 63–81.

Mertus, Julie, and Simon Heller. 1992. "Norplant Meets the New Eugenicists: The Impermissibility of Coerced Contraception." *Saint Louis University Public Law Review* 11: 359–83.

Meyer, Roger. 1995. "Biology of Psychoactive Substance Dependence Disorders: Opiates, Cocaine, and Ethanol." In *The American Psychiatric Press Textbook of Psychopharmacology*, edited by Alan Schatzberg and Charles Nemeroff, chap. 26. Washington, D.C.: American Psychiatric Press.

Michie, Helena, and Naomi Cahn. 1997. *Confinements: Fertility and Infertility in Contemporary Culture.* New Brunswick, N.J.: Rutgers University Press.

Miller, Jerome. 1996. *Search and Destroy: African-American Males in the Criminal Justice System.* New York: Cambridge University Press.

Miller, Kenneth. 1996. "Together Forever." *Life*, April, 44–47+.

Mink, Gwendolyn. 1998. *Welfare's End.* Ithaca, N.Y.: Cornell University Press.

Minnesota. 1998. Fetal Alcohol Syndrome Web site at http://www.fas.state.mn.us

Minow, Martha. 1990. *Making All the Difference: Inclusion, Exclusion, and American Law.* Ithaca, N.Y.: Cornell University Press.

Mitchell, Cynthia. 1990. "Woman Is Told to Stay Sober While Pregnant: Tennessee Judge Slaps Ban on Alcohol, Illegal Drugs." *Atlanta Constitution*, 11 January, A1.

Mitchell, Lisa, and Eugenia Georges. 1997. "Cross-Cultural Cyborgs: Greek and Canadian Women's Discourses on Fetal Ultrasound." *Feminist Studies* 23, no. 2: 373–401.

MMWR: Morbidity and Mortality Weekly Report. 1998. "Maternal Mortality—United States, 1982–1996" 47, no. 34 (4 September): 705–707.

Moore, Kathryn Glovier. 1990. "Substance Abuse and Pregnancy: State Lawmakers Respond with Punitive and Public Health Measures." *ACOG Legisletter* 9, no. 3.

Moore, Marat. 1990. "Hard Labor: Voices of Women from the Appalachian Coal Fields." *Yale Journal of Law and Feminism* 2: 199–238.

Moran, Eileen Geil. 1993. "Domestic Violence and Pregnancy." In *Encyclopedia of Childbearing: Critical Perspectives*, edited by Barbara Katz Rothman, 110–12. Phoenix: Oryx Press.

Morgan, Lynn. 1996. "Fetal Relationality in Feminist Philosophy: An Anthropological Critique." *Hypatia* 11, no. 3: 47–70.

———. 1997. "Imagining the Unborn in the Ecuadorian Andes." *Feminist Studies* 23, no. 2: 323–50.

Morris, Anne, and Susan Nott. 1995. "The Law's Engagement with Pregnancy." In *Law and Body Politics: Regulating the Female Body*, edited by Jo Bridgeman and Susan Millns, chap. 3. Aldershot, England: Dartmouth Publishing.

Moss, Debra. 1988. "Pregnant? Go Directly to Jail." *American Bar Association Journal* (November): 20.

Moss, Kary. 1990. "Substance Abuse during Pregnancy." *Harvard Women's Law Journal* 13: 278–99.

———. 1991. "Forced Drug or Alcohol Treatment for Pregnant and Postpartum Women: Part of the Solution or Part of the Problem?" *New England Journal on Criminal and Civil Confinement* 17: 1–16.

Mulholland, Kristin. 1987. "A Time to Be Born and a Time to Die: A Pregnant Woman's Right to Die with Dignity." *Indiana Law Review* 20: 859–78.

Mullings, Leith. 1984. "Minority Women, Work, and Health." In *Double Exposure: Women's Health Hazards on the Job and at Home*, edited by Wendy Chavkin, chap. 6. New York: Monthly Review Press.

Murphy, Patrick. 1996. "Protect the Innocent" (op-ed). *New York Times*, 30 July.

Murray, Charles. 1984. *Losing Ground: American Social Policy, 1950–1980*. New York: Basic Books.

———. 1993. "The Coming White Underclass." *Wall Street Journal*, 29 October.

National Committee on Pay Equity (NCPE). 1998. "The Wage Gap over Time: In Real Dollars, Women See Little Change." Fact sheet. Washington, D.C.: NCPE.

National Law Journal. 1996. "Abuse of Viable Fetus Ruled a Crime," 29 July, A8.

National Public Radio. 1996. *All Things Considered*, 13 September.

Neimann, Linda. 1990. *Boomer: Railroad Memoirs*. Berkeley: University of California Press.

New York Times. 1983. "Drug Case Stresses Fetus Rights," 27 April, A18.

———. 1989. "Missouri Fetus Unlawfully Jailed, Suit Says," 11 August, B5.

———. 1991. "The Cost of Not Treating Crack" (editorial), 24 December.

———. 1992. "Mothers' Smoking Is Linked to Child," 8 September, C9.

———. 1994a. "Behind a Boy's Decision to Forgo Treatment," 13 June, A12.

———. 1994b. "Youth Who Refused Drug for Transplant Dies at 15 in Florida," 22 August, A14.

———. 1996. "Prenatal Drug Use Is Ruled Child Abuse," 17 July, A10.

———. 1998a. "The Partial-Birth Strategem" (editorial), 16 May, A28.

———. 1998b. "Pregnant Drinkers Face a Crackdown," 24 May, A16.

———. 1998c. "Judge Intends Prison Time to Block Abortion," 11 October, A30.

Newman, Karen. 1996. *Fetal Positions: Individualism, Science, Visuality*. Stanford, Calif.: Stanford University Press.

Norton, Constance. 1990. "Legislators Should Not Have Feared Title VII Pre-Emption of California's Temporary Transfer Alternative to Discriminatory Fetal Protection Policies." *Golden Gate University Law Review* 19: 463–506.

Nozick, Robert. 1974. *Anarchy, State, Utopia*. New York: Basic Books.

Nurmi, Joy, and Vincent Leclair. 1990. "Fetal Rights Spurs Judge's Decision." *Rockville Gazette*, 7 February, A1.

Nyberg, Cheryl. 1991–92. *Subject Compilations of State Laws: An Annotated Bibliography*. Urbana, Ill.: Carol Boast and Cheryl Nyberg.

Oakley, Ann. 1984. *The Captured Womb: A History of the Medical Care of Pregnant Women*. Oxford: Basil Blackwell.

Okin, Susan Moller. 1989. *Justice, Gender, and the Family*. New York: Basic Books.

Olen, Helaine. 1991. "Racial Tinge to Drug Testing of New Moms." *Chicago Tribune*, 19 December, C14.

Oren, Laura. 1996. "Protection, Patriarchy, and Capitalism: The Politics and Theory of Gender-Specific Regulation in the Workplace." *UCLA Women's Law Journal* 6: 321–73.

Paltrow, Lynn. 1988. "A Matter of Conscience." *National Law Journal*, 7 November, 13.

———. 1992. *Criminal Prosecutions against Pregnant Women: National Update and Overview.* New York: Reproductive Freedom Project, American Civil Liberties Union.

Parness, Jeffrey A. 1992. "Arming the Pregnancy Police: More Outlandish Concoctions?" *Louisiana Law Review* 53: 427–48.

Pateman, Carole. 1988. "The Patriarchal Welfare State." In *Democracy and the Welfare State*, edited by Amy Gutmann, chap. 10. Princeton, N.J.: Princeton University Press.

Paul, Maureen; Cynthia Daniels; and Robert Rosofsky. 1989. "Corporate Response to Reproductive Hazards in the Workplace: Results of the Family, Work, and Health Survey." *American Journal of Industrial Medicine* 16: 267–80.

Pediatrics. 1990. "Drug-Exposed Infants" (Statement of the Committee on Substance Abuse of the American Academy of Pediatrics) 86, no. 4 (October): 639–42.

Perry, Ruth. 1993. "Engendering Environmental Thinking: A Feminist Analysis of the Present Crisis." *Yale Journal of Criticism* 6, no. 2: 1–16.

Petchesky, Rosalind. 1979. "Workers, Reproductive Hazards, and the Politics of Protection: An Introduction." *Feminist Studies* 5, no. 2: 233–45.

———. 1984. *Abortion and Woman's Choice: The State, Sexuality, and Reproductive Freedom.* Boston: Northeastern University Press.

———. 1987. "Foetal Images: The Power of Visual Culture in the Politics of Reproduction." In *Reproductive Technologies: Gender, Motherhood, and Medicine*, edited by Michelle Stanworth, chap. 3. Minneapolis: University of Minnesota Press.

Phelan, Jeffrey. 1991. "The Maternal Abdominal Wall: A Fortress against Fetal Health Care?" *Southern California Law Review* 65: 461–90.

Poland, Marilyn, et al. 1993. "Punishing Pregnant Drug Users: Enhancing the Flight from Care." *Drug and Alcohol Dependence* 31: 199–203.

Pollitt, Katha. 1990. "'Fetal Rights': A New Assault on Feminism." *The Nation*, 26 March, 409–18.

Priston, Terry. 1997. "New Jersey Daily Briefing; Fetal Abuse Charge Rejected." *New York Times*, 4 January, A25.

Purdum, Todd. 1996. "Speaking to Veterans' Groups, Clinton Orders an Expansion of Agent Orange Benefits." *New York Times*, 29 May, B7.

Purnick, Joyce. 1996. "Elisa's Death: A Year Later, Hints of Hope." *New York Times*, 21 November, B1.

Purvis, Andrew. 1990. "The Sins of the Fathers: Both Parents May Be Vulnerable to Toxins That Cause Birth Defects." *Time*, 26 November, 90.

Quayle, Dan. 1992. "Restoring Basic Values: Strengthening the Family." *Vital Speeches of the Day* 58 (15 June): 517–20.

Quindlen, Anna. 1994. "The Baby Bill." *New York Times*, 8 June, A25.

Rabb, William. 1998. "Jail Pregnant Cocaine Users Says Panel on Juvenile Crime." *Mobile Register*, 9 June.

Raeder, Myrna. 1993. "Gender and Sentencing: Single Moms, Battered Women, and Other Sex-Based Anomalies in the Gender-Free World of the Federal Sentencing Guidelines." *Pepperdine Law Review* 20: 905–90.

Raines, Elvoy. 1984. Editorial Comment to Ronna Jurow and Richard H. Paul, "Cesarean Delivery for Fetal Distress without Maternal Consent." *Obstetrics & Gynecology* 63, no. 4 (April): 598–99.

Rawls, John. 1971. *A Theory of Justice*. Cambridge, Mass.: Harvard University Press.

Reed, Adolph. 1990. "The Underclass as Myth and Symbol: The Poverty of Discourse about Poverty." *Radical America* 24, no. 1: 21–40.

Remnick, David. 1988. "Whose Life Is It, Anyway? Angie Carder Lived a Very Simple Life . . . and Died a Very Complicated Death." *Washington Post*, 21 February, W14.

Reproductive Freedom News. 1994. "Woman Who Refused C-Section Delivers Healthy Baby," 3, no. 1 (14 January): 6. New York: Center for Reproductive Law and Policy.

———. 1996a. "Legislation to Punish Crimes against Pregnant Women May Portend Broader Anti-Choice Agenda," 5, no. 4 (23 February): 4–6. New York: Center for Reproductive Law and Policy.

———. 1996b. "Washington Appeals Panel Affirms Dismissal of Charges against Woman for Behavior during Pregnancy," 5, no. 11 (28 June): 3. New York: Center for Reproductive Law and Policy.

———. 1996c. "Canadian Appeals Court Finds Pregnant Woman Cannot Be Forced into Drug Treatment," 5, no. 16 (11 October): 8. New York: Center for Reproductive Law and Policy.

The Responsive Community. 1991. "Sterilization—the Solution to Crack Babies," 1, no. 1: 72.

Rhoden, Nancy K. 1986. "The Judge in the Delivery Room: The Emergence of Court-Ordered Cesareans." *California Law Review* 74: 1951–2030.

Rich, Marney. 1988. "A Question of Rights: Birth and Death Decisions Put Women in the Middle of Legal Conflict." *Chicago Tribune*, 18 September, C1.

Richardson, Lynda. 1998. "Doctors Criticize Delays in Receiving Newborns' H.I.V. Data." *New York Times*, 14 May, B1.

Roberts, Dorothy. 1991. "Punishing Drug Addicts Who Have Babies: Women of Color, Equality, and the Right of Privacy." *Harvard Law Review* 104: 1419–82.

Robertson, John. 1983. "Procreative Liberty and the Control of Conception, Pregnancy, and Childbirth." *Virginia Law Review* 69: 405–64.

Robin-Vergeer, Bonnie. 1990. "The Problem of the Drug-Exposed Newborn: A Return to Principled Intervention." *Stanford Law Review* 42: 745–809.

Rodriguez, Pablo. 1998. "The Doctor in the Bulletproof Vest" (op-ed). *New York Times*, 28 October, A29.

Rosen, Ruth. 1991. "What Feminist Victory in the Court?" (op-ed). *New York Times*, 1 April, sec. A.

Rosenbaum, Marsha. 1981. *Women on Heroin*. New Brunswick, N.J.: Rutgers University Press.

Rosenthal, Elisabeth. 1990. "When a Pregnant Woman Drinks." *New York Times Magazine*, 4 February, 30+.

———. 1997. "A New York Study Finds Uninsured Are on the Rise." *New York Times*, 25 February, A21.

Rosner, Fred, et al. 1989. "Fetal Therapy and Surgery: Fetal Rights and Maternal Obligations." *New York State Journal of Medicine* 89, no. 2 (February): 80–84.

Roth, Rachel. 1997. At Women's Expense: The Costs of Fetal Rights. Ph.D. Diss., Yale University.

Rothstein, Laura. 1992 and 1993 Supp. *Disabilities and the Law*. Colorado Springs, Colo.: Shepard's/McGraw-Hill.

Samuels, Suzanne Uttaro. 1995. *Fetal Rights, Women's Rights: Gender Equality in the Workplace*. Madison: University of Wisconsin Press.

San Diego Union-Tribune. 1989. "Mom Gets Probation in Drugged Delivery, Deaths of Twin Boys," 9 June, A11.

Sandel, Michael. 1982. *Liberalism and the Limits of Justice*. Cambridge: Cambridge University Press.

Schlichtmann, Laura. 1994. "Accommodation of Pregnancy-Related Disabilities on the Job." *Berkeley Journal of Employment and Labor Law* 15: 335–410.

Schrag, Peter. 1995. "Problems Deferred Haunt UC and CSU." *Sacramento Bee*, 9 July, F1.

Schroedel, Jean. 1985. *Alone in a Crowd: Women in the Trades Tell Their Stories*. Philadelphia: Temple University Press.

Science News. 1994. "Country Kids: No Letup from Lead" 146 (30 July): 79.

———. 1998. "Cesarean + AZT = Almost No HIV Transmission" 153 (27 June): 405.

Scott, Judith. 1984. "Keeping Women in Their Place: Exclusionary Policies and Reproduction." In *Double Exposure: Women's Health Hazards on the Job and at Home*, edited by Wendy Chavkin, chap. 9. New York: Monthly Review Press.

Segal, Elizabeth. 1991. "Social Policy Intervention with Chemically Dependent Women and Their Children." *Child and Adolescent Social Work* 8, no. 4: 285–95.

Segers, Mary. 1995. "The Pro-Choice Movement after *Casey*: Preserving Access." In *Abortion Politics in American States*, edited by Mary Segers and Timothy Byrnes, chap. 12. Armonk, N.Y.: M. E. Sharpe.

Shaw, Margery. 1984. "Conditional Prospective Rights of the Fetus." *Journal of Legal Medicine* 5, no. 1: 63–116.

Shearer, Beth. 1993. "Cesarean Birth: Indications and Consequences." In *Encyclopedia of Childbearing: Critical Perspectives*, ed. Barbara Katz Rothman, 56–59. Phoenix: Oryx Press.

Shellenbarger, Sue. 1993. "As More Pregnant Women Work, Bias Complaints Rise." *Wall Street Journal*, 6 December, B1.

Sherman, Rorie. 1991. "Bioethics Debate: Americans Polled on Bioethics." *National Law Journal*, 13 May, 1.

Shirk, Martha. 1991. "Hospital Tried to Force Caesarean for Second Time in 3-1/2 Years; Deaconess Asked Court to Order Surgical Procedure." *St. Louis Post-Dispatch*, 2 February, A3.

Shriner, Thomas L. 1979. "Maternal versus Fetal Rights: A Clinical Dilemma" (editorial). *Obstetrics & Gynecology* 53, no. 4 (April): 518–19.

Siegal, Nina. 1997. "Hope for Change: State Settles Federal Class-Action Suit That Charged Inadequate Medical Care in Women's Prisons." *San Francisco Bay Guardian*, 13 August, 10.

Simpson, Elizabeth. 1999. "Drugs Bond Mother, Child in Illness; Families Find that Charging Abuse is Difficult before a Baby's Birth, But New Law Offers Hope." *Virginian Pilot*, 25 April, A1.

Singer, Cathy. 1990. "The Pretty Good Mother." *Long Island Monthly*, January, 46+.

Skelton, George. 1996. "Capitol Journal: Three Strikes and You're Out of Room." *Los Angeles Times*, 25 April, A3.

Skelton, George, and Daniel Weintraub. 1991. "Most Support Norplant for Teens, Drug Addicts." *Los Angeles Times*, 27 May, A1.

Smith, George Bundy, and Gloria M. Dabiri. 1991. "Prenatal Drug Exposure: The Constitutional Implications of Three Governmental Approaches." *Seton Hall Constitutional Law Journal* 2: 53–126.

Smith, Lynn. 1998. "The $200 Question." *Los Angeles Times*, 3 April, E1.

Snitow, Ann. 1990. "A Gender Diary." In *Conflicts in Feminism*, edited by Marianne Hirsch and Evelyn Fox Keller, chap. 1. New York: Routledge.

Solinger, Rickie. 1992. *Wake Up Little Susie: Single Pregnancy and Race before "Roe v. Wade."* New York: Routledge.

———. 1993. "'A Complete Disaster': Abortion and the Politics of Hospital Abortion Committees, 1950–1970." *Feminist Studies* 19, no. 2: 241–68.

———. 1994. *The Abortionist: A Woman against the Law.* New York: The Free Press.

Sollom, Terry. 1993. "State Legislation on Reproductive Health in 1992: What Was Proposed and Enacted." *Family Planning Perspectives* 25, no. 2: 87–90.

Solomon, Renee. 1991. "Future Fear: Prenatal Duties Imposed by Private Parties." *American Journal of Law and Medicine* 17, no. 4: 411–34.

Sor, Yvonne. 1986–87. "Fertility or Unemployment: Should You Have to Choose?," *Journal of Law and Health* 1: 141–228.

———. 1991. "The Right to Say No" (editorial), 1 February, B2.

Stabile, Carol. 1992. "Shooting the Mother: Fetal Photography and the Politics of Disappearance." *Camera Obscura* 28, 178–205.

Stanworth, Michelle, ed. 1987. *Reproductive Technologies: Gender, Motherhood, and Medicine.* Minneapolis: University of Minnesota Press.

Staples, Brent. 1995. "The Chain Gang Show: Humiliating Prisoners, for Political Profit." *New York Times Magazine*, 17 September, 62–63.

State Legislatures. 1993. "Norplant Approval in Michigan Unmarred by Controversy," 19, no. 5: 7.

Stattmann, Ed. 1989. "Ill., La., N.H.: Bennett Hears Experts on Fetal Drug Effects." United Press International, 9 October.

Steckenrider, Janie S. 1996. "Aging as a Female Phenomenon: The Plight of Older Women." Paper presented at the Annual Meeting of the American Political Science Association, San Francisco, 30 August.

Stein, Loren, and Veronique Mistiaen. 1988. "Mothers behind Bars." *Boston Sunday Herald Magazine*, 30 October.

Stein, Theodore. 1998. *The Social Welfare of Women and Children with HIV and AIDS: Legal Protections, Policy, and Programs*. New York: Oxford University Press.

Stellman, Jeanne, and Mary Sue Henifin. 1982. "No Fertile Women Need Apply: Employment Discrimination and Reproductive Hazards in the Workplace." In *Biological Woman: The Convenient Myth*, edited by Ruth Hubbard, Mary Sue Henifin, and Barbara Fried, 117–45. Cambridge, Mass.: Schenkman Publishing.

St. Louis Post-Dispatch. 1990. "Women Count as Full-Fledged Human Beings" (editorial), 8 May, B2.

Stoddard, Kathy. 1990. "Fetal Rights, Fetal Wrongs: The Courts and Legislatures Respond to the Fetal Rights Hysteria." *New Haven Advocate*, 16 July, 25.

Taub, Nadine. 1996. "At the Intersection of Reproductive Freedom and Gender Equality: Problems in Addressing Reproductive Hazards in the Workplace." *UCLA Women's Law Journal* 6: 443–56.

Taylor, Avril. 1993. *Women Drug Users: An Ethnography of a Female Injecting Community*. Oxford: Clarendon Press.

Taylor, Janelle. 1992. "The Public Fetus and the Family Car: From Abortion Politics to a Volvo Advertisement." *Public Culture* 4, no. 2: 67–80.

Teare, Catherine. 1995. "Prenatal Drug Effects Still Uncertain." *Youth Law News* 17, nos. 4–5: 20–25.

Terry, Don. 1993. "Illinois Is Seeking to Force Woman to Have Cesarean." *New York Times*, 15 December, A22.

———. 1996. "In Wisconsin, a Rarity of a Fetal-Harm Case." *New York Times*, 17 August, A6.

Thornton, Terry, and Lynn Paltrow. 1991. "The Rights of Pregnant Patients: Carder Case Brings Bold Policy Initiatives." *HealthSpan* 8, no. 5: 10–16.

Toufexis, Anastasia. 1991. "Innocent Victims." *Time*, 13 May, 56–60.

Tribe, Laurence. 1988. *American Constitutional Law* (2d ed.). Mineola, N.Y.: The Foundation Press.

———. 1992. *Abortion: The Clash of Absolutes* (2d ed.). New York: Norton.

Tsing, Anna. 1990. "Monster Stories: Women Charged with Perinatal Endangerment." In *Uncertain Terms: Negotiating Gender in American Culture*, edited by Faye Ginsburg and Anna Tsing, chap. 17. Boston: Beacon Press.

Turner, Maureen. 1999. "Pregnancy and Privacy: Should a Woman Have to Compromise One for the Other?" *Valley Advocate*, 11 March, 14–17.

Uniform Laws Annotated. "Uniform Rights of the Terminally Ill Act (1989)" (West 1994 Supp.).

United Press International (UPI). 1991. "Parma Man to Be Sentenced in Death of Newborn," 26 March.

U.S. Congress. House. Education and Labor Committee. 1990. "A Report by the Majority Staff on the EEOC, Title VII, and Workplace Fetal Protection Policies in the 1980s." 101st Cong., 2d sess.

U.S. Congress. Office of Technology Assessment. 1985. *Reproductive Hazards in the Workplace*. Washington, D.C.: U.S. Government Printing Office.

———. 1991. *Medical Monitoring and Screening in the Workplace: Results of a Survey — Background Paper*. Washington, D.C.: U.S. Government Printing Office.

U.S. Department of Health and Human Services. n.d. *State Resources and Services Re-*

lated to Alcohol and Other Drug Abuse Problems, Fiscal Year 1990. Written by the National Association of State Alcohol and Substance Abuse Directors.

———. 1993. *Pregnant, Substance-Using Women: Treatment Improvement Protocol Series.* Publication No. 93-1998.

U.S. Public Health Service, Region IX. 1991. *Assessment of Services for Substance-Exposed Infants and Their Families in the San Francisco Bay Area.* Cathy Levine, Project Officer, and Claire Brindis, Project Director. San Francisco, California.

Van Biema, David. 1995. "Abandoned to Her Fate." *Time,* 11 December, 32–36.

Wagner, Eileen. 1991. "The Alcoholic Beverages Labeling Act of 1988: A Preemptive Shield against Fetal Alcohol Syndrome Claims?" *Journal of Legal Medicine* 12, no. 2: 167–200.

Walzer, Michael. 1983. *Spheres of Justice: A Defense of Pluralism and Equality.* New York: Basic Books.

Warren, Jennifer. 1987. "Case against Woman in Baby Death Thrown Out." *New York Times,* 27 February, sec. A.

Weinbaum, Eve. 1997. "Transforming Democracy: Rural Women and Labor Resistance." In *Women Transforming Politics: An Alternative Reader,* edited by Cathy Cohen, Kathleen Jones, and Joan Tronto, chap. 19. New York: New York University Press.

Williams, Patricia. 1990. "Fetal Fictions: An Exploration of Property Archetypes in Racial and Gendered Contexts." *Florida Law Review* 42: 81–94.

Williams, Wendy. 1993. "Equality's Riddle: Pregnancy and the Equal Treatment/Special Treatment Debate." In *Feminist Legal Theory: Foundations,* edited by D. Kelly Weisberg, 128–55. Philadelphia: Temple University Press.

Williams Obstetrics (13th ed.). 1966. New York: Appleton-Century-Crofts.

Wilson, William Julius. 1987. *The Truly Disadvantaged: The Inner City, the Underclass, and Public Policy.* Chicago: University of Chicago Press.

Wilczynski, Ania, and Allison Morris. 1993. "Parents Who Kill Their Children." *Criminal Law Review* (January): 31–36.

Wisconsin State Journal. 1996. "Baby Born Drunk Has Related Defects," 5 July.

Wright, Michael. 1979. "Reproductive Hazards and 'Protective' Discrimination." *Feminist Studies* 5, no. 2: 302–25.

Young, Iris. 1990. *Justice and the Politics of Difference.* Princeton, N.J.: Princeton University Press.

———. 1995. "Punishment, Treatment, Empowerment: Three Approaches to Policy for Pregnant Addicts." In *Expecting Trouble: Surrogacy, Fetal Abuse, and New Reproductive Technologies,* edited by Patricia Boling, chap. 6. Boulder, Colo.: Westview Press.

Youth Law News. 1985. "County Jail Miscarriage Rate 50 Times State Average," 6, no. 6: 4.

———. 1990. "One Drug-Using Mother's Story," 11, no. 1: 19.

———. 1991. "Dollars Invested in Children Save Money," 12, no. 2: 9.

Zeller, Shawn. 1998. "Fetal Abuse Laws Gain Favor." *National Journal,* 25 May, 1758.

Zent, Jeff. 1998. "Minot Planning Commission Rejects Treatment Center Plan." *Minot Daily News,* 25 August.

Zuckerman, Barry, and Deborah Frank. 1992. "'Crack Kids': Not Broken." *Pediatrics* 89, no. 2, 337–39.

Court Opinions and Documents

In re A.C. 533 A.2d 611 (D.C. App. 1987).

In the Matter of A.C. 539 A.2d 203 (D.C. App. 1988).

In re A.C. 573 A.2d 1235 (D.C. App. 1990).

Adkins v. Children's Hospital 261 U.S. 525 (1923).

Ashley v. Florida 701 50.2d 338 (Fla. 1997).

Beal v. Doe 97 S.Ct. 2366 (1977).

Brigham and Women's Hospital v. Britto Civil Action No. 84532, Suffolk Superior Court, unpublished order, 16 July 1986. Excerpted in *Massachusetts Lawyers Weekly*, 28 July 1986, 21.

In re Fetus Brown 689 N.E.2d 397 (Ill. 1997).

People of California v. Jaurigue No. 23611, transcript of oral argument, 21 August 1992.

People of California v. Zaring 8 Cal.App.4th 362 (1992).

California Department of Fair Employment and Housing v. Save Mart 1992 WL 223887.

Crouse Irving Memorial Hospital, Inc. v. Paddock 485 N.Y.S.2d 443 (Sup. 1985).

Cruzan v. Missouri Department of Health 497 U.S. 261 (1990).

Curran v. Bosze 566 N.E.2d 1319 (Ill. 1990).

DeNino v. State Ex Rel. Gorton 684 P.2d 1297 (Wash. 1984).

DSS v. Felicia B. 543 N.Y.S.2d 637 (Fam.Ct. 1989).

Dothard v. Rawlinson 97 S.Ct. 2720 (1977).

In re Dubreuil 629 So.2d 819 (Fla. 1993).

Dunning v. National Industries 720 F.Supp. 924 (M.D. Ala. 1989).

Elaine W. v. Joint Diseases North General Hospital 613 N.E.2d 523 (N.Y. 1993).

Estelle v. Gamble 429 U.S. 97 (1976).

EEOC v. Corinth, Inc. 824 F.Supp. 1302 (N.D. Ind. 1993).

Fenn Manufacturing v. Commission on Human Rights and Opportunities 1994 WL 51143 (Conn. Super.).

Fenn Manufacturing v. Commission on Human Rights and Opportunities 652 A.2d 1011 (Conn. 1995).

Fosmire v. Nicoleau 536 N.Y.S.2d 492 (A.D. 2 Dept. 1989).

Fosmire v. Nicoleau 551 N.E.2d 77 (N.Y. 1990).

Geduldig v. Aiello 417 U.S. 484 (1974).

General Electric v. Martha Gilbert et al. 97 S.Ct. 401 (1976).

Application of the President and Directors of Georgetown College 331 F.2d 1000 (1964).

Gloria C. v. William C. 476 N.Y.S.2d 991 (Fam.Ct. 1984).

Grant v. General Motors Corporation 743 F.Supp. 1260 (N.D. Ohio 1989).

Grant v. General Motors Corporation 908 F.2d 1303 (6th Cir. 1990).

Harris v. McRae 100 S.Ct. 2647 (1980).

Hayes v. Shelby Memorial Hospital 546 F.Supp. 259 (N.D. Ala. 1982).

Hayes v. Shelby Memorial Hospital 726 F.2d 1543 (11th Cir. 1984).

Jackson v. State 833 S.W.2d 220 (Tex. Ct. App. 1992).

In re Jamaica Hospital 491 N.Y.S.2d 898 (Sup. 1985).

Jefferson v. Griffin Spalding County Hospital Authority 274 S.E.2d 457 (Ga. 1981).

Johnson v. State 578 So.2d 419 (Fla. App. 5 Dist. 1991).

Johnson v. Florida 602 So.2d 1288 (Fla. 1992).

Johnson Controls, Inc. v. California Fair Employment and Housing Commission 218 Cal. App. 3d 517 (1990).

Keeler v. Superior Court 2 Cal.3d 619 (1970).

Khalifa v. G.X. Corporation 408 N.W.2d 221 (Minn. App. 1987).

McFall v. Shimp 10 Pa. D. & C. 3d 90 Allegheny Ct. Comm. Pleas (1978).

In re Madyun Misc. No. 189-86 of the Superior Court of the District of Columbia Civil Division, appended to *In re A.C.* 573 A.2d 1253 (D.C. App. 1990).

In re Melideo 390 N.Y.S.2d 523 (1976).

Mercy Hospital v. Jackson 489 A.2d 1130 (Md. App. 1985).

Mercy Hospital v. Jackson 510 A.2d 562 (Md. 1986).

Muller v. Oregon 208 U.S. 412 (1908).

Oil, Chemical and Atomic Workers, International Union v. American Cyanamid Co. 741 F.2d 444 (D.C. Cir. 1984).

Planned Parenthood of Southeastern Pennsylvania v. Casey 112 S.Ct. 2791 (1992).

Raleigh Fitkin-Paul Morgan Memorial Hospital v. Anderson 201 A.2d 537 (N.J. 1964).

Reyes v. California 75 Cal.App.3d 214 (1977).

Robinson v. California 370 U.S. 660 (1962).

Roe v. Wade 410 U.S. 113 (1973).

Santa Clara Pueblo v. Martinez 436 U.S. 49 (1978).

Schloendorff v. Society of New York Hospital 105 N.E.2d 92 (1914).

Secretary of Labor v. American Cyanamid. Occupational Safety and Health Review Commission Docket No. 79-2438, 20 August 1980.

Secretary of Labor v. American Cyanamid. Occupational Safety and Health Review Commission Docket No. 79-5762, 15 July 1980.

Secretary of Labor v. American Cyanamid. 9 O.S.H. Cas. (BNA) 1596 (1981).

Security National Bank v. Chloride 602 F.Supp. 294 (D.Kan. 1985).

Shady Grove Adventist Hospital v. Tawanda Walters. Docket *In re Tawanda Walters and Unborn Fetus*, No. 52658: Petition for Emergency Services, 12 January 1990; Response of Tawanda Walters and Her Counsel to Petition for Emergency Protective Services, 12 January 1990; Order Granting Emergency Protective Services, 12 January 1990; Report of Temporary Emergency Guardian, 15 January 1990.

Stamford Hospital v. Vega 674 A.2d 821 (Conn. 1996).

In re Steven S. 178 Cal. Rptr. 525 (Cal. Ct. App. 1981).

Taft v. Taft 446 N.E.2d 395 (Mass. 1983).

Thornburg v. American College of Obstetricians and Gynecologists 106 S.Ct. 2169 (1986).

Union Pacific Railway Company v. Botsford 141 U.S. 250 (1891).

United Auto Workers v. Johnson Controls, Inc. 680 F.Supp. 309 (E.D. Wis. 1988).

United Auto Workers v. Johnson Controls, Inc. 866 F.2d 871 (1989).

United Auto Workers v. Johnson Controls, Inc. 111 S.Ct. 1196 (1991).

United States v. Vaughn Daily Washington Law Reporter, 7 March 1989, 441, 446–47.

In re Valerie D. 613 A.2d 748 (Conn. 1992).

Whitner v. South Carolina 492 S.E.2d 777 (S.C. 1997).

Winston v. Lee 105 S.Ct. 1611 (1985).

Wright v. Olin Corporation 697 F.2d 1172 (4th Cir. 1982).

Wright v. Olin Corporation 585 F.Supp. 1447 (W.D. N.C. 1984).

State of Wyoming v. Dianne Pfannenstiel. Docket: Criminal Complaint, 5 January 1990; Motion to Dismiss for Insufficiency of Criminal Complaint, 26 January 1990; Brief in Support of Defendant's Motion to Dismiss on Insufficiency of Criminal Complaint, 26 January 1990.

Zuniga v. Kleberg County Hospital 692 F.2d 986 (5th Cir. 1982).

State Statutes as of December 31, 1992

Alabama Code § 22-8A-4(a) (1990). "Natural Death Act."

Alaska Stat. Ann. § 04.21.065 (b) (Oct. 1994 Supp.). "Alcoholic Beverages: Posting of Warning Signs."

Alaska Stat. Ann. § 18.05.037 (Oct. 1994 Supp.). "Fetal Health Effects Information."

Alaska Stat. Ann. § 18.12.040 (c) (Oct. 1994 Supp.). "Rights of the Terminally Ill Act."

Arizona Rev. Stat. Ann. § 4-261 (1993 Supp.). "Alcoholic Beverages: Warning Signs."

Arizona Rev. Stat. Ann. § 36-141 (B) (1993). "Services to Pregnant Women; Priority."

Arizona Rev. Stat. Ann. § 36-3262, Statement 3 (1993). "Medical Treatment Decisions Act."

Arkansas Code Ann. § 20-17-206 (c) (Michie 1993). "Rights of the Terminally Ill or Permanently Unconscious Act."

California Business & Professions Code § 2191 (f), (g) (West 1994 Supp.). "Continuing Medical Education."

California Education Code § 51203 (West 1994 Supp.). "Instruction on Alcohol, Narcotics, and Restricted Dangerous Drugs" (K-12).

California Government Code § 12945 (c)(1) and (2) and § 12945.5 (West 1992 and 1996 Supp.). "Fair Employment and Housing Act" (pregnancy and sterilization).

California Health & Safety Code § 7189.5 (c) (West 1994 Supp.). "Natural Death Act."

California Health & Safety Code §§ 10900–10902 (West 1991). "Perinatal Substance Abuse" (model needs assessment protocol).

California Health & Safety Code § 11781 et. seq. (West 1991). "Accessing Alcohol and Drug Recovery Programs for the Disenfranchised."

California Health & Safety Code §§ 11757.50 to 11757.66 (West 1991). "The Alcohol and Drug Affected Mothers and Infants Act of 1990."

California Health & Safety Code § 11998.1 (f) (9) (of Division 10.6) (West 1991). "Drug and Alcohol Abuse" (priority for pregnant women).

California Penal Code § 11165.13 and § 11166 (g) (West 1992). "Maternal Substance Abuse; Positive Toxicology Screen at Time of Delivery."

California Welfare & Institutions Code § 14132.21 (West 1991 and 1994 Supp.). "Perinatal Substance Abuse."

California Welfare & Institutions Code § 14132.36 (West 1994 Supp.). "Residential Care Programs for Alcohol and Drug Exposed Pregnant and Postpartum Perinatal Women."

Colorado Rev. Stat. Ann. § 15-18-104 (2) (West 1989). "Medical Treatment Decision Act."

Colorado Rev. Stat. Ann. § 19-3.5-105 (f) and 19-3.5-107 (1) (West 1990 and 1994 Supp.). "Children's Trust Fund."

Colorado Rev. Stat. Ann. § 25-1-203 (g) (West 1990 and 1994 Supp.). "Grants for Public Programs."

Colorado Rev. Stat. Ann. §§ 25-1-212 to 25-1-215 (West 1990 and 1994 Supp.). "Treatment Programs for High-Risk Pregnant Women."

Colorado Rev. Stat. Ann. § 26-4-302 (1)(s) (West 1990 and 1994 Supp.). "Basic Services for the Categorically Needy—Optional Services."

Colorado Rev. Stat. Ann. § 26-4-508.2 (West 1990 and 1994 Supp.). "Pregnant Women—Needs Assessment—Referral to Treatment Program."

Connecticut Gen. Stat. Ann. § 17a-644 (West 1992). "Substance Abuse Treatment Programs for Pregnant Women and Their Children."

Connecticut Gen. Stat. Ann. § 17a-659 (West 1992). "Task Force on Substance-Abusing Women and Their Children."

Connecticut Gen. Stat. Ann. §§ 17a-660 and 17a-661 (West 1992). "Awareness Programs for Health Care Providers Re Substance Abuse during Pregnancy."

Connecticut Gen. Stat. Ann. § 19a-574 (West 1994 Supp.). "Removal of Life Support Systems Act."

Connecticut Gen. Stat. Ann. § 31-40 (g)–(i) (West 1987). "Employment Regulation."

Connecticut Gen. Stat. Ann. § 46a-60 (a) (7) (E) (West 1987). "The Human Rights and Opportunities Act."

Delaware Code Ann. tit. 16, § 190 and tit., 24 § 1770 (1992 Supp.). "Required Warning" (verbal warnings and signs for medical offices).

Delaware Code Ann. tit. 16, § 2503 (d) (1995). "Patient's Right to Terminate Treatment Act" (also known as the "Death with Dignity Act").

District of Columbia Code Ann. § 6-2421 to 6-2430 (1995). "Natural Death Act."

District of Columbia Code Ann. § 25-147 (1991). "Alcoholic Beverages: Warning Signs."

District of Columbia Code Ann. § 32-1602 (b) (1993). "Eligibility for Treatment for Substance Abuse."

Florida Stat. Ann. § 415.501 to § 415.608, esp. § 415.503 (3), § 415.503 (4), and §§ 415.503 (9) (a) (2) and (g) (West 1993). "Protection from Abuse and Neglect" (defines terms).

Florida Stat. Ann. § 415.5082 to § 415.5089 (West 1993) and Juvenile Procedure Rule § 8.705 et. seq. (West 1992). "Guardian Advocates for Drug Dependent Newborns."

Florida Stat. Ann. § 765.101 et. seq. (West 1994 Supp.). "Health Care Advance Directives Act."

Georgia Code Ann. § 3-1-5 (a) (1990). "Alcoholic Beverages: Warning Signs."

Georgia Code Ann. § 26-5-5 (10), § 26-5-20, and § 37-7-2 (6) (1994 Supp.). "Priority Admissions for Drug Dependent Pregnant Females."

Georgia Code Ann. § 31-32-3, 5 (1994 Supp.). "Living Wills Act."

Hawaii Rev. Stat. § 327D-6 (1991). "Medical Treatment Decisions."

Idaho Code § 39-4504 (4) (1993). "Natural Death Act."

20 Illinois Comp. Stat. Ann. 305/4-103 to 305/5-103-1 (West 1993). "Model Programs; List of Providers; Subcommittee on Women's Treatment."

20 Illinois Comp. Stat. Ann. 305/9-101 (West 1993). "Special Services" (treatment).

20 Illinois Comp. Stat. Ann. 305/13-101 to 305/13-105 (West 1993). "Services for Pregnant Women and Mothers" (treatment).

20 Illinois Comp. Stat. Ann. 2310/55.54 and 2310/55.59 (West 1993). "Educational Program" (for pregnant women) and "Residential Care—Addicted Pregnant Women."

235 Illinois Comp. Stat. Ann. 5/6-24a (West 1993). "Liquor Control Act: Display of Birth Defects Warning Signs."

305 Illinois Comp. Stat. Ann. 5/5-5 (West 1993). "Medical Services for Welfare Recipients" (referrals to substance abuse treatment).

325 Illinois Comp. Stat. Ann. 5/3 and 5/4 (West 1993). "Abused and Neglected Child Reporting Act." See also 705 Illinois Comp. Stat. Ann. 405/2-3 (West 1992). "Juvenile Court Act: Abused, Neglected, or Dependent Minors."

325 Illinois Comp. Stat. Ann. 5/7.3b (West 1993). "Referral of Addicted Pregnant Persons—Services."

755 Illinois Comp. Stat. Ann. 35/3 § 3 (c) (West 1992). "Living Will Act."

Indiana Code Ann. § 16-8-11-11 (d) (Burns 1993). "Living Will Act."

Indiana Code Ann. § 31-6-4-3.1 (Burns 1994 Supp.). "Child in Need of Services" (juvenile law).

Indiana Code Ann. § 31-6-11-2.1 (2) (Burns 1994 Supp.). "Child Abuse Definitions."

Iowa Code Ann. § 125.32A (West 1994 Supp.). "Discrimination Prohibited" (treatment programs).

Iowa Code Ann. § 144A. 6. par. 2 (West 1989). "Life-Sustaining Procedures Act."

Iowa Code Ann. § 232.77 (2) (West 1994). "Photographs, Xrays, and Medically Relevant Tests" (juvenile justice).

Iowa Code Ann. § 235C.1 to 235C.3 (West 1994). "Council on Chemically Exposed Infants and Children."

Kansas Stat. Ann. § 65-1,160 to § 65-1,167 (1992). "Preconception and Perinatal Programs."

Kansas Stat. Ann. § 65-28,103 (a) (1992). "Natural Death Act."

Kentucky Rev. Stat. Ann. § 214.160 and § 214.175 (Michie 1994 Supp.). "Substance Abuse Tests of Pregnant Women and Newborn Infants" and "Anonymous Surveys of Substance Abuse during Pregnancy."

Kentucky Rev. Stat. Ann. § 222.021 and § 222.037 (Michie 1994 Supp.). "Substance Abuse and Pregnancy Work Group" and "Pilot Projects for Services to Prevent Substance Abuse during Pregnancy."

Kentucky Rev. Stat. Ann. § 243.895 and § 311.378 (Michie 1994 Supp.). (Alcohol warning signs.)

Kentucky Rev. Stat. Ann. § 311.622 et. seq. (Michie 1994 Supp.). "Living Will Act."

Louisiana Rev. Stat. Ann. § 23:1008 A (3) and (4) (West 1993 Supp.).

Louisiana Rev. Stat. Ann. § 40:1299.58.1 et. seq. (West 1992). "Declarations concerning Life-Sustaining Procedures Act."

Louisiana Rev. Stat. Ann. § 46:2505 (West 1994 Supp.). "State Substance Abuse Plan."

Louisiana Rev. Stat. Ann. § 46:2511 to § 46:2514 (West 1994 Supp.). "The Council to Prevent Chemically Exposed Infants."

Maine Rev. Stat. Ann. tit. 18-A, § 5-711 (West). "Uniform Rights of the Terminally Ill Act." (1989 session laws, c. 830, and 1991, c. 441 and 719.)

Maine 1991 Me. Resolves, chap. 49 (HP 174/LD 259). "Child Care Vouchers for Children of Substance Abusers."

Maryland Code Ann. Health-Gen. § 5-605. "Life-Sustaining Procedures Act."

Massachusetts Gen. Laws Ann. chap. 119, § 51A (West 1993). "Injured Children; Reports."

Minnesota Stat. Ann. § 144.3871 (West 1994 Supp.). (Alcohol warning signs.)

Minnesota Stat. Ann. § 145.9265 (West 1994 Supp.). "Fetal Alcohol Syndrome and Effects and Drug-Exposed Infant Prevention."

Minnesota Stat. Ann. § 145B.13 (3) (West 1988). "Living Will Act."

Minnesota Stat. Ann. § 254A.17 Subd. 1(a) (West 1994). "Programs for Pregnant Women and Women with Children."

Minnesota Stat. Ann. § 253B.02 Subd. 2 (West 1994). "Civil Commitment Act."

Minnesota Stat. Ann. § 363.02 Subd. 1 (8) (v) and § 363.03 Subd. 1 (5), (6) (West 1991). "Human Rights Act" (employment practices).

Minnesota Stat. Ann. § 626.556 Subd. 2 (c), § 626.5561, and § 626.5562 (West 1994 Supp.). "Reporting of Neglect" (criminal procedure; prenatal exposure to controlled substances).

Mississippi Code Ann. § 41-41-107 (1993). "Withdrawal of Life-Saving Mechanisms Act."

Missouri Ann. Stat. § 191.725 to § 191.745 (Vernon 1994 Supp.). "An Act Relating to the Protection of Certain Children."

Missouri Ann. Stat. § 459.025 (Vernon 1992). "Life Support Declarations Act."

Montana Code Ann. § 50-9-106 (6) and § 50-9-202 (3) (1993). "Rights of the Terminally Ill Act."

Nebraska Rev. Stat. § 20-408 (3) (1992 Supp.). "Rights of the Terminally Ill Act."

Nebraska Rev. Stat. § 53-148.01 (1993). "Liquor Control Act: Warning Sign."

Nevada Rev. Stat. Ann. § 432B.330 1 (b) (Michie 1991). "Protection of Children from Abuse and Neglect."

Nevada Rev. Stat. Ann. § 449.624 4 (Michie 1991). "Withholding or Withdrawal of Life-Sustaining Treatment Act."

New Hampshire Rev. Stat. Ann. § 132:19 to 132:21 (1994 Supp.). "Prenatal Chemical Dependency Task Force."

New Hampshire Rev. Stat. Ann. § 137-H:14 (1990). "Living Wills Act."

New Hampshire Rev. Stat. Ann. § 175:4, IV (1994). "Alcoholic Beverages: Advertising" (warning signs).

New Hampshire Rev. Stat. Ann. § 457:23, II (1992). "Marriage: Requirements" (fetal alcohol syndrome brochures to marriage license applicants).

New Jersey Stat. Ann. § 26:2H-56 (West 1994 Supp.). "Advanced Directives for Health Care Act."

New Mexico Stat. Ann. § 24-7-1 et. seq. (Michie 1994 Supp.). "Right to Die Act."

New Mexico Stat. Ann. § 60-6A-30 (Michie 1994 Supp.). "Business Licenses: Posting of Warnings" (alcohol and birth defects).

New York Alcoholic Beverage Control Law § 105-b (Consol. 1994 Supp.).

New York Mental Hygiene Law §§ 19.01 and 19.07 (Consol. 1994 Supp.).

North Carolina Gen. Stat. § 90-320 et. seq. "Right to Natural Death Act."

North Dakota Century Code § 23-06.4-7, 4 and § 23-06.4-03, 3.a.3 (1991). "Uniform Rights of the Terminally Ill Act."

Ohio Rev. Code Ann. § 2133.06 (B) (Anderson 1994). "Modified Uniform Rights of the Terminally Ill Act."

Ohio Rev. Code Ann. § 3793.15 and § 3793.02 (D) (Anderson 1992). "Program concerning Addicted Pregnant Women and their Children" and "Duties of Department" (mandate to define "intervention").

Oklahoma Stat. Ann. tit. 10, § 1101, 4 (West 1987). "Delinquent, Deprived, Neglected Children" (defines terms).

Oklahoma Stat. Ann. tit. 21, § 846 A.2 (West 1994 Supp.). "Crimes and Punishments: Child Abuse" (reporting drug-exposed newborns).

Oklahoma Stat. Ann. tit. 63, § 3101.8, C (West 1994 Supp.). "Rights of the Terminally Ill or Persistently Unconscious Act."

Oklahoma HJR 1032 (1991 session laws). (Task Force on Substance Abuse during Pregnancy.)

Oregon Rev. Stat. § 127.505 to 127.660, and esp. § 127.540 (5) (1991). "Health Care Decisions Act."

Oregon Rev. Stat. § 430.560 (2) (1994 Supp., Part 6). "Treatment Programs" (synthetic opiates).

Oregon Rev. Stat. §§ 430.900 to 430.955 (1994 Supp., Part 6). "Alcohol and Drug Treatment for Pregnant Users."

Oregon Rev. Stat. § 431.825 and § 106.081 (1992). "County Clerk to Distribute Fetal Alcohol Syndrome Pamphlets to Marriage License Applicants."

Oregon Rev. Stat. § 471.551 (1994 Supp., Part 6). "Warning Signs Related to Alcohol and Pregnancy."

Oregon Rev. Stat. § 659.389 (1994 Supp., Part 8). "Employment Practices Affecting Pregnant Employees."

20 Pennsylvania Cons. Stat. Ann. § 5414 (1994 Supp.). "Advance Directive for Health Care Act."

Rhode Island Gen. Laws § 15-2-3.1 (1988). "Marriage Licenses: Fetal Alcohol Syndrome Warning Law."

Rhode Island Gen. Laws § 23-4.11-6 (c) (1994 Supp.). "Rights of the Terminally Ill Act."

Rhode Island Gen. Laws § 23-13-18 (b) (7) (1989). "Maternity Care Payor of Last Resort" (substance abuse counseling).

Rhode Island Gen. Laws § 42-72-5 (b)(24) (1993). "Department of Children, Youth, and Families" (hospital discharge plans for drug-exposed newborns).

South Carolina Code Ann. § 44-77-70 (Law. Co-op. 1993 Supp.). "Death with Dignity Act."

South Dakota Codified Laws Ann. § 34-12D-10 (1994). "Living Will Act."

South Dakota Codified Laws Ann. § 35-4-99 and 35-4-100 (1992). "Alcoholic Beverages: Display of Health Warning Sign."

Tennessee Code Ann. § 32-11-101 et. seq. (1993 Supp.) "Right to Natural Death Act."

Tennessee Code Ann. § 68-24-104 (e) (1994 Supp.). "Abuse Prevention Pilot Programs."

Texas Health & Safety Code Ann. § 672.004 (3) and § 672.019 (West 1992). "Natural Death Act."

Utah Code Ann. § 62A-4a-404; see also § 62A-4a-101 and § 62A-4a-411 (1993 and 1994 Supps.). "Child Abuse or Neglect Reporting Requirements."

Utah Code Ann. § 75-2-1109 (1993). "Personal Choice and Living Will Act."

Vermont Stat. Ann. tit. 18, § 5251-5262 (1987). "Terminal Care Documents Act."

Virginia Code Ann. § 2.1-51.15:1 (Michie 1994 Supp.). "Secretary of Health and Human Resources to Develop Certain Criteria" (relating to pregnant women and to drug-exposed babies).

Virginia Code Ann. § 37.1-182.1 (Michie 1994 Supp.). "Regulations on Treating Pregnant Substance Abusers."

Virginia Code Ann. § 54.1-2403.1 (Michie 1994 Supp.). "Protocol for Certain Medical History Screening Required" (pregnant women and substance abuse).

Virginia Code Ann. § 54.1-2981 et. seq. (Michie 1994 Supp.). "Health Care Decisions Act."

Virginia Senate Joint Resolution No. 11 and House Joint Resolution No. 41 (1990 session laws, pp. 2447–50; continued by HJR No. 387, 1991 session laws, pp. 1920–22); HJR No. 388 (1991 session laws, pp. 1922–23); HJR No. 389 (1991 session laws, pp. 1923–24). (Task force study committees.)

Washington Rev. Code Ann. § 70.122.030 (1) (c) (West 1992 and 1994 Supp.). "Natural Death Act."

Washington Rev. Code Ann. § 74.09.790 (6) (West 1994 Supp.). "Maternity Care Access Program" (substance abuse treatment).

West Virginia Code § 16-30-1 et. seq. (1998) "Natural Death Act."

Wisconsin Stat. Ann. § 46.03 (West 1994 Supp.). "Fetal Alcohol Syndrome and Drug Danger Pamphlets."

Wisconsin Stat. Ann. § 46.55 (West 1994 Supp.). "Grants for Services to Persons in Treatment" (child care).

Wisconsin Stat. Ann. § 46.86 (West 1994 Supp.). "Treatment Programs."

Wisconsin Stat. Ann. § 46.238 (West 1994 Supp.). "Infants Whose Mothers Abuse Controlled Substances" (service provision).

Wisconsin Stat. Ann. § 146.0255 (West 1994 Supp.). "Testing Infants for Controlled Substances."

Wisconsin Stat. Ann. §§ 146.183-184 (West 1994 Supp.). "High-Risk Pregnancy Grants" (alcohol- or drug-related).

Wisconsin Stat. Ann. § 154.03 (2) 1.3 (West 1989). "Natural Death Act."

Wyoming Stat. Ann. § 35-22-102(b) (July 1994 Supp.). "Living Will Act."

Miscellaneous Federal and State Statutes and Regulations

Pregnancy Discrimination Act of Title VII of the Civil Rights Act. 42 U.S.C.A. 2000e et. seq.

45 *CFR* 96.131. "Alcohol and Drug Abuse and Mental Health Services Block Grant."

California Penal Code § 187 (a) and (b) (3) (West 1988) (homicide).

Florida Stat. Ann. § 782.09 (West 1992) (manslaughter).

Georgia Code Ann. § 31-9-7 (1991). "Medical Consent Law."

New Jersey Stat. Ann. § 30:4C-11 (West 1981). "Division of Youth and Family Services."

North Dakota Century Code § 50-08.1-01 (1993 Supp.). Statement of Legislative Policy on "Aid to Pregnant Women."

Virginia Code Ann. § 16.1-241.3 Advanced Legislative Service 1998 (child abuse reporting).

Index

Abortion, 17, 18–21
  access to, 22–23, 155
  and decision making, 70
  and equality, 19, 185, 194
  and fetal rights politics, 1, 32, 194–95
  and gender roles, 25
  pressures for, 30–31
  See also Anti-abortion movement; *Roe v. Wade*
Abortion providers, illegal, 18, 182–83
ACLU. *See* American Civil Liberties Union
Act Relating to the Protection of Certain Children, An (Missouri), 165
ADA. *See* Americans with Disabilities Act
ADAMHA. *See* Alcohol, Drug Abuse, and Mental Health Administration
Addiction, defined, 139. *See also* Drug and alcohol use in pregnancy
Adkins v. Children's Hospital, 43
Administrative substance abuse legislation, 174–75, 176
Adoption, pressure to relinquish children for, 22
AFDC. *See* Welfare
African American women
  disproportionate prosecutions against, 146–47
  employment discrimination against, 65, 81
  and fetal abuse legislation, 172
  and fetal protection policies, 41–42
  HIV status of, 129
  medical coercion against, 96
  reproductive control of, 22, 23, 147
  stereotypes about, 28n, 143–44, 152–53
  See also Race
Agent Orange, 86
Agrelo, Benny, 133

Aid to Families with Dependent Children (AFDC). *See* Welfare
Alabama, 95n, 164
  fetal rights politics in, 195
  living wills in, 123–24
Alaska, 146n
  abortion reform in, 18
  fetal abuse legislation in, 164, 165, 166, 170n, 171n, 178
  living wills in, 123, 197–98
Alcohol, Drug Abuse, and Mental Health Administration (ADAMHA), 141, 169
Alcohol use in pregnancy, 28n, 139n, 142, 148–49, 189
  consumer education regarding, 170–71, 177, 201
  See also Drug and alcohol use in pregnancy
Alderman, Ellen, 4
Allied Chemicals, 46
All Things Considered, 3–4
AMA. *See* American Medical Association
American Academy of Pediatrics, 129, 155
American Civil Liberties Union (ACLU), 128, 146n
American College of Obstetricians and Gynecologists, 105, 121, 129, 155, 162n
American Cyanamid Company, 14, 37, 46–47, 50–51, 74–75
  occupational safety and health charge against, 52–57, 85
  sex discrimination suit against, 57n
American Medical Association (AMA), 121, 129, 139, 155, 178
American Public Health Association, 155
Americans United for Life, 20

Americans with Disabilities Act (ADA), 5–6, 85
Anderson, Willimina, 108
Andrews, Lori, 95
Anti-abortion movement, 1, 12, 20, 22, 124, 194–95. *See also* Abortion
Application of the President and Directors of Georgetown College, 107–8, 111, 113n
Arizona
  fetal abuse legislation in, 164, 168n, 170n, 199
  living wills in, 123, 198
Arkansas, 164
  living wills in, 123
Arney, William, 32–33
ASARCO, 46
Ashley, Kawana, 186
Ashley v. Florida, 186
Asian and Asian American women, medical coercion against, 96. *See also* Race
Attempted murder, women who used alcohol during pregnancy charged with, 189–90
At Women's Expense: State Power and the Politics of Fetal Rights (Daniels), 9–11
Australia
  fetal rights cases in, 34
  prenatal technology in, 34
AZT, 129, 130

B. F. Goodrich, 46, 50
Baer, Judith, 42
Balisy, Sam, 181
Barnett, Ruth, 182–83
Battery production. *See* Lead exposure
Beal v. Doe, 120
Becker, Barrie, 156, 162, 179
Becker, Mary, 49, 85, 87
Belson, James, 119–20
Bennett, Belinda, 34
Bertin, Joan, 14, 85
BFOQ. *See* Bona fide occupational qualification
Bill of Rights. *See* Constitution, U.S.
Birth, social vs. biological, 35
Birth control. *See* Contraception; Sterilization
Birth defects
  causes of, 47–48, 49, 68, 194
  proposed compensation fund for, 83
  seen as parental malpractice, 31
  See also Fetal protection policies

Birth outcomes
  in jail and prison, 154
  and men, 144, 169
  and poverty, 12
  of pregnant drug users, 137, 139, 143, 144, 154, 169
  in jail, 156
  in other countries, 144
  and refusal of medical interventions, 96–97
  and violence against pregnant women, 178
Blackmun, Harry, 19, 36, 73
Black women. *See* African American women
Blank, Robert, 7, 32, 83–84
Blood transfusions, 71
  conflicts over, 107–8, 109–14, 128
"Boarder babies," 161
Bodily integrity, right to, 181. *See also* Patients' rights
Boesin, Richard, 145–46, 178n
Boland, Paul, 163
Boling, Patricia, 7
Bona fide occupational qualification (BFOQ), 60, 62, 63, 75
  in *UAW v. Johnson Controls*, 70–71, 72, 73–74
Bone marrow donation, refusal upheld, 105
Bork, Robert, 55, 74–75
Boyd, Susan, 34, 144
Bradley, Joseph, 42
Brennan, William, 71
Bricci, Tabita, 127–28
Brigham and Women's Hospital v. Britto, 115–16
Britto, Dolores, 115–16
Broadman, Howard, 156
Broken Cord, The (Dorris), 142
Brown, Darlene, 128
Bunker Hill Company, 14, 46, 47, 50
Bush administration, 21, 39
Business necessity defense, 60, 63, 64, 65
  and general societal interests, 62, 69

Cadmium, 45n, 46n
Cahn, Naomi, 26
California
  criminal prosecutions in, 135–36, 146n, 156
  drug-exposed infant abuse and neglect cases in, 161–62
  employee protection legislation in, 76–77, 81, 85–86

and drug testing and reporting, 143,
147–48
and fetal abuse legislation, 172
and fetal abuse mythology, 28n, 143–
44, 152–53
and fetal protection policies, 41–42
and medical coercion, 91–92, 96
and reproductive control of women,
22, 23
Race discrimination in employment,
65, 81
*Raleigh Fitkin-Paul Morgan Memorial Hospi-
tal v. Anderson*, 108, 110, 118
Ramsey, Michael, 151
Rand Corporation, 145n
Reagan, Ronald, 52, 55, 139
Reagan administration, 21, 39, 57
Reasonable efforts, in child abuse and
neglect proceedings, 162, 193
Reed, Adolph, 24
Rehnquist, William, 73n, 75
Religious freedom, 103–4, 115
and forced blood transfusions, 107–8,
109–14, 128
and forced cesareans, 92–93, 117
Reno, Janet, 147
Reproduction, women's disproportionate responsibility for, 2, 5, 8,
12–13, 25, 43, 62, 63–64, 70,
107, 113
and employment/motherhood conflict,
38, 42–43
and fetal protection policies, 38, 39, 48,
69–70, 75
Reproductive capacity–based discrimination. *See* Fetal protection policies;
Sex discrimination in employment
Reproductive health, 54, 75
and Occupational Safety and Health
Act, 57, 85
research on, 48, 66, 68
and workers' compensation, 84
See also Birth defects; Fetal protection
policies
Reproductive leave, 83–84
Reproductive politics, 17–18, 194–96
historical context of, 21–25
since *Roe v. Wade*, 18–21
See also Anti-abortion movement; Fetal
rights politics
Reproductive technology, 24–25, 34
Re S (England), 34
Rescue, question of duty to, 104–5

Reyes, Margaret Velasquez, 145
Reyes v. California, 145
Rhode Island
fetal abuse legislation in, 164, 166
abuse/neglect oriented, 174
administration oriented, 175n
education oriented, 171
treatment oriented, 168n, 202
living wills in, 123
Rhoden, Nancy, 7, 32, 105n
Riggs, Betty, 47, 74–75
Right to die, 122–26
Right-to-life movement. *See* Anti-abortion
movement
Roberts, Dorothy, 19n, 147
Robertson, John, 29–31, 106, 181
Robinson v. California, 139
Robin-Vergeer, Bonnie, 161
Roe v. Wade, 2, 17, 30, 36
and criminal prosecution of women,
135
framework of, 18–20, 21, 106–7
and medical coercion, 93, 106–7, 110,
117–18, 120, 122
Rose, Janeen, 78–80, 85
Rosen, Judith, 178n
Rosner, Fred, 3
Ryan White Comprehensive AIDS
Resources Emergency (CARE)
Act, 129

St. Joe's Minerals, 46
Sanger, Margaret, 23
Santa Clara Pueblo v. Martinez, 149
Scalia, Antonin, 73n
Schlichtmann, Laura, 77n, 80, 85
Schloendorff v. Society of New York Hospital,
103, 108
Scott, Judith, 86n
Secretary of Labor v. American Cyanamid,
54–57
Security National Bank v. Chloride, 49n
Sentencing Commission, U.S., 147
Separation of powers, 151
Serious threat defense to employment
discrimination, 78
Service-sector employment, 41
Sex discrimination in employment, 14,
44–45, 59–60
and accommodation of pregnant
workers, 77–82, 83–84, 85–86
American Cyanamid case, 58n
and equality/difference debate, 9–10

Taft, Lawrence, 114–15
Taft, Susan, 114–15
Taft, William Howard, 43
Taft v. Taft, 114–15
Tague, Tony, 182
Task forces, on prenatal drug exposure, 175, 176
Taylor, Avril, 34, 162n
Taylor, Janelle, 6–7
Technology, and fetal rights politics, 31–36
Tennessee, 95n
  fetal abuse legislation in, 164, 166, 168n
  living wills in, 123
Texas, 95n, 146n, 164
  living wills in, 123
Thirteenth Amendment, 103
Title VII, Civil Rights Act of 1964, 44–45, 58n, 59–60, 86, 185
  and accommodation of pregnant workers, 80–82, 85
  court opinions under
    General Elecric v. Gilbert, 44
    Grant v. GM Corp., 45, 72–73
    Hayes v. Shelby Memorial Hospital, 64–66, 67–68
    Wright v. Olin, 47, 61–63, 67, 69
    Zuniga v. Kleberg County Hospital, 64
  and reproductive capacity, 85
  and state employee protection legislation, 76, 77
  and workplace safety, 82
  See also Equal Employment Opportunity Commission; Pregnancy Discrimination Act; Sex discrimination in employment; *United Auto Workers v. Johnson Controls*
Tobacco use, 144, 158–59
Tort liability, 13n
  of employers, 49, 72, 73–74, 82
  and patients' rights, 104, 132
  of pregnant women, 30, 31, 186–87
Toxic substances, 45–46n, 47–48, 78–79
  OSHA standard setting for, 52
  See also Fetal protection policies; Lead exposure
Toxic Substances Control Act, 86
Treatment programs
  access to, 138–41, 153, 166–69, 174, 176, 202
  benefits of, 141, 179–80
  and criminal prosecutions, 151–52, 155, 157

involuntary commitment to, 148, 172–73, 194, 195
  proposals to mandate, 155
  public opinion regarding, 158
Tribe, Laurence, 18, 104, 108, 121n
Tsing, Anna, 190
Turner, Belle, 151

UAW. *See* United Auto Workers
Ultrasound, 34, 36n, 118
"Underclass," and stereotypes about women, 24, 152–53. *See also* Class; Race
Union Carbide, 46
Union Pacific Railway Company v. Botsford, 103, 108
Unions, 41, 49, 50–51, 81. *See also specific unions*
United Auto Workers (UAW), 49
United Auto Workers v. Johnson Controls, 66–70, 85
  BFOQ analysis in, 70–71
  dissents in, 72–73
  fetal personification in, 68–69, 71–72
  impact of, 87–88
  Supreme Court decision in, 60, 73–74, 82
United States v. Vaughn, 152
United Steelworkers of America (USWA), 50
Urban drug use, stereotypes about, 28n, 147. *See also* Class; Race
USWA. *See* United Steelworkers of America
Utah
  fetal abuse legislation in, 164, 166, 172, 202
  living wills in, 122–23

Vaughn, Brenda, 152–53, 156
Vermont, 164
  health insurance in, 39n
  living wills in, 123
Vinyl chloride, 45n
Violence, against pregnant women, 11, 135–36, 150, 153, 165, 177–78
Virginia, 146n
  fetal abuse legislation in, 164, 166
    abuse/neglect oriented, 173, 174, 195
    administration oriented, 175n
    treatment oriented, 167
  health insurance in, 39n
  living wills in, 123
Voluntary motherhood movement, 23